MICHA]

Michael Pavelka studied Theati
under the guidance of designers
assisted Barry Kay at the Royal C
embarking on his early freelance ~~~~~~ ~~~ ~ ~~~~-year residency at the
Warehouse Theatre Company with director Ted Craig, designing many
premieres of new plays and musicals.

Early in his career he designed two productions for Lindsay Anderson,
including Philip Barry's *Holiday* at the Old Vic, and over the last thirty
years he has designed over a hundred and sixty productions both
nationally and internationally along with a dozen London West End plays
and musicals, including *Twelve Angry Men*, *Absurd Person Singular*, *The
Constant Wife*, *How the Other Half Loves*, *Leonardo the Musical*, *Other
People's Money*, *Blues in the Night* (also in New York), *Rose Rage*, *A
Midsummer Night's Dream*, *A Few Good Men* and *Macbeth*.

He designed many Brecht and Shakespeare productions at the Library
Theatre Company, winning the Manchester Evening News Award for Best
Design for *Galileo*, then later at the National Theatre of Uganda, the first
Brecht play translated into an African language; *Mother Courage and Her
Children*, which then transferred to the Grahamstown Festival, South
Africa and Kennedy Center, Washington DC. In the United States his
designs include *Twelfe Night* at Seattle Rep and *Rose Rage* at the Chicago
Shakespeare Theater, which transferred to New York and for which he
was nominated for Best Costume Design at Chicago's Jeff Awards. More
recently he designed the world premieres of Richard Taylor and David
Wood's chamber opera *The Go-Between* at West Yorkshire Playhouse, and
Frank McGuinness's *The Hanging Gardens* at the Abbey Theatre, Dublin.

For dance he designed *Siamese Twins*, a pilot project with The Cure;
Revelations at the Queen Elizabeth Hall; and *Off the Wall* with Liam Steel
and Robert Tannion's Stan Won't Dance company, which relaunched the
Royal Festival Hall in 2007. His designs subsequently represented the UK
at the Prague Quadrennial 2011.

A founder member of Propeller Theatre Company, he has designed nearly
all of their many award-winning, world-touring ensemble Shakespeare
productions. Michael won the Theatre UK's Best Design 2009 for
Propeller's *The Merchant of Venice* and his designs for *Richard III* were
exhibited to critical acclaim at World Stage Design 2013.

For the RSC he designed *The Odyssey*, *The Two Gentlemen of Verona*,
Henry V and *Julius Caesar*; and for the National Theatre, *Edmond*, with
Kenneth Branagh on the Olivier stage.

He lives in London and Northern France and his three children are all
working in the performing arts.

Other titles in this series

SO YOU WANT TO BE A THEATRE DESIGNER?

Michael Pavelka

Foreword by Alison Chitty

NICK HERN BOOKS

London

www.nickhernbooks.co.uk

A Nick Hern Book

SO YOU WANT TO BE A THEATRE DESIGNER?
first published in Great Britain in 2015
by Nick Hern Books Limited
The Glasshouse, 49a Goldhawk Road, London W12 8QP

Copyright © 2015 Michael Pavelka
Foreword copyright © 2015 Alison Chitty

Michael Pavelka has asserted his
moral right to be identified as the author of this work

Cover designed by Peter Bennett
Author photo by Simon Richards

Typeset by Nick Hern Books, London
Printed and bound in Great Britain by
Ashford Colour Press, Gosport, Hampshire

A CIP catalogue record for this book
is available from the British Library

ISBN 978 1 84842 354 1

'Magicians should do their magic to enchant us,
then they should teach us their tricks.'

Augusto Boal

Contents

CONTENTS

Foreword

Theatre designers work from original material, be it written, composed, devised or improvised. Together with the director we interpret the material and design a physical world that frames the action and holds the performers. We must be artists, sculptors, painters and architects. We must be collaborators and negotiators, practical, determined, always keeping a sense of humour.

I have worked all my life in the theatre, starting in repertory theatre in Stoke-on-Trent in the 1970s. I learned my craft with extremely limited resources over the course of eight years. I worked on a great range of plays and documentaries. The work was political and it made sense to me. Stoke is a theatre-in-the-round where the focus is on the actors and what they say; this led me first and foremost to respect the writer and his material and secondly the performers. This philosophy has been the basis of all my work. After Stoke, I was resident designer at the National Theatre for eight years and subsequently I have worked in the UK and all over the world in theatre, opera and film.

Michael Pavelka has also worked all over the world in all forms of theatre and is also an experienced educator, running courses at BA and MA levels. He has written a book that is a comprehensive introduction and guide to the world of the professional theatre designer, a key book for anyone contemplating entering the profession and embarking on a career in theatre design. Before anything else, students of theatre design should read this book, and I wish it had been available for the students of the postgraduate Motley Theatre Design Course, where I was director for twenty years.

However, this is much more than a book for beginners. I would also urge those designers who have already started working to read it to get the benefit of Michael's overview and his many years of experience.

So You Want To Be A Theatre Designer? puts theatre design in its context. It helps us to understand our heritage and where we are in the evolution of the ever-changing and developing art of theatre design. It inspires us to embrace all that is good that has gone before, while encouraging us to look forward, relishing innovation and change where it can enhance the way we tell our stories. There is no single way to design a production. We develop our own ways of working, shaped by our careers, our aesthetics, our values and our passions.

This book is one in a series about making theatre, complementing those written by (and for) directors, producers, writers and others. It will also be very useful for those other practitioners as an introduction to how designers are creative, and to our ways of thinking and working. This should become the standard textbook on the world of the theatre designer. And, above all, it is a very entertaining read!

Alison Chitty

Prologue:
Theatre Design in the Modern Age

In a sense, since the theatre was first produced, there has always been theatre design; although it hasn't always been called that. In fact, the theatre designer, as a distinct role in the making of a show, has only existed for about a hundred and twenty years.

In England, the first buildings specifically constructed for the presentation of plays were 'state-of-the-art' theatres such as the Rose and later the Globe in London's off-limits pleasure district on the South Bank of the Thames. The architecture of the theatre *was* the scenic design and the costumes were often extremely valuable hand-me-downs from wealthy patrons. Stage props were, more often than not, the real thing… but all in all, it must have been a radical, immersive experience giving substance to the fact that the word 'theatre' describes both the art form and the place that it is conceived for.

The most lavish bespoke sets and costumes had been the domain of court masques: for the elite, not the general public. Design for plays really began to flourish when theatre performances moved indoors. The first acknowledged English 'designer' of such events is Inigo Jones, whose early seventeenth-century drawings give us a vivid impression of their scale and sumptuousness. Shakespeare too, mid-career, started to write for stages which were no longer at the mercy of the weather or unruly crowds, and which must have relied on a lesser suspension of disbelief in the actors' surroundings, opening up the possibility of more visual storytelling and so scene-craft.

The development of the court masque in England was ambushed by the Civil War and a Puritan backlash. But with the restoration of the monarchy, and the resurgence of theatregoing later called 'Restoration Drama', a century after Marlowe, Greene and Shakespeare, playhouses began to spring up for the public's entertainment and, with it, theatres modelled on classical buildings, with picture-framed stages and scenic machinery to deliver an array of special effects.

Until the late 1700s, an audience would go to 'hear' a show. By this time, however, theatre productions had become entertaining spectacles as much as a place for listening to stories. Even Shakespeare's plays were being given new treatments to make them a visual as well as a verbal event. Interludes, like variety acts, were shoehorned into the story, allowing for music and dance to play a part in livening up an otherwise well-worn classical text. The theatregoing public demanded more and more lavishly produced shows; particularly in London's expanding West End society. Richard Cumberland, one of many successful pioneers among eighteenth-century showmen, declared in his memoirs of 1806 that the age of going to 'see' a theatre performance had begun and, with it, the beginnings of design as a vital part of the audience's experience:

> ...henceforward, theatres for spectators rather than playhouses for hearers.

For the following hundred more years, the scenic world of a stage show was imagined by theatre producers and crafted by scenic carpenters and painters. They remain the unsung fathers of theatre design, much like the stonemasons and stained-glass makers of medieval churches and cathedrals, who now would be credited with the vision and title of an architect. Theatre designers today still often have a practical skill under their belt, such as prop-making or dressmaking, but that is certainly not an essential requirement since the responsibilities that design brings often outweighs the urge to muck in and get their hands dirty. It's also useful to have a degree of detachment from the making process to be able to make difficult editorial decisions for the sake of getting the production right, rather than insisting on that favourite hat or luscious wall. Designers began to emerge as those craftsmen with more and more editorial control over their work, 'cheek by jowl' with the producers.

With the dawn of the twentieth century came new technologies powered by electricity – this changed everything. Theatre artists could immediately see the potential of controlled electric light, rather than the ambient glow of gas limelight. With the possibilities of lighting instruments that could be focused came a more three-dimensional world on stage, which might cast shadow, look and feel somehow 'real', full of subtlety or strikingly abstract. The more sophisticated manipulation of stage light, in combination with mechanical engineering, could then create dynamic and fantastical worlds of transformation and revelation.

Without doubt, the acknowledged forefathers of design in the modern age are Adolphe Appia and Edward Gordon Craig, although there were, of course, other pioneers, such as the prolific Joseph Urban. They are all, in essence, the first acclaimed theatre designers, although they would just as likely have been called stage decorators at the time. The billing for design on posters between the two world wars, if there was any acknowledgement at all of who might be responsible for how a production looked, would read: 'Decor by…' This implied that the designer dallied around the edges, chose the colours of the soft furnishings, perhaps decided on the position of the doors and left the rest up to the director of the show (themselves often called the 'actor manager' or simply the 'producer', as the term 'director' was also in its infancy). These theatre artists were significant by way of the fact that they had a complete vision for the stage event: crossing or breaking boundaries. Even the more recent 'setting by…' suggests the outmoded notion of a fixed idea.

Edward Gordon Craig, however, had far more to say and do than that. He drew up what has become something of a manifesto for theatre-making that remains valid to this day, a useful checklist of ideas and principles for directors, designers and performers alike. His essay 'On the Art of the Theatre' published in 1911 argues that all the elements on stage should work as a harmonious whole and should knit together words, movement, scenery and sound into a single composition – what we might call today a modernist's 'total theatre'. Craig's starting point was that theatre is, by definition, a stylised art form in contrast to the rigorously naturalistic methods demanded by late-nineteenth-century theatre heavyweights, such as Stanislavsky.

Craig constructed systems and experimented with space using models to create symbolic theatrical worlds that were ahead of his time in that many of his ideas could not yet be realised successfully: it took another half-century or so before they would be. In simple terms, he was both ambitious and innovative in pursuit of his 'vision', a quality shared with all the most influential designers since.

The vibrant, turbulent, twenty-year period of revolutionary art and social movements during the interwar period brought women designers to the foreground. Growing emancipation was echoed in the emergence of brilliant, radical and socially committed architects and interior designers such as Grete Schütte-Lihotzky or Eileen Gray, and the clothes designers Schiaparelli and Chanel. Their work and artistry married form and function in a clean but sensual aesthetic – a model for the future. In post-revolutionary Russia, and for at least a decade, women avant-garde artists were spearheading the radical reappraisal of theatre's role in

Soviet society.[1] So too in British theatre, women were beginning to make a mark on design and on design education that would last through World War Two and into the late-twentieth century – the trio of Margaret Harris, Sophie Harris and Elizabeth Montgomery Wilmot, otherwise known as 'Motley', probably being the most influential.[2]

After the war, the deconstruction and reconstruction of what was the British Empire, and the massive reconfiguration of urban communities around the country, were echoed in the presentation of the world on stage – theatre designers made that drama visible and increasingly dynamic. Advances in affordable electronic technologies, engineering (hydraulics, for example), various synthetic materials and, crucially, an explosion of new architectural ideas all contributed towards designers deconstructing the fabric of stage space and recalibrating it – realising the experiments of Craig, and beyond. The ambitious designs of innovators such as Josef Svoboda (Laterna magika, Prague) set a high benchmark for world scenography, integrating structures, light and projected imagery. Following groundbreaking work by Sean Kenny, whose career and life were cut short but whose legacy was continued by Ralph Koltai (*Metropolis*), Maria Björnson (*The Phantom of the Opera*), John Napier (*Cats, Time, Les Misérables*) and the 'lift and tilt' distortions of Richard Hudson, what became known as the 'designer's theatre', inspired a generation of directors and audiences. British design produced exciting theatrical worlds which drove and transformed a story through stage 'magic', and which were undoubtedly a major factor in the dominance of the British musical in the West End, on Broadway and across the world during the 1980s and '90s.

Meanwhile, whether in the playhouse of the Royal Court, the pioneering architecture of Manchester's Royal Exchange or in Denys Lasdun and Peter Softley's brutal National Theatre building on London's South Bank, designers such as Jocelyn Herbert, John Bury or Alison Chitty pursued a more restrained, minimal and, many would say, refined aesthetic. They captured, simply and powerfully, the disturbing worlds of visionaries such as Samuel Beckett and Harrison Birtwistle that pulled apart the post-war human psyche. They left us with iconic stage images that served the story and defined an era.

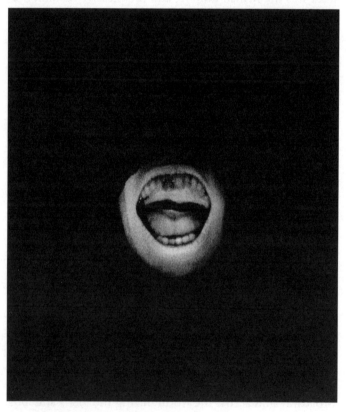

Samuel Becket's *Not I* designed by Jocelyn Herbert.
Photo John Haynes/Lebrecht Music & Arts.

The UK has had its fair share of experimental theatre companies, although they are possibly more likely to have been celebrated in culturally assured mainland Europe, or even further afield, and sit comfortably alongside the likes of Yukio Ninagawa, Peter Stein or Pina Bausch, than in their homeland. Peter Brook found it impossible to stay in England to pursue his grand project of researching and fusing cross-cultural theatrical forms, instead decamping to Paris and teaming up with designer Jean-Guy Lecat to redefine his 'empty space'. Hesitate and Demonstrate, Impact Theatre Company, Forced Entertainment and a host of others have pushed the boundaries of visual theatre-making over the last thirty years or so. Perhaps the most prolific of these has been Complicite, whose founder and leading light, Simon McBurney, would never consider himself a designer but continues to produce some of the most inventive and arresting images of recent times. Likewise, Lloyd Newson and his company DV8 push the envelope of physicality and spatial illusion. Both mix a fascinating and powerful cocktail of traditional forms and up-to-the-minute visual media.

We are now in a digital whirlwind. The best contemporary designers scoop up their legacy and, using everything at their disposal, are constantly playful, artful, and wistfully reflect on our post-postmodern lives. Theatricality infiltrates everything and everywhere. No one can count on being safely tucked up in a theatre balcony expecting to be spoon-fed a play... Everything is an 'experience'. Directors, choreographers and designers now have to be aware that their work will be seen across a range of media and spaces other than those of the spoken word, aria or movement in an auditorium. Theatre-makers now work across all platforms: stage, screen and virtual environment. The universe of scenography is expanding each day, and determined stage designers are up for it.

PART ONE

What is Contemporary Theatre Design?

1

Theatre Design or Scenography?

Increasingly, British and American theatre designers are also describing themselves as 'scenographers', although the word still doesn't sit comfortably in the profession and remains tinged with academic or at least overly conceptual ways of approaching theatrical ideas and production. On continental mainland Europe, theatre design *is* scenography: the term is more widely and comfortably used, so it can be defined lucidly by theatre-makers on the job in the context of a noun or verb.

Its origins are in mid-seventeenth-century France: *scénographie*. That word evolved via Latin, which, in turn, came from the Greek *skēnographia* ('scene-painting', or the art of portraying objects or scenes in perspective). Of course, scene-painting has a far longer tradition than theatre design. Many a designer honed their skills doing just that, Jocelyn Herbert for one, but the dictionary definition goes only a small way to describing the scope of scenographic practice – particularly in a contemporary context – which is probably why it is an unstable word in a continual state of flux.

Pamela Howard's book *What is Scenography?* is an excellent way for you to start unpicking the language of scenography and give you some real substance to hang your opinions on. Everyone has a nuanced definition of his or her own, and through making work you, the reader, will have yours. In the main, as a designer, I avoid using the term on a daily basis as it tends to create a twinge of panic in directors (because they might perhaps think you're stomping through their intellectual space), in a design team (because it smacks of pulling rank and could sound pretentious/competitive) or to technicians (because they probably don't care what you *call* what you do... and they're probably right!).[3]

If, by the time you're a designer in the field, you are asked by family or friends, '...and what do you do?' I challenge you to say, 'I'm a scenographer.' Watch their eyes glaze over, and then breathe a sigh of relief when they realise, or you mercifully tell them, that it means you're a theatre designer. My advice is to use the label that a non-specialist recognises and you'll have a far easier and rewarding conversation. Chiefly, you're unlikely to argue the toss about all this unless you're in a scholarly situation, in which case you may (or may not) find the following passage useful. I'll attempt to describe how, in my view, the two terms jostle for position in the knowledge that as soon as I do, there will be a hundred more alternatives from others, and probably ten from myself before long; but here goes:

Scenography describes a context in which theatre can be made, and hints at a method of achieving it. This can be applied to a full range of phenomenological circumstances, from grand opera to making a meal at home in your kitchen; the scenography itself is not theatrical until it's presented as such. If, as spectators, we're focused on any such mundane action through the 'lens' of theatrical representation, scenography will have captured and shaped the moment.

Theatre design puts the human need of storytelling first. A theatre designer's craft is to position the audience's visual and spatial relationship to the actors, singers or dancers who are central to the narrative. If the furniture designer Charles Eames' definition of design is close to the mark, that it's 'a plan for arranging elements in such a way as best to accomplish a particular purpose', then 'theatre design', in performance terms, 'does what it says on the tin'.

Scenography is a set of circumstances; theatre design shapes them. Both terms harmonise, or at least overlap, through making things. What we do in our profession is, above all, tested using practical methods, in tangible (even if virtual) spaces, with real people. We make, reflect, and make again, collaboratively. Josef Svoboda uses a rather more holistic term for the aim of the activity itself, rather than the means by which we get there:

> We don't promote any [particular] artistic discipline. We synthesise, that is we choose the artistic principle that corresponds to our theatrical concept... priority on stage belongs to the '*theatrician*' and only then to the designer.

In the UK, theatre designers will usually design all the visual aspects of a production: settings, properties and costumes. Designers abroad will usually specialise in one or two of these elements. Occasionally, European or North American designers might couple both set and lighting design, and in doing so may be more comfortable with the defining themselves as the production's scenographer. For the purposes of staking out what a designer has responsibility for in each of these distinct but integrated disciplines, there now follows a thumbnail sketch of the principle elements of theatre design and what designers usually focus on when tackling their particular challenges. The checklist for each area is unpacked more fully in later chapters, but it's worth saying here in the first instance that in each case the specialist designer needs to have a general appreciation of literature, visual culture and contemporary social concerns.

2

Set and Prop Design

Scenic design usually involves creating and harmonising both the space and the objects within it. It invariably means that designers in this area have to be most acutely aware of the form and function of both architecture and product design in all its variations. Composition (incorporating aesthetics), as a primary aspect of design, underpins the arrangement of all things in both a conceptual and physical frame. Like all practical subjects, knowledge of a range of materials is important, although it's also crucial that an appreciation of a material's properties doesn't constrain a good idea – but rather supports or enhances it.

Set design used to be underpinned by needing to know a range of construction and treatment techniques that 'faked' the real thing. This was chiefly for reasons of budget or transportability. While it's always useful to make your designs as practical as possible in a range of circumstances, such as touring, the fact is that the relatively lower cost of materials today such as steel, aluminium and its fabrication has liberated the designer from 'artifice'. Special effects can now be used for particular purposes and are usually 'read' by the audience as a layer of theatricality in a world of more familiar actual structures and objects.

Drawing practice is essential – it is a way of making your thoughts material that also helps you look, plan and communicate. Obviously drawing spaces is paramount both in terms of measurable accuracy (technical drawing) and offering an impression for fellow theatre-makers (imaginative and observational drawing). The combination of these is drawing in one- or two-point perspective, which is useful, but something of a dying art as software now makes such views, and the ability to fly through them, increasingly easy. It's always useful to know what the computer is doing with your data, however, so learning the rudiments by hand gives your use of computers an authority when your design leaves the screen and becomes real, full-scale and in need of adjustment with the naked eye as the audience will see it. Drawing a sequence of moments in a narrative (storyboarding) is also important – you can do this by mimicking the artistry of a graphic novel or strip cartoon, or maybe taking it to a further level with slide shows, animatics and animations.

Architecture is often misleadingly thought of as being the design of structures and partitions for bodies to inhabit, rather than framing the air around people: actors and audiences are no different. Manipulating spaces and rudimentary ergonomics are essential to the set and property designer. Although drawing in a technical scale is key to accurate design, the human scale of the work is fundamental. Stage designers cannot afford to forget that storytelling is a primal, human activity and that the audience will probably need to be focused on that ninety per cent of the time. Performers have to feel supported both physically and conceptually in order to be able to do their work, and inappropriately distracting design can be counterproductive to the quality of a complete theatrical experience.

Having said that, there are always exceptions: an obvious one is the overture or entr'acte of an opera. These often lengthy passages of music introduce themes and motifs that will leave plenty of scope for the designer and director to make a string of rolling powerful visual statements. The music fills the space and immerses the audience with sensations that can be more extravagantly matched by movement and design. Other specialist considerations can impact on design, such as the classical ballet's need for plenty of floor space with the design chiefly providing a context for the dance, around and above the space.

But, by and large, a chair is a chair, and if the designer has not taken into account that it has to be able to get on stage by fitting through a door, to be light enough to be carried by a performer whilst acting, and to be the right height to comfortably sit on (e.g. the length of the lower part of the human leg), then the story could be compromised, and the design will be noticed for all the wrong reasons.

Top tip: *Never underestimate the power of domestic detail – the smallest everyday object aptly chosen and perfectly placed, either singularly or repeated to make huge visual impact, can echo William Blake's poetic maxim of helping the audience 'see a world in a grain of sand'.*

Set- and prop-design reference checklist:

- Architecture.

- Painting.

- Sculpture.

- Geometrical drawing.

- Observational drawing.

- Storyboarding.

- Interior design including furniture and other domestic objects.

3

Costume Design

In many respects, a costume designer's process is similar to an actor's in rehearsal. It starts with the text and looking for clues in the writing that help build depth to the characterisation when brought to life on stage. Sometimes that can be what the character themselves says and sometimes what other characters say about them. The most common and simplistic mistake that design can make is to *describe* the character, leaving no scope for the actor or, worse, 'telegraphing' what the character is about to play out. For example, whether we previously know the story of *Macbeth* or not, why would he be dressed in anything signalling his slide into evil (e.g. black leather) before he gets there – we wouldn't need the three witches' prophecy in Act One for a start! Other sins include upstaging a performance with an outrageously flamboyant shape or colour that overwhelms both actor and character. All this sounds like a recipe for tame naturalism at best and mundane sloppiness at worst, but the job of the costume designer for drama is to take the recognisable and shape it into a convincing *context* for the story.

Actors sometimes have a temptation to invent a backstory for their character that has no substance in the author's writing. The deeper these intricate inventions pervade the actor's 'method', the harder it is for the costume designer (and indeed often the director) to track and respond to. Quite often, however convoluted the path an actor takes, it will rightly lead them back to the face-value story, so both patience and diplomacy are high on a successful costume designer's credentials en route. Whether it's the designer or the actor who runs away with their own ideas about the text, the best policy is a transparent process of show 'n' tell so that ideas have the best chance of coming together and a third, collectively made, idea can surface.

Jocelyn Herbert's costume design for Dandy Nichols as Marjorie in *Home* at the National Theatre.

The continually shifting impression of a costume on stage is fascinating and exciting. Actors use clothes in unexpected ways, and lighting can change a material from a dull sack to vibrant couture.

When embarking on a project, an early question might be whether you will be designing what are essentially regarded as 'clothes' or what could be more aptly termed 'costumes'. Of course, under presentational stage conditions, clothes philosophically become costumes, so the definition may describe the designer's *attitude* to realising the work, rather than the product itself. Likewise, if the framing of a production is convincing to the eye and mind, costumes can become accepted as the character's clothes for an hour or two. The reality is that often these decisions are shaped by budget: shopping is often far less costly than making from scratch, while hiring falls somewhere in between the two depending on how long the production will run for. There is no doubt that, usually, the costume designer's preferred choice is to have full control of the fabrics and cut – to fully realise a drawn idea within a fully considered idea.

Like the set designer's need to keep the story moving through a sequence of changing spaces, so the costume designer has to be aware of the journey a character makes through the arc of the narrative. This may result in the character making a gear-change, literally and metaphorically, as their story develops. For example, clothes may have to go through a process of ageing as stage time 'fast-forwards' over months or years, or 'jump-cuts' in film. Also, as with set design, there is a tussle between imagining a big concept or scheme for the world of the play, and the logic of individual parts. One of the earliest decisions the creative team can make is whether the production can be framed by and exist within an overall colour palette or historical period. Sometimes a tightly designed aesthetic is very satisfying for the audience to 'buy in to' and on other occasions it can be seen as overbearing and overblown. The truth is that this may not be revealed until it is too late and all you can do is put it down to experience. The main thing is that, collaboratively with the actors, everyone has pursued their 'look' with the same purpose and that the costume idea will be robust enough to sustain the shifts a performer might make in the development of a role.

The extremities of the body are crucial for an actor. Heads, hands and feet frame an actor's physical presence and are critical not only to the power of their silhouette in a theatrical image, but are also a key to defining their gestures and posture. This in turn comments on what they say as a character or influence how they feel as a performer in the act of performance. For these reasons, decisions about how to deal with the design of such elements have to be carried out with great precision and sensitivity on behalf of the designer and costume-maker: always ensuring that everyone involved in the process understands each other's concerns every step of the way.

Starting from the top down, hats for actors will often serve the function of helping to establish their character's social status. Once the hat has achieved that task, however, usually after a matter of minutes, if not seconds, the hat can outstay its purpose and therefore its welcome. Hats and lighting are not comfortable bedfellows – brims can cause shadows across the face, so try to be aware of their sustainability in performance. An artful design and a skilled milliner can overcome most technical hat-related obstacles, but, if not, the hat can often be reduced to completing the costume's authentic look for the moment of an entrance or the silhouette of an exit, and otherwise either carried or hung up somewhere. Scenically, hats can be useful to establish codes of etiquette, culture or transitions but, because of their close proximity to the eyes, they need to mould to the actor's persona unlike some other items of clothing.

For the actor, director and others, practical factors soon kick in: 'Is it secure when I'm dancing?' 'Is it "upstaging" someone else in the scene?' 'If I take it off, can I put it back on in the scene easily?' Another useful function of hats is to describe, with no need for scenic effects, whether the scene is set in an interior or exterior space, and what the weather's like. But again, once that is established for the audience, questions about the hats' dramatic validity may soon emerge, usually at the technical rehearsal.

Wigs and facial hair, being an extension of the body, carry all the same considerations of a hat but, because they are often fixed there (usually with glue), have to be approached with double the attentiveness to the actor. They can be fiddly to arrange and uncomfortable to wear – so it has to be worth the trouble. A designer might draw an impression of the character assuming a wig is needed but finally discover, through negotiation and clever hairstyling, that the disadvantages of a wig can be outweighed by the advantages of actor-security and a more natural look. Wigs have the ability to subtly morph an actor's appearance, enhance their beauty or subvert it. Alternatively they can transport a drama into another epoch, change an actor's gender, or through extreme exaggeration, transform the genre of a production from a simple play to, for example, a pantomime.

Good wigs are understandably expensive and, with other qualities of wig, you usually get what you pay for! Not only are they extraordinarily time-consuming to make, the decision to use them for a run of performances also carries an inevitable maintenance issue, in that once the wig's style is achieved, it will probably have to be reset every night by someone who is properly trained. Actors occasionally feel confident enough to do this themselves, and a few might prefer to, but this sort of multitasking increasingly belongs to a bygone age of performers being more technically self-contained and perhaps less designer-dependent on their overall appearance.

Glove-makers are now a rarity. Bespoke gloves, like many time-consuming specialist objects, are relatively expensive in comparison to shop-bought. Vintage sourcing for gloves is almost impossible, as originals have usually taken too much wear and tear, plus the fact that, because of better health over the last century, people's bodies, and particularly women's hands and feet, have got bigger. There are online companies that supply theatre-costume basics, including gloves, corsets and so forth, but, for a designer, there is nothing like revelling in the expertise and craft of a top-class milliner, glove- or shoemaker.

Gloves, like hats, establish and complete a character's image – they also make technical demands of an actor: their ease of putting on and taking off, either onstage or making a quick change in the wings. Gloves are particularly challenging for actor-musicians, as good manual grip is, of course, fundamental to the playing of many instruments. There are some costumes that just can't be conceived without the inclusion of gloves, from a burlesque dancer to, say, a welder in a factory, but again, actors may be keen to keep their options open when playing a scene and discard them in a pocket or bag as part of the action.

For some actors, the shoes are often the most important part their costume. Shoes are the actor's most direct connection to the set, can support or even model the way they move and bookend their body, counterpointing, complementing or distracting from figure, head and speech. To help with all this, actors, particularly those of an older generation,[4] will occasionally be very keen to use shoes that they are familiar with, have broken in or simply want to use their own. Designers have to be sensitive to this and reassure the actor that if all their needs and fears are taken into account, the design's cohesion is, thereafter, paramount. There is also a safety issue here in that actors have to be secure in their footing and, at least in the early stages of a production, scenery contributes to an unfamiliar and potentially hazardous environment. It may be that both designer and costume supervisor have to make doubly sure that the actor has their new shoes in rehearsal as soon as possible, and therefore well in advance of having to confront all the other demands of being on stage in front of an audience – particularly if they also will have to cope with a raked (sloping) or uneven floor on your set.

Top tip: *Be prepared to make more detailed separate drawings for these separate elements, or at least find clear visual references for them. This gives you a far more informed starting point for discussion: signalling to an actor, costume supervisor, maker, and ultimately the director, that you have thought it through.*

Costume-design reference checklist:

- History of fashion.

- Painting and portraiture.

- Soft sculpture.

- Knowledge of the properties of textiles.

- An appreciation of pattern-cutting.

- Observational drawing.

4

Masks and Make-Up

Masks have an ancient role and significance in many types of performance, stretching back to 'prehistory'. They have often been regarded as an essentially non-European phenomenon, with the exception of the occasional and frivolous use of half- and full masks in various carnivals. There is, though, in Europe too, a darker shamanistic history of the use of masks in pre-Christian rituals: chiefly celebrating annual cycles, sabbats and changes of seasonal weather. In terms of dramatic narrative, however, *commedia dell'arte*, a cornerstone of Western European theatre culture, uses masks extensively in the portrayal of archetypes that confirmed familiar and recognisable domestic character traits, rather than the modern tendency of masks representing 'otherness'.

In the first half of the twentieth century, masks enjoyed something of a comeback in the theatre, a possible trigger for this being greater access to hitherto impenetrable cultures, such as those of Japan and Africa. This resurgence was brought into the public's consciousness through the early work of Picasso's 'African Period' paintings[5] and later designs for the stage. Edward Gordon Craig speculated on notions of transforming actors into automata to suppress the performer's urge to 'feel' the part, so he surmised, compromising theatre's conceptual integrity: these Über-marionettes[6] thereby handing ultimate control to the director. Brecht dabbled with the use of masks to distance the audience and demonstrate un-naturalistic dual reality,[7] and Oskar Schlemmer's designs for Bauhaus events[8] 'masked' and extended the entire body based on geometrical formulae, without any obvious metaphorical meaning: changing the figure from a vehicle for narrative, to one of pure composition, tension and kinesis.

This legacy gives theatre designers and directors a diverse 'language' of a mask's purpose and meaning in relation to other theatrical conventions in use today. Drawing on *commedia*'s prescribed 'family' of characters, some that should be masked and others that should not, along with the purpose of Greek mask unifying the chorus as a social group ('the people'), creative teams should feel they can continue to reinvent these traditions of striking theatrical storytelling for either classical or contemporary subjects.

Outside of ballet, however, the power of masks is quite rightly treated with caution. Obvious exemptions to this are revivals of the Greek dramas themselves – Peter Hall with, at first, Jocelyn Herbert, and then later Alison Chitty, on the National Theatre's aptly shaped, epic, Olivier arena stage spring to mind. Hall was also responsible for a notable example in modern drama with his stage adaptation of Orwell's *Animal Farm*. Julie Taymor's designs for *The Lion King* have gone some way to successfully popularising the mask in commercial musical theatre; although the anthropomorphic nature of the subject leant itself to their obvious use. She has, however, established herself as perhaps the west's greatest exponent of applying mask work and imagery to all manner of subjects, including her extraordinary interpretations of Shakespearean tragedy.

Nowadays, with the increasing popularity of theatre festivals that attract companies from across the globe, there are many opportunities to see masks in action, and like forms of movement (Butoh, for example), puppetry (Bunraku, for example), and other musical forms (Beijing Opera, for example, or kabuki), the temptation can be to appropriate their appearance, rather than inhabit their ethos. So theatre designers and directors must beware the extraordinary technical, if not cultural, immersion an actor has to undergo to even begin to use any mask effectively, and before being seduced by its 'exotic' imagery.

Mask-making checklist:

- Masks should add to, and not distract from, the performance.
- Keep weight to a minimum.
- Ensure a comfortable fit.
- Be mindful of not hampering an actor's ability to see, hear, speak or sing clearly.

Make-up is, of course, closely connected to masks as it is used to enhance, or even transform, an actor's appearance: in essence, it is, and can have, a 'special effect'. Make-up can also be used in conjunction with a mask to extend its decoration or blend it into the flesh tones of the face. In this regard, then, make-up can bridge the gap between a mask and a prosthetic, or a wig/facial hair, and the skin. Actors have often had some training and practice in doing their own make-up or even prosthetics (such as false noses, scars and tattoos), but this will vary from person to person. The designer will, at some point in a production process, be needed to step in and coordinate a consistent approach to make-up and clarify its particular use or effect in a project. It may be necessary to bring a specialist make-up designer into a project to work closely with, particularly, the costume designer and, again if appropriate, a specialist wig designer. The more fantastical worlds of, say, *Cats* or *Starlight Express* are obvious examples whereby additional expert knowledge and creative input could be welcome.

Though make-up is, of course, less rigid than a mask, both materially and conceptually, a designer's discussions with an actor about its pros and cons can be very similar. Fundamental questions include: '*Are we using it for a naturalistic or stylised effect?*' '*Do we want the audience, therefore, to notice it or not?*' '*How might the design's prevailing physical conditions; the audience's proximity, the lighting, etc., affect how we intend to use make up?*' Practical considerations might include: '*If the performance action is very physical, is sweat or smudging likely to be a factor?*' '*What if it gets on the clothes – can we clean them?*' Then, there might also be a discussion, firstly with the director and then the actors, about an authentic 'period look' if you are designing a historical piece – and by 'historical', I mean anything from Restoration Comedy to punk.

Whatever the extent of its use, a designer should have an opinion about make-up's contribution to the production. Often, the great detail required in a designer's drawing of make-up is such that finding some other form of reference, from a book or the internet, is more useful. As I've already mentioned, a designer's role is also to have an overview and coordinate what can become an eclectic mix of influences: particularly when actors make their own suggestions, bring in photographs or offer you clippings of images from magazines. Actors often, and understandably so, simply want to look their best, but their interpretation of what that actually means in the context of your design concept may cause some friction. This, as in every collaborative art, is where your prowess as a diplomat and communicator plays a vital role. You must take on board both an actor's vulnerability and the fact that they know their body better than anyone else: *has your design really embraced who they are as people first, and dramatic character second?* If not, it may be time to take another look at that costume drawing you made before the start of rehearsal!

5

Design for Opera:
Music, Voice and Image

What's so special about opera?

> All art constantly aspires to the condition of music.
>
> *Walter Pater, essayist, aesthete and critic*

Design for opera needs to be… well, what could be plainer: *operatic!* If you want to pursue a career as an opera designer it's simply not going to happen unless you absolutely *love* music. Music and the voice are the beginning and end of the form; design, direction, lighting and even acting are, finally, subordinate.[9] The orchestra and performers, under the leadership of the conductor, produce audible volume, while the designer has to fill spatial volume – they have to match each other and both are immense. Designers aspire to the 'grand gesture': a broad brushstroke of a statement that may look overstated on paper until coupled with the reality of full orchestral sound and singers who possess an unbelievable inner jet-propulsion. Its demands are colossal, but so too are its rewards. Opera always was the perfect vehicle for 'designer theatre', given the extreme abstract and stylistic nature of its conventions – here staged naturalism is most certainly surplus to requirements. Echoing Pater's words, here's an opera designer's view:

> Having the music to respond to is the most incredible thing. You never have to think about colour – the music just gives it to you.
>
> *Ashley Martin-Davis, designer*

In opera, everything about both the design process and the result is longer, larger and more expensive. The planning of operas takes years, not weeks or months, so the opera designer's time on the job is stretched to six, seven or more times than for a designer of, for example, a play at even the largest UK theatres, such as the National or the Royal Shakespeare Company. There are a number of understandable reasons for this state of affairs, many of them logistical but some that lie deeper, in respect of and for its weighty history.

Opera is a world art form, not unlike ballet. You don't just work in one country, or one continent; you work in *the world*. Opera's domain is surprisingly and paradoxically small, but you are nevertheless working on a world stage for a worldly audience. The design process is tricky because, like most theatre design, you want to be true both to yourself and the work by not being influenced by other productions, but it's no good being naive and not acknowledging what has previously happened elsewhere – you have to be in control of what *you* are doing. The opera 'community' is tightly knit and they are also therefore familiar with each other's work, talk to each other a lot with a common language and understand what's current – to some extent jostling and influencing each other.

Opera productions have a far longer gestation period because generally everyone's dealing with a large project and the money issues are bigger. Designers tend to have substantial but not, relatively speaking, more generous budgets than, say, West End musicals. There are other complications; for example, fitting comfortably into a season of other opera productions in repertoire and in the same theatre space. Opera companies want the design delivered a long way in advance to gauge the feasibility of how to achieve it in the context of a programme of work. The scale white-card model or maquette of the set design is vital to show your concept to the company through the critical eyes and mind of the theatre's intendant (the general director of the opera house), and there then follows all the long-winded process of costing and budgeting before you can get on with the final design. Opera theatre spaces are usually far bigger than that of drama (perhaps twice the size, up to 2,500 or more seats), unless you're designing an experimental premiere in a 'festival' environment, for example. A lot is expected of you from the intendant, who will want a design embracing that notion of the 'grand gesture'.

Putting an opera design together

Perhaps the major difference between designing a drama and an opera is that the music makes you design very much with time in mind: the scenery has to fit dynamically with the timing of the music's overtures, entr'actes and phrases. With a play it's possible to extend transitional moments by slowing down, speeding up or even adding dialogue or 'stage business' to make that change as long as dramatically sustainable. Opera designers understand that the key to an effective and practical design is that you discipline yourself to sit with the model and listen to the music, working out in your mind whether it's possible within that time frame. A huge advantage that opera has over designing a scripted play is that you have the recording – you have the libretto and the music score in front of you and then you actually have it sung to you! If ever you get stuck, you can listen again and again for inspiration. It's not crucial that the designer can read music, but it certainly helps.

Opera designers and directors spend much more time conceptually envisioning not just the scenic locations but also the detail of every dramatic moment. Some directors want to almost 'block' (plan) all the singer's moves in relation to the scenic space in model form with the designer before rehearsals, partly because many principal singers' availabilities are restricted (they move from role to role, travelling sometimes fleetingly between opera houses). Pre-planning is often therefore a very exacting process for the director, more than for a Shakespeare play, for example, when the creative team can usually give themselves both a more fluid scenic space and a more sustained creative process to explore its potential, much of which will unfold in rehearsals with the actors over a number of weeks, not days.

Planning the design involves taking on board more opinions than for drama – the creative team can extend to six or seven, each with their own disciplines and perspectives. There are at least three of you at the beginning of the process, a designer, director and conductor – and sometimes four if you include a choreographer. Design itself is frequently subdivided between set and costume, and direction can also include not only a choreographer, but also a fight director and the theatre's staff directors. The conductor is a key player for all involved, very often having had many previous experiences of tackling a particular opera (or at least other works by the same composer), while the lighting designer will make a huge contribution later in the process… and then, of course, there's the intendant of the theatre.

You will have to present your concept in its early stages to the company's intendant, and they have power of veto. They have an oversight of the previous productions of that opera at their theatre and are quite within their rights to demand a redesign because, for example, your plans look strikingly similar to something they've produced before, or indeed similar to a production in another opera house. They have, after all, hired you to invent something new (although perhaps not too alarmingly radical!). Sometimes their productions will have been repeated over many years and so a design from say, forty years ago, can be current and in conflict with your own new production. It's therefore very important that when you are undertaking the first stages of the design process, you know as much about the agenda for

that company and as many of the other renowned productions of that opera as is possible, both recent (say, in the last
ten years) and not so recent. You have to know where to
'place' your production in relation to what's happening in
today's opera scene. If you want to be an opera designer,
you'll need to be a total fanatic.

At the first and critical design presentation you may or may
not be accompanied by your director – in either case, it's
your job to sell your creative team's vision for the piece to
the opera company in as powerful and convincing a way as
possible. To argue your point to the best of your ability it's
crucial that you are super-organised – for example, showing a complete photo storyboard of the whole model in the
form of a PowerPoint presentation along with the physical
model itself.

Whatever the production budget, it's always wise not to let
that shape what you do artistically.[10] If through your presentation you convince the intendant that you and your
director have an extraordinary vision for the opera, so that
they completely believe in what you want to do, an artistic
case can override a financial one, and more money just may
be found to realise your work.

Then there's the orchestra – they are a powerful (unionised)
group and have an influence on design decisions. Designers
have to respect the orchestra's artistic and physical space: the
orchestra pit. If you want to build out anything over or
around the pit, you have to go through many channels to get
that to happen, and you can expect the orchestra to be very
resistant to design decisions that might disrupt their traditional relationship to the stage, the singers, and the
audience. More radical design decisions, such as putting the
orchestra onstage, obviously changes both the orchestra's
spatial and aural relationships with all concerned. For example, in big opera houses the distance between the front of the
stage and the first-row seats can be immense. Designers will

frequently try to bridge the yawning gap between audience and singer which, of course, means closing over the part of the orchestra pit. Progress is negotiated through both the conductor and the particular opera house's resident head of orchestra, and it's obviously of prime importance to have the conductor on your side. Unconventional decisions have to be argued for and a compelling case put forward that has the good of the production foregrounded to avoid the accusation of gratuitous design.

The best conductors are very much involved with the director's rehearsal process and are also really interested in the designer's visual response to the music through the connectedness of tone, shape and colour. They will also be experienced in the practicalities of singers and singing, the performer's physical relationship and view of the conductor at critical moments in an aria, and their relationship with the mass of chorus. They may also advise on architectural acoustics – both of the building and the impact your design has in it. Acoustics is not an exact science but designers have to be aware of certain dos and don'ts that are partly addressed through an accumulation of experience (including, of course, the errors) and common sense. The voice travels roughly in straight lines and will project and reflect like light, so it stands to reason that if you have gaping spaces in your design, particularly at the sides of the stage, the voice could disappear into them to be lost for ever from the ears of the audience. Heavy, textured drapery will absorb the voice (as it will light) and muffle it. Sometimes you'll get strange surprises – acoustics can be a minefield of anomalies. A performer can stand in a particular position where their voice will reverberate or echo and no one can put their finger on why. The voice requires a 'springboard', or at least to not be impeded; a hard surface behind the singers will usually help.[11]

In the production week, i.e. the last remaining rehearsals on stage before opening, over the course of any one day you may be sharing stage time with an evening performance of an opera currently in rep. This is so the opera house doesn't lose revenue and the resident performers, for example the orchestra and chorus, are fully occupied.[12] This means that your set design will have to come down midway through the afternoon in order for the technical crew to reinstate the evening's scenery. The knock-on effect is that these rehearsals can be dense and intense so as to achieve more in less time than drama, and, once again, they contribute to opera's time and expense. This, in what is usually a continuously intensive production period for drama productions, is often therefore fragmented in opera productions and can span weeks rather than days.

When designing a brand-new opera, the creative journey is far more open and in that sense more like designing a play. It's also a great adventure musically, in that all you are likely to have to work with, as you try to conceive of your design, is a voice and piano accompaniment.

> Nobody's ever heard it before; nobody knows what it actually *is* yet, and you're trying to unravel it. The most exciting moment is when you hear the full orchestra play it for the first time (only when your design is already in front of you on stage) – it's an absolute revelation… a 'So *that's* what it is!' moment.
>
> *Ashley Martin-Davis, designer*

Surtitles in the language native to the opera house can be a blessing for those who need to follow the nuances of the narrative, but also, on occasion, a trap for conceptual creative teams. I recall director Deborah Warner's mid-1990s *Don Giovanni* at Glyndebourne, designed by Hildegard Bechtler (set designer) and Sue Blane (costume designer), presenting us with a striking image of the Last Supper complete with the breaking of bread and the sipping of wine, only for it to be undermined by descriptions of other foodstuffs running across the top of the proscenium – it's not that I couldn't appreciate the staging's metaphor, it's just that Mozart's dead – can't we change the rules?

Operatic ritual has it that on opening night the designer is afforded the opportunity to take a bow with the director and conductor. This can be either wonderfully celebratory or embarrassing, depending on your constitution and whether the audience is armed with a barrage of boos (paradoxically acknowledged by some as a sign of approval) or cheers.

Opera design is not for the faint-hearted: it requires stamina in the process and bravado in its execution. If, however, you enjoy a somewhat nomadic lifestyle and your aesthetic lends itself to metaphor or abstraction, the strangeness and power of the form consistently offers designers the chance to let their inner artistic ambitions free. It's no wonder that so many eminent painters have had a crack at it!

What do opera singers need?

Opera singers are in many respects a breed apart – it's staggering what they can do with the human voice; and the fact that they cope with a multitude of languages, are on the move from country to country and have to keep in top condition vocally, puts design and designers in a respectful place. Opera allows for visual statements on an epic scale to take flight, and costuming is a major part of that. Large opera companies often have a resident chorus that can even be augmented from project to project. This mass of performers offers a fantastic opportunity to paint flowing pictures on stage with the movement of costumes. The chorus also lends the costume designer the chance to help create a whole community from which the story unfolds, so designing both a unity and particularity for the group can give clarity, believability and integrity to the central narrative, matching their volume (both physically and audibly) with a bold visual identity.

The big difference with singers is that they are fascinated by the idea of doing another production of, say, *Carmen*, in yet another different way, having already done twelve productions of *Carmen* in twelve different ways beforehand. Actors, on the other hand, are usually doing the role for the first time, and that's sufficient a journey of discovery in itself.

Singers come with quite a lot of baggage: they know the pitfalls and they know what works – but on the whole they're very generous and 'game'. They really can walk a tightrope and sing at the same time! They very much like to be directed because they are really concentrating on the technique of singing. They're like athletes in their dealing with the voice, because the voice rules, so they quite like working within a clear framework created by the director and designer.

In the main, opera singers are very tolerant of grand designs. They will often scale impossible sets and wear the strangest of costume creations in an effort to be part of an extraordinary visual and aural experience. They tend to be less concerned with a 'backstory' to their character than an actor in a drama: concentrating their efforts on being true to the composer's and librettist's intentions, and working closely with the orchestra's conductor to this end. Sometimes even the director can be of secondary importance to this goal, and the visual concepts of the production may also weigh less heavily on their part. Singers, though, do need to know that their costume will allow them to do what they do best – sing. If they can do that, they will feel confident that they can match any image a costume designer will fling at them. This means in practical terms that their throat area has to be kept free and that the torso (the diaphragm and lungs to be precise) is allowed the space to move, expand or contract comfortably. This, though, doesn't always mean a loose cut: some singers like to physically 'push against' their clothing, even a corset. Again, hats should be accessorised with caution, as with drama but for different reasons. The whole head contributes to the tone and impact of the human voice, so covering it in fabric may alter the skull's characteristics as a natural amplifier. Like any artist, they need to have full control of the tools of their trade, so talking about their individual technical preferences is vital.

The cliché of the opera singer's silhouette is that they are big... sometimes very big. This is increasingly not the case, so you will find the variety of body shapes and sizes is unpredictable. For this reason, although it's always good practice anyway, knowing who is cast in a role will be crucial as you conceive the costume for them. It's no good hanging on to your mind's-eye wish for a sylph-like Lady Macbeth if the singer is clearly not! Bodies are the canvas on which to paint your ideas, and their characteristics are a given reality to be embraced (metaphorically, of course!). That is not to say that a costume and wig cannot transform someone from the everyday to the operatic, indeed they must, but knowing your material is key to a successful result that everyone will be happy with. This is often tricky given the preparation time for opera, so designs may have to change deep into your design process. Operas can also find their way into a company's repertoire over a number of years, sometimes decades, so the original production's design will have to adapt to cast changes and possibly need a radical technical costume redesign.

Top tip: *Understandably, opera and musical-theatre singers' necks expand after their warm-up and during a show, so collar shapes and sizes are vital to their comfort.*

Opera terms during final rehearsals

Opera has a unique technical language that everyone, no matter what their nationality, will understand. Here are some key terms:

Bauprobe: A rehearsal session at which the set designer, lighting designer and production manager can see the set's moving parts under stage light – to test that any transitions will work with the score in real time.

Sitzprobe (*prova all'italiana*): A rehearsal session at which the singers sing with the orchestra, with the focus on integrating the two groups. It is often the first rehearsal whereby the orchestra and singers rehearse together.

Stage and orchestra: These are final rehearsal sessions on stage in the production week which are dedicated to the conductor, orchestral players and singers. The director and designer can step back for these sessions.

Stage and piano: These are final rehearsal sessions on stage in the production week which are dedicated to the director, design team and singers. The conductor may be present but not the orchestra.

[Note: For more theatrical terms, see the glossary at the end of this book.]

6

Design for Dance:
Space, Body and Image

Design and dance were made for each other. Dance is at once both primal and disciplined, which is echoed by a designer's response to it. The experience of seeing dance is highly visceral and, when at its best, exquisitely inventive. The dance-design symbiosis demands that there is nothing spare: shifting shapes, compositions and rhythms compound to form a visual language to which a designer can make a dynamic contribution in collaboration with a choreographer and dancers. By interpreting human movement into design, a visual artist can introduce objects into spaces that prompt or sometimes interestingly resist and challenge dance movement. Design can create both a physical playground for performance and add a metaphorical layer to the work as a whole.

Designers in this field don't need to be able to read dance notation or 'dance score', as might be useful for a designer of opera to read music. There are many different systems of dance notation and any one of them is evidence of how visual the art form is. Many choreographers have their own way of making notes, both in preparation for and during the rehearsal process. Some choreographers make extraordinary drawings, and their notebooks are a graphic wonderland of images, marks and maps.

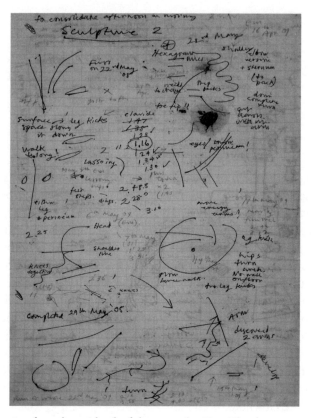

Notation from the notebook of choreographer Tony Thatcher.

This drawing by Tony Thatcher gives the impression of a cross between García Lorca's surreal poetic, figurative graphic work (he also being a director) and the chalkboard of Niels Bohr – it's both enigmatic and pragmatic.

Designers should devote some time to drawing dancers as they work in order to study the human body in motion, to get used to fundamentally relying on what they see or hear in a space and to find personal ways of integrating a sequence of flowing figurative moments into the work – it's also really enjoyable in its own right!

Classical ballet

Classical ballet tends to be divided into narrative and non-narrative works. These two forms often require slightly different approaches to conceiving the design.

Narrative ballets, much like dramas, bring prerequisites, interior or exterior locations that the choreographer and designer will find references for and build around a somewhat formulaic series of musical and therefore choreographic passages. These would involve a number of opportunities for a ballet company ranging from solos, to pas de deux, to episodes written specifically for the corps de ballet such as the Flower corps in Tchaikovsky's *The Nutcracker*. Each requires the choreographer and designer to agree the space that the dancers need and how the costume distinguishes between or unifies groups in a single, shifting image. The narratives are also often structured into three acts, much like classical dramas, with intervals in between; or perhaps like the movements in a classical symphony, giving the designer a clean break, during which the stage can be transformed out of view of the audience.

New ballet work tends to be non-narrative, conceptual or abstract, as choreographers have become more interested in making work around a preoccupation with formal movement or social theme. This work, much like contemporary dance (see below), will have a more fluid design process that draws on multiple reference points and personal interpretations rather than on an architectural place or landscape. Other sorts of visual artists, such as painters and sculptors rather than established theatre designers, are often engaged for this more single-minded approach. Paradoxically though, an ongoing process of devising something unique ultimately demands a greater 'unity of purpose' across the creative team, including the composer, as the visual language adjusts itself throughout the production's evolution.

Costume design by Yolanda Sonnabend for *La Bayadère* (1989), choreographed by Natalia Makarova for the Royal Opera House.

In either of these forms, there are essentially two contrasting choreographer-designer processes, with the designer being either reactive or proactive. Both rely on the vision of the choreographer at the outset, but hinge on whether the choreographer has a clear idea of what the movement will be, asking a designer to respond to that; or whether the choreographer is looking to form ideas for the movement through tackling design concerns *with* the designer.

> This specialism begins with giving the dancers room to dance! Initially, when you don't know what the

choreography actually is, you design at the edges and
in the air and at the back.

Peter Farley, designer

Choreographers and designers for ballet complement and
rely on each other in so far as both, like the dance form, are
highly specialised.

The ideas for a drama are only preserved in the written
script which, unless it's a devised work, exists separately
from the particular production: the physicality of the shows
are unrecorded.[13] Ballet's precise movements, and therefore
its ideas, are notated using the vocabulary of steps according to which academy the dance form has originated from
or are working within (even if the choreographer chooses to
break that vocabulary).[14] This means that complete productions from many decades ago can be reproduced with most
of their 'production values' still intact, including the design.
Designers for ballet are therefore far more aware of their
own design traditions in much the same way as are choreographers and dancers.

How do you make a start? Established ballet companies
often work from a building base that's attached to a particular theatre. Their scale of operation means that, unlike
contemporary dance, shadowing and assisting is a possible
way to break into ballet design. Designers for these major
companies often use assistants to make the models for
designs planned in advance of rehearsal, unlike their contemporary dance counterparts who design more
spontaneously. There may also be assistant choreographers
attached to companies that are your possible future creative
partner. Know your dance – it's something of a niche area,
so you'll be expected to be passionate about it and be up to
speed on both its long history and the latest movers and
shakers. Ballet and dance in general communicate across the
frontiers of language, so your knowledge should preferably
extend to other countries.

Contemporary dance

There are a number of clear-cut differences for a designer between the lengthy heritage of classical ballet and the relative newcomer of mid- to late-twentieth-century contemporary dance. Classical ballet may be more often than not involved or concerned with the reconstruction of previous works in a repertoire, usually to well-established musical scores by widely recognised classical composers, and requires a knowledge base accumulated through research of the past in order to make new work in the present, even if the piece is a world premiere. In general, contemporary dance is concerned with making new works, although often still within a tradition of academic training,[15] but often to a shorter time frame and usually in much more modest circumstances – particularly financial.

New work demands a new design and perhaps a new way of designing. Contemporary-dance designers therefore need to be continually challenging themselves and their process so that there is minimal reliance on what has already become a vernacular visual language for dance – contemporary design doesn't necessarily mean new design.

Dance designer Suzie Holmes, based at the Trinity Laban Conservatoire, came from a family background of fashion design mixed with an English and Drama education. She recalls what first attracted her to working with contemporary dancers and movement, rather than actors and scripts:

> Everything I wasn't mad about in text-based theatre is
> resolved by the more abstract nature of dance. It was
> more liberating and closer to the potential that
> fashion had for taking risks with design.

To make a start in design for dance, and if you're not on a course that specialises in the field, it's obviously a good idea to seek out centres of professional dance that support smaller working partnerships of choreographers, designers and dancers. In London, for example, that would mean seeing as much work as you can at venues like Trinity Laban, London Contemporary Dance School at The Place, Sadler's Wells and Rambert on the South Bank; or, in other parts of the UK, the Wales Millennium Centre and Scottish School of Contemporary Dance in Dundee.

In this day and age, however, you're less likely to meet and form a relationship with a choreographer by staying late in the bar and meeting socially. Dancers and aspiring choreographers are now more aware of taking care of their bodies – the climate and competition is now such that the body is far more of a hallowed place, and performers are far more respectful of the way they treat it. Gone are the days of hooking up over a pint and a cigarette! So, much like other forms of networking in the twenty-first century, following up a connection through social media, websites and blogs tends to be perceived as far more professional and effective. Likewise – and perhaps more so than in other areas of design for performance – owing to relatively poor formal funding, you will most likely have to make your first work without any payment... and it's worth emphasising that this will be true of the choreographer and performers as well. The chicken-and-egg paradox of needing to have some realised work under your belt and in your folio in order to get work with a young choreographer in the first place is doubly true of dance. The physical and devised nature of the form raises the level of risk in a creative partnership, so it's best to start modestly, creating solo pieces or duets in non-commercial venues, such as dance schools, before making the assumption that you're equipped for the job.

The process of making a contemporary-dance piece is very often fluid and instinctive for all contributors. The nature of the work can change radically from hour to hour in rehearsal so everyone has to be exceedingly flexible and sensitive to how the work is forming, shifting and then reforming. Sometimes the work will have a musical framework (live or recorded); sometimes the spoken or sung word is very much a part of the mix. Designers need to be aware of aural as well as visual opportunities – to respond to the sound that dancers and objects make… including the power of the absence of sound. Some designers respond to aural stimuli in terms of shape, some in textures and others through colour; they're all different and equally valid – the important quality for an artist, whether you acquire it or possess it instinctively, is the sensitivity to be able to interpret in an imaginative way what you think, see or hear.

The design process in dance has to be shared, and finding a common language amongst everyone involved is paramount. Choreographers bring a wide vocabulary of movement, and designers bring a wide vocabulary of imagery. They meet through either, but there is no doubt that the reading and choice of images can steer a creative process. This means plenty of show-'n'-tell sessions: discussion can only make limited progress before the interpretation of descriptive language falls short of what's physical or visually needed… For example, everyone has different mental pictures and reference points for the colour purple. Even drawings can fall short of what's required and can even mislead. At this stage, response time is crucial, and, for many, plunging into working with actual materials in real time and space knits an idea together more dynamically. This way of integrated working makes logistical demands of the designer, in that they have to carefully plan how to get materials into the dance studio at a point when both choreographers and company will be able to spend quality time testing the ideas.

It's also important to bear in mind the lighting conditions the bodies and objects might be under – how do fabrics react to coloured lighting, how do skin tones read next to certain textiles? I once used a muted non-metallic gold fabric for a figure-hugging costume, only to realise on stage (and too late) that the performer looked totally naked at a distance, such was the similarity of the fabric's tone to that of her own skin.

Texture and transparency is also important to consider in terms of dance lighting, which often has a key source from side to side of the stage ('cross lighting'). Cross lighting emphasises the profile and shapes of the dancers by casting light on one side of their bodies at the expense of the other, which is in greater shadow or a complementary/contrasting colour. This in turn 'pulls out' the surface qualities or density of costume fabrics, so it's important to be aware of and anticipate a textile's properties under these conditions. Talk with the lighting designer at an early stage about what to avoid or what to take advantage of in the final outcome. Perhaps using some rudimentary lighting in rehearsal will help all the creative team see the design's potential.

Many choreographers would like the designer in rehearsal for more time than they can possibly spare... and far more than a designer of drama, for example. Having said that, it's vital for the designer to be engaged with the research and development process as much as possible: the more familiarity you have with how the ideas form, the more likely it is that design decisions will have a conceptual unity with the piece and an aesthetic integrity.

Authorship of contemporary dance is as thorny a subject as any other form of creativity. Dance pieces are widely recognised first and foremost as works of choreography, and projects may well have been initiated by a choreographer to attract funding. If that's the case, then there is certainly every argument that says it's fundamentally their work, and the traditional hierarchies will remain undisturbed – designers will contribute towards the success of that work along with other creative artists and performers, but they cannot claim authorship. If, on the other hand, the project is set up as a speculative joint venture, it's a designer's role to continue to challenge the direction a piece is taking and not simply to settle into a passive relationship with the choreographer – in fact, the choreographer should expect it and regard the designer's view as an important factor in the creative vision.

If the project is not local to you, then timing your visits to rehearsal is vital, and making video recordings whilst you're there is also a key strategy in making an unrushed and careful analysis of choreographic movements. Alternatively, live webcams or uploaded recorded 'scratch' movie footage from rehearsal can be very useful for creative discussion – it's important to ensure this is only shared between a minimum of participants, however, so that the integrity of the rehearsal room as a place for artistic risk is fully respected and kept 'in house'.

Having said that, good final production shots for your folio are essential to get ahead in dance design. The visual and sensual nature of dance lends itself to striking photographic images. You certainly need a good-quality camera to be able to do this effectively yourself – or leave it to a professional. Dancers frozen in mid-flight or formation never fail to satisfy if caught successfully in a still, and are usually more memorable as images than video footage – although a snappy ninety-second video edit of a piece's essence can often be equally compelling and persuasive.

Top tip: *Don't get hooked on your first or favourite design idea – learn to enjoy the roller-coaster ride of making a piece of figurative, live kinetic art!*

What do dancers need?

The fitting room is the designer's rehearsal studio. In dance, for all the reasons outlined above, the practical, face-to-face getting to grips with the material in hand is critical to a successful outcome that everyone is happy with.

The first fitting is usually the most challenging and revelatory for both the dancer, in terms of how they foresee their performance might be evolving, and for the designer, in that their material ideas are being fully tested at an experimental stage. There are many challenges in the fitting-room situation that require all concerned to take colossal leaps of faith in each other. Being incomplete or even just pieces of fabric, the costume ideas never look their best; the situation is always removed from the context of the final production; and the room itself is often not in the most glamorous of surroundings (being sometimes an improvised corner of a studio). Like rehearsal, making a record of the different stages is useful for yourself, the costume-makers and the choreographer... but use your common sense about how exposing it can feel for the performer (and designer), who will also want strictly restricted access and distribution.

The circumstances of modern dance can lead designers into an over-reliance on contemporary, affordable, off-the-peg clothing, providing dancers with non-durable but trendy high-street fashion or forms of sportswear. However, designers at the forefront of their field are continually looking for new textiles, plastics, elastics and other unprecedented substrates to work with and anticipating how they will behave in performance: in fact, practice-based research. The fitting room is a sort of living laboratory where these ideas are bench-tested. The test soon needs to extend beyond the confines of the fitting and into the action of rehearsal where it can be put through its paces. The early trials of these experiments need everyone concerned to be open to risk, trusting, practical and often as clinical as a scientist or as objective as an engineer. Having said that, for the performer, the experience of feeling the costume is often crucial as a tactile extension of their physical being and stage presence. Dancers will understand that their costume will respond to movement and, along with its colour, for example, will combine with choreographic composition to make a definitive theatrical image.

Practically speaking, dancers need to be supported by their costume. Fit is essential – if the costume isn't compatible with the irrefutable reality of a particular dancer's stretching, contracting, sweaty body, then chances are it's not going to make it through the fitting stage. The costume also has to be durable enough to take enormous amounts of stress and maintenance over the course of a run of performances. The bodies of contemporary dancers tend to be more diverse than those of classical ballet, so working with, if not flattering, a dancer's physique is important. Suzie Holmes:

> It's not fair to a dancer to not be aware of how the body functions. A designer owes it to a performer to make that individual look as good as he or she possibly can in relation to the work.

They may not like the idea of what they're wearing, but as long as they feel the fit is secure and they are appropriately covered, they will perform with greater confidence. Modern-dance costumes can often be minimal but are by no means simple to execute, given these requirements and how exposed dancers are on stage. Having been used to being physically manipulated all their working lives, they, unlike some actors, will also not resist being pulled about in fittings to anticipate the most extreme physical conditions the costume might be subjected to. For example, asking them to stretch the torso, squat or make a deep plié tests out the support and comfort a dancer needs in the grounded lower portion of their bodies.

As the technical prowess of ballet dancers improved over the mid-twentieth century, there was less and less need to decorate the body and, coupled with an acceptance of the near-naked (and subsequently completely naked) form on stage in the swinging sixties, dance costume quickly evolved into a minimal art form. Body stockings became a canvas that, with the occasional addition, allowed the designer to express their 'inner-abstract painter' – and that is still the case. There is no doubt that the extended formal actions of a classical dancer demand an appreciation of the freedoms that their limbs need – particularly if your ideas set out to consciously challenge their movement. For instance, and obviously, work *sur les pointes* usually requires a floor with a precise amount of grip and an even horizontal surface. As with most dance costume, the performers will probably need to hold, lift or catch each other cleanly, so beware of a costume's elements that could cause a mistake or even accident. Headdresses need to be as light as possible and masks have as open a view as possible – dancers need all their peripheral vision. Fabrics in a dancer's costume need to have dynamic properties that not only don't inhibit their movements but actively complement action in some specific way, as well as making a visual statement without the benefit of speech to comply or contrast with.

Dancers view and review every move they make in studio mirrors, not just relying on the choreographer for feedback as an actor might of a director. They are often therefore their own worst critics and, unlike the rest of us, have to examine and confront their physical idiosyncrasies in detail on a daily basis. On the whole, dancers are disarmingly humble and impressively frank about their needs, which is what can be so utterly refreshing about costume design for dance.

Top tip: *Listen to the performers about how they view their bodies in relation to the piece. They know themselves better than you ever can, so be attuned to this and empathise at the same time as asserting your own ideas!*

7

Site-Specific Theatre

The building is my text.

Geraldine Pilgrim

To begin this section we have to be clear about what site-specific theatre actually is. Although the label given to this form of theatrical event should clearly describe how it comes about and what makes it different from theatre made in purpose-built buildings, there are some obvious but frequently misunderstood assumptions about its premise.

Theatre in and of spaces that are not built for that purpose has a long heritage. Early forms of storytelling, oral histories, spring from myths and legends, true or fantastical, surrounding specific locations and their communities. Theatre-makers down the ages have used their buildings to tell stories in a form that the audience could easily decipher, by adhering to universally understood spatial arrangements coupled with particular local architectural aesthetics. In other words, they responded to their environment: a specific site. However, site-specific performance as a distinct genre began in the late 1960s and early 1970s. It was born of the avant-garde site-specific art work movement in an attempt to make and show art outside of what was becoming felt and thought to be the artificial, pretentious and 'loaded' gallery and theatre environments; to open up and occupy a more varied and relevant range of interior and exterior venues.

Site-specific performance could be said to have emerged from the mood swing of 1968's student unrest and a response to find a more equitable art form in a belief that the spectator is of equal significance and meaning to the event as the performers themselves: site-specific events recalibrated the audience-performer, and audience-location, relationship. Performers (not always trained actors) and spectators both reached a more profound depth of empathy with an event than within a traditional theatre space, where the audiences were separated from the performers, often repeating what was beginning to be perceived as over-worn, elitist, dogmatic dramas – designers also having to serve them by producing a convincing but artificially structured setting. In some senses, then, site-specific work also redefined the role of theatre designers and their methods.

Over the last twenty to thirty years, many exciting theatre pieces have been produced in buildings other than theatres, but not all these productions can claim to be site-specific. Epic dramas, dance pieces and other spectacles have been played out in anything from abandoned factories to bus depots and power stations, but very often they are *staged* in alternative locations to challenge the play or to add a metaphorical or symbolic layer to the producer's concept of a previously written text. There is no doubt that, to a greater or lesser degree, many of these events have challenged the theatregoing public's preconceptions about a particular play and the way it had been previously produced. Using abandoned locations has provided creative teams with monumental spaces that are concurrently in some way familiar through their everyday use, but usually only subtly adding a single layer to what the director or designer wanted to 'say' about the text: using the site merely as an overarching framing devise.

Likewise, film-makers use sites to shoot scenes 'on location'. That too is rarely what we would call site-specific. The purpose of the building, garden or other landscape in this context is to mimic where the action took place if based on historical fact, or simply to make it more convincing if designed for a fictional drama.

In the case of classical texts, a non-theatre space can infuse the play with a fresh atmosphere and wrap a well-worn story in a sometimes fascinating anachronistic skin; but one that runs in parallel, rather than being completely integrated. Not only can these productions be exciting conceptually, they also provide a provocatively unconventional physical space for a designer and director to exploit. Nevertheless, this sort of event still cannot be classified in any way as site-specific: these are examples of theatre *in*, but not *of*, a specific space.

What I've so far described is, broadly speaking, theatre in a 'found' space. Therefore, conversely, true site-specific theatre involves work that has generated a devised narrative, often highly visual or sensational (meaning affecting all the senses), *directly* from a unique location. The theatre-maker in this context, whether an architectural structure or a topographical landscape, draws creative inspiration solely from that space and no other; harnessing its form, history and (usually previous) function. That is not to say that a theatre can't be a building that a site-specific theatre-maker can respond to – on the contrary, a theatre piece in but also of that theatre could be truly site-specific, even if the piece also adapts some elements of theatrical text as a vehicle for the visual narrative.

Because of its open, devised form, site-specific theatre-makers tend to have leanings towards, or indeed have their origins in, a blend of theatre and fine-art performance, or even sculpture. Its appeal is that it can test the limits of theatrical convention from whichever of these angles it's tackled. The distinctions between director and designer are blurred, questioned and sometimes dispensed with altogether in favour of more universal titles such as 'theatre-maker', 'theatre artist', and so forth.

By definition, this work is also often rooted in the society in which the building is situated and has, over perhaps tens of decades, become a part of. The richest sites, artistically speaking, are often those with residents close by or workers and other users of a space that have a deep-seated connection with it – their histories being inextricably linked – and the equation of poetry over function, or vice versa, can equate to striking and moving theatre in the right hands. Primary research in the form of interviews and sifting through archives to tease out images and stories nudge some site-specific work close to forms of verbatim theatre or docudramas; the linking factor being that the building is always central to a site-specific piece. Occasionally and when at its best, local participants and audiences can have life-transforming experiences taking part in such projects, giving them a greater sense of identity and pride in their community, whilst for others a performance can simply reveal hidden nearby treasures in a vivid, perhaps haunting, and unforgettable form.

There are often opportunities to work on site-specific projects in many theatre-design-related programmes, but the best way to gain real experience is to assist on a large-scale project or start a small project of your own.

Geraldine Pilgrim, one of site-specific theatre's innovators and leading practitioners, describes what inspires and sustains her work:

> You have to find and fall in love with a site first. I believe that places and people need acknowledgement of their existence… I have to feel that a building wants me there… sometimes I know a building doesn't: I have to 'listen' to the building. Then I think it's a privilege and my responsibility to take the opportunity to bring the building – albeit temporarily – back to life.

Site-specific work doesn't only take place in abandoned places, buildings in limbo between disuse and reuse or demolition. There are events that respond to sites that are still in use whether that use has changed or not, such as London's

Imperial War Museum, originally built as an asylum. This is a hybrid form that nudges against 'interventions', 'happenings' and other seemingly (but actually carefully managed) feral performance activity. What might have these to do with design, I hear you ask? Design in a pure form deals with space, people and impact, so there's no more challenging an environment than when all these factors are shifting. Theatre design also relies to a great degree on observing and using the rituals and patterns of human activity, so a designed theatrical reality that mirrors or counterpoints the 'scenography of the everyday' can be a fascinating cocktail for performers and audience, given the premise that humans habitually, consciously and subconsciously, both act and look.

As a designer of an 'on-site' event (*Off the Wall*, 2007) and being given a vast and (then) gloomy location to transform (the piazza and surrounding Brutalist buildings of London's South Bank's Royal Festival Hall and Hayward Gallery), I *learned* to love it over time by working in and with it. We took the approach that the architecture presented a series of pure masses of concrete, volumes of air and that walls were not so much enclosing spaces but presenting a series of exciting vertical surfaces to perform on – celebrating the modernist spirit and challenging the audience to see the area in a different light.

On occasion, the ambitious projects of the type that Geraldine Pilgrim initiates can bring a possible 'stay of execution' to what might have been a significant building condemned to a planner's death. The effectiveness of the project, including its appreciation of designers past, can awaken awareness of its importance to the people who used it in its glory days and those who have inherited perhaps only a glimpse of it as a familiar landmark. For connoisseurs of the effectiveness of 'design for living', from fiction to reality and back again, site-specific work is for you.

Site-specific theatre: the practicalities

Site-specific work brings with it a huge number of logistical and technical hurdles. Geraldine Pilgrim believes that 'practicalities begin with "health and safety" regulations.' These will vary tremendously depending on whom you consult and where you are geographically, but as a professional artist and designer you have to be genuinely committed to their importance.

> You can have the most brilliant ideas in the world but, if you don't check the relevant H&S and fire regulations all of those ideas may be prohibited and it will break your heart. Therefore it's important to bring in a production manager at the earliest stage who is experienced in site work, to be your advisor as to what you can do, what you can't do, and what you may be able to do.

> Also as the creator/designer of a site-specific performance, it is crucial to check that the site has the following basic but vital amenities:

> *Water* – for cleaning, toilets, drinking.

> *Electricity supply* – for lighting, sound, heating (in winter), etc. If there is no mains supply, how many (silent) generators will you need?

> The lighting designer is also an important part of the creative equation: they can tell you what is possible given the spaces and power at your disposal and how lighting design for site performance is a very different style from that of theatres.

> Other considerations include:

> *Disabled access* – in old buildings, full disabled access may be impossible. Therefore your publicity must state this, but as much as is practical should be done to fulfil access requirements – perhaps including a projected live feed of inaccessible images in an accessible area.

Marketing – the best word-of-mouth marketing will come from the community local to the site, as long as they feel included in the project. Social networking amongst participants and their personal invitations to friends and family can be a strong basis for good audience numbers.

Press and publicity – this is a complex issue as, although you may not want to expose volunteers to professional criticism, the participants and the project deserve recognition, so it is best to invite the press and reviewers.

In designer-director terms, there then follows a period of engagement with the whole site, inside and out. If you are to create a theatrical moment of transition without any specific change other than the audience's imaginings, then it is crucial you have analysed the space to appreciate its dynamics so that you can place objects and people in the most effective position – this all sounds rather abstract until, of course, you have the specific site to respond to! Suffice to say that if you have found an empathy with the space, it will give you the answer to any of the questions you ask of it. Geraldine's process involves:

Frequent visits and getting to know the site like the back of your hand, drawing maps, discovering exits and entrances, plotting routes and making models if necessary. You should make time to allow the building to gradually reveal its imagery and ghosts.

Some of the practical steps you might take to understand your site can include: making a personal drawing;[16] measuring both its vital features and more subtle nuances; and researching the history and former life of the building. All of this is unlike the way you would approach a ubiquitous theatre space into which your designs could fit quite comfortably.

Bringing your ideas to life in the most economical way is at the heart of the process, especially given that the project and spaces could be vast. So, model-making, though the most powerful way to understand a given space, may need to be reduced to a minimum; just concentrate on the areas that will need a precise design 'fit' so that constructed elements are understood by technicians.

Researching the history of your site can involve a number of strategic approaches, all valid but judged to be more or less appropriate by carefully considering the presence of the site in the locality and the community around it. Of course, museums, the internet, parish records, and local council and library archives can tell you much about the broad sweep of the site's history, including imagery in, say, newspaper reports. But Geraldine believes that:

> the best source for research material for a site project will first come through finding and talking to people who are or were connected to the building and the locality and who have memories and experience of being involved with the site and the area.

> Leafleting and putting up notices in community centres, doctor's surgeries, libraries, lunch clubs, cafés, pubs, etc., explaining the project and asking people to contact you with their experiences of your chosen site, as you want to bring it temporarily back to life, is a good place to start. Often the best source of initial practical information on an empty building is that of the security guards who will know whom to contact about permission to use it and the detailed physical layout of the site.

Site-specific work has an exciting future through the use of digital media. The use of audio, video, Bluetooth technology and GPS can bind audiences together and navigate them through buildings, open sites or complete cities. Performances in these contexts integrate or intervene with the everyday environment and unsuspecting witnesses, rather than an 'audience'. Companies such as Rimini Protocol (*Remote Avignon, Radioortung – 10 kilometres of files Dresden*) and Seven Sisters (*Atalanta*) continue to devise work that not only challenges our sense of ourselves in time and place, but also empowers the audience to choose, edit or construct the images they see from physical to virtual; from moment to moment.

As with pursuing any particular theatre specialism, I recommend going to see as much of this work as possible to be able to understand and have your own opinions about the nuances of different artists' engagement with a specific site, paying particular attention to how the design of a theatrical fiction responds to existing environments and 'real life'.

8

Original Practices:
Theatre or Museum?

The term original practices (OP) here refers to productions at the heart of Shakespeare's Globe, a full-scale reproduction of the original Globe built in 1598 on a site close to the present theatre on London's South Bank. It was there, when the new Globe opened in 1997, that designer Jenny Tiramani began to pioneer its strategy for design and realisation. You can watch recordings of her later work (Tim Carroll's productions of *Richard III* and *Twelfth Night*) on DVD to appreciate some of its care and exactitude. However, like all theatre, original-practice productions are there to be witnessed and for the audience to believe for a moment that they have been transported to another time whilst remaining on (or at least close to) the spot where the plays were first performed. Either seeing or, if you get the chance, working on an OP show is theatre heaven for those who are passionate about history, or inspired by research.

Each of these major projects has become a test case for mounting an English Renaissance-period show as authentically as possible, using the latest available knowledge: in many instances being at the forefront of research. That said, the artistic and production team at Shakespeare's Globe are not the only practitioners exploring traditional methods and materials. Christine Edzard and Sands Films, her film production company in London's East End, have built a worldwide reputation for making both scenery and costume using traditional techniques. You can almost smell Victorian London in her epic films of *Little Dorrit* and *The Fool*. For the purposes of this book, however, I'll stick with theatre techniques and staging – although there is, as is often the case, a great deal of transferrable production expertise between theatre and film.

The main reason for OP is to learn through experimentation and discovery. For those who are interested in historical performance practice, instrumentation or historical costume, it's fascinating to be able to explore, through action, how people hundreds of years ago may have behaved, and to speculate on how that behaviour could have been informed by their environment. The work deepens our existing knowledge even if the audience on the night don't fully appreciate the effort, yet it is still a contentious area in that many theatre professionals either love it or hate it – but for similar reasons.

The division centres on whether our present-day theatre needs to invest time and money in what could be viewed as a museum piece, however spectacular, which is of academic rather than theatrical merit. These productions need huge resources behind them, some say disproportionate to the value of the experience on stage, and sometimes the producers of the shows have to draw a line under the funding and use more conventional methods as a last resort. Their value, though, has to be measured holistically, beyond the show itself, and be recognised for satisfying our natural curiosity about how English culture has evolved and how that might feed future developments, such as the complementary indoor Jacobean theatre on the site of the Globe that opened in 2014 and the new playhouses for Shakespeare in Stratford-upon-Avon. The cynical view is that the work is closer to the many re-enactment societies that cater for laypeople's interest in historical detail rather than to a vital engagement with the here and now. Whatever your opinion of the Globe, there is no doubt that this independently financed organisation is a major success story, the shows are well attended by an appreciative and enthusiastic audience, and have become the basis for an outstanding educational and archival resource for designers.

OP drives many aspects of a production, including the fact that usually there is very little scenery on stage: the Globe itself, with its established three entrances, balcony above and trap doors over and below the stage, being used to the full. This means that decisions about where the actors move can be left in a more fluid state through rehearsals and can change through performance. That in turn throws the emphasis of the design onto the costumes and props. The complex costume changes are often made in view of the audience; so the backstage skills both in preparation and during performances are driven by what materials are used and by the details of construction, such as the clothes' fastenings. Female roles are often played by (not always young) men and the designer therefore has to make decisions about to what extent their masculinity is revealed, which in turn radically dictates the fit of the clothes, the authenticity of their foundation garments, and so on. Unfortunately, given the vast expense and very long time frame involved with making costumes without modern technology or materials, not to mention the extremely high level of skill and precision needed by those doing the construction, 'original practices' is, like most high-grade, practice-based research in any field, only able to be indulged in by a very fortunate and exclusive few – but doesn't that add to its tenuous value?

The chances of designing an original-practice production at Shakespeare's Globe are extremely slim, and so, having not done one myself, I'm hugely indebted to Hannah Lobelson (who, over many years, was the wardrobe manager and a costume supervisor at the Globe) for this account of what it takes to mount a production and the artistic and technical stamina needed to maintain an OP show.

[55]

The team of costume-makers are assembled from the best and most experienced throughout Europe, and so you have cutters from France and Germany working together with costume-makers from England. Fabrics hand woven in Italy are combined with antique lace bought from private collections. Of course, as there are so few people working at this level, the knowledge, skills and techniques have evolved over the years of making costumes in this way, resulting in what is now probably the peak of 'original practice'. Nothing is overlooked – silk thread, pewter buttons, doublets padded with horsehair.

Naturally, as everything is made by hand, the costume must be started very early on, which means that many design decisions must be made before casting is finalised, giving the actors little opportunity to contribute many ideas to their costume. For an actor, performing in an original-practice production could either be an inspiring and rewarding experience – informing their way of being on stage and giving insight into their historical character – or it could be restrictive and frustrating. The actual experience of wearing the clothing would be unlike any other performance experience. The cutting of the costumes is extremely tight compared to what is worn today, and so an original-practice doublet would feel completely unfamiliar to an actor in 2014 who is used to wearing T-shirts and suits. Of course, this totally affects how they move on stage and should give an authenticity and structure to their performance, but it can also be hot and uncomfortable and some actors really struggle.

In addition to this, the way the costumes are made means that they take longer to put on before the performance, and also that the actor needs help getting dressed and undressed, making them quite dependent on whomever is assisting them. Again, some actors enjoy this process of getting ready before the performance and the care the wardrobe assistant must take with dressing the actor to ensure that the perfectly made costume transfers successfully to the stage. Some actors find the early dressing call before the performance and the lack of independence – needing help even to undress at the interval to go to the bathroom – quite frustrating.

Hannah goes on to describe the knock-on effect that these techniques and materials have on the show-to-show management of the clothes. The pressure of being faithful to the period's methods is exacerbated by the fact the costume department are often also preparing for other productions in the season, such as education or touring projects.

For the wardrobe department that is striving to maintain the costumes the way the designer intended and to dress the actors for each performance, there are hours and hours of work involved. The main garments cannot be laundered (just as in the sixteenth century), as the fabrics, construction and dyes are not stable enough. So each actor is wearing a linen undershirt or smock, which is washed and ironed after each performance. Fortunately some concessions to speed are made, and washing machines and electric irons are used. But the white starched ruffs and cuffs which the Elizabethan period is so well known by are laundered by hand, starched using rice starch and then pressed and folded over hot-iron pokers to get the intricate curls and twirls. Woollen and silk stockings are also washed by hand and then squeezed through an antique mangle before drying to prevent any shrinking or stretching. Any damage that a garment experiences during the performance is carefully repaired. The skill and speed of the wardrobe-maintenance team really come into play when you have two performances on one day and only ninety minutes to turn the show around before starting it all again. Everything is second to getting the show on stage looking spectacular, and this is why you absolutely have to have a wardrobe team that cares as much about the costumes as the designer and makers – because wardrobe are the ones, night after night, getting it right.

For designers, the research of an OP show begins with a decision about precisely which year the production will refer back to. Other, non-OP, productions at Shakespeare's Globe or RSC have a much freer attitude to 'period costume': often settling loosely for late Elizabethan or Jacobean. In many respects the fluidity of these decisions might actually reflect the mix of clothes in any given era – a snapshot of any urban street now will reveal an image of how our eclectic contemporary world is smattered with all manner of past fashions and styles that overlap and would confound definitive descriptions by future historians. Having said that, OP is a living laboratory and so a particular production can set its conditions. Hannah again:

> Usually the designer doesn't go anywhere near the level of research required for an original-practice production, because it just isn't important to them. Issues such as silhouette, colour schemes and character tend to take precedence rather than, for instance, what style of sleeve the English court was wearing in 1617! The skill in an original-practice production is that these considerations of character and shape are still very much present, but always tempered and served by what was actually occurring in that chosen period in history and at that level of society.

A starting point for aspiring 'original practitioners' is to visit the best archives and museums that stock original clothing, such as the Victoria and Albert Museum, or the School of Historical Dress that houses the Janet Arnold archive. Janet Arnold's series of books, *Patterns of Fashion*, remains an authoritative guide for pattern-making and cutting of historical clothes, and for the Elizabethan/Jacobean period the fourth in the series, which deals with elementary garments and accessories, is particularly absorbing and useful for both

OP aficionados and designers who need expert reference material. However hard designers strive for authenticity, researchers only have to take one look into the archives of the Royal Shakespeare Company's past productions' costume designs at the Shakespeare's Birthplace Trust to realise how inescapably knotted up we are in the aesthetic our own times. 'Original practice' represents a unique and genuine attempt to escape our Zeitgeist.

9

Lighting and Video Design

I've elected to put both these disciplines in the same section. At the turn of the century there would have been no sense in doing this, but lighting designers now assume that video projection is likely to be considered for any production, and not only big-budget musicals. The working relationship between video and lighting design is vital so that one doesn't compete with the other, cancelling out each other's effectiveness.

Career lighting designers emerge from a range of starting points. Some will come through a technical-theatre training, usually in a course affiliated to a drama school. Others may work their way to designing through being an electrician in a lighting department, progress to being a production electrician, find they are offered opportunities to light modest events or small shows and then get a taste for it. Lighting-desk programmers are indispensible to a lighting designer during the production week when the 'paper' design is applied to the reality on stage. Sometimes the operator's experience of this critical phase of the process – constantly listening in to the interchange of ideas between the director and designers – will develop into taking on the design of a project or two of their own, until they find their niche as a fully fledged designer. Being an assistant to a seasoned lighting designer, and then perhaps becoming an associate, is not unlike the career path (if you can call it that) of a set or costume designer – but as with most theatre activities, having your share of good fortune and networking can define what you will do and the speed at which you advance, no matter which route you take.

The new generation of lighting (and set) designers are familiar with video's language, strengths and weaknesses in a live
show. Likewise, directors have a more sophisticated and
fearless approach to moving images, whether recorded or
live feed, in relation to the presence of an actor on stage.
How the disciplines knit together is now in many ways more
complex as the technical possibilities multiply and their layered use proliferates, but communication between the
members of the creative team is increasingly swift and efficient by smartphone and media exchange, so a balance
between them is crucial.

Lighting designer Tim Lutkin recalls the ingredients of a
particularly ideal working partnership between designers,
director and video artist:

> There was a real equality and calmness about us
> working together, and anybody could suggest
> anything right form the start. Each morning, I'd be
> genuinely excited about getting back into the theatre.

Lighting designers can sometimes feel a little marginalised
from the inner circle of director, set and costume designers.
There is a perfectly innocuous reason for that: they are frequently the last to be hired in a creative team. With a little
experience, most LDs relax about this common situation
and have the wisdom to ease their way into a project, knowing that often they can't make a concrete contribution until
the physical design starts to take shape. Lighting is, after all,
chiefly concerned with adding tone and hue to something
actual, transforming shapes and revealing a space by changing intensities: the timing of lighting transitions also being
of the essence, of course. A lighting designer's task is also
inevitably to ensure the audience can see the actors: so
before having the subject and object to light, anticipation
and preparation are the order of the day.

Lighting is not simply a layer of gloss to be added at the last
minute, however. The LD has to study the play as intensely

as any in the creative team in order to gauge the mood swings in its narrative, perhaps use naturalistic phenomena, such as weather conditions, to enhance their metaphorical values (as in *King Lear*, for instance), or immerse the audience in an wonderland of abstracted pattern and intense colour. The study of the works of fine-art painters, both classical and contemporary, is an excellent way to find inspiration, and this can intersect with a theatre designer's visual references.

What the theatre designer aims for, in a two-dimensional image, needs experienced technical know-how to realise it faithfully on stage. Lighting can be at its most spectacular and ethereal when used to enhance atmospheric effects. Water, smoke or haze, dry ice and other amorphous elements all come into their own with a well-positioned lantern, and each substance requiring specific expert treatment. Costume designers would be wise to show the lighting designer the range of fabric samples they might use, along with the designs on paper, before going ahead with construction. It is extraordinary how coloured lighting filters, gels and now LEDs can react differently with what might seem similarly coloured textiles: particularly those in a range of blacks. Theatre lighting can suddenly reveal underlying hues in a dyed weave, transforming what the designer thought in natural light were a selection of carefully chosen solid blacks, to chocolate browns, or perhaps, even maroon.

Moving light, once hand operated (in the form of a follow spot, for example) but now fully computerised and programmed, dovetails with the moving images of a video projection and, when interchangeable, can build an extraordinarily unsettling and shifting environment. A musical or opera production is inconceivable without the integration of light that reflects the life and soul of the sound.

It is in the crossover between all these disciplines that the term scenography comfortably sits – an integrated harmonious or, alternatively, fractured theatrical landscape, waiting for the performer's presence to inhabit its territory and give it full meaning. It is for this reason that further references to lighting in this book will be woven through all the other aspects of design for the stage.

Unsurprisingly, video designers usually come from having had some interest or training in designing for film, motion graphics or animation. Mixing the projection of images in live events has an exceedingly long history stretching back into the Victorian times – for instance, in magic lantern shows at both commercial fairs and in the domestic parlour – or, in a wider cultural context, shadow puppetry. Blending cinema and theatre now has a century-old tradition, and with every technological advance the mix becomes more and more fluid and integrated. Video design in a live context, however, has now surpassed the simplistic approach of projecting images onto screens, once positioned way behind the action, or in front of it on a flown gauze cloth, for example.

Designers who work exclusively as video artists emerged in the 1990s when equipment became more technically efficient and affordable. The digital technology in lighting systems at that time and computer technology in the form of increasingly easy-to-use software (such as editing programmes) accelerated the proliferation of projected images in live performance. A decade later, projected imagery was an option open to any production from the smallest fringe show to the major stages of London's West End. Crucially, these advances reduced the time it took to edit and render movie footage, so that when all the elements of a production came together, the creative team could work with video in as responsive and flexible a way as they could with performers, and with lighting, sound and other design elements. Mapping software, with increasing accuracy, allowed set and video designers to work together more closely: fusing projection and physical objects, often appearing on materials other than a projection screen. The whole stage became a possible surface on which to project still and moving images, or more abstract, sensual, broken light – object, image and light each commenting on the other, creating metaphors, layers and richness.

When used to best effect, video enhances what's on stage rather than dominates it. Creating a balance between the two is vital and can only really be blended in a meaningful and sophisticated way through trial and error in real time and space.

Devotees of this interdisciplinary approach to theatre-making have to understand both the possibilities and limits of the technology: and have to have a genuine appreciation of how live theatre works, particularly the primacy of the performer's presence. What's more, video artists in collaboration with designers and directors have begun to develop a new visual language – which has moved beyond a twenty-first-century equivalent to the nineteenth-century backdrop. When video was first used it became very popular very quickly, and the early practitioners from film backgrounds attempted with varying degrees of success to integrate it into theatre events, sometimes not appreciating the difference between theatrical conventions and those of recorded, cinematic events. Their biggest mistake was to assume that an interesting projected graphic automatically makes interesting theatre – it can, of course, but the live context and the way it's produced is everything! It's of paramount importance that video designers understand that theatre takes place in a live, three-dimensional space, and that they, along with the rest of the creative team, can't be precious about their images – the process has to remain flexible and changeable in response to these fundamentals. The difficulty that the video designer has with this is that he or she may have invested a good many hours shooting, editing and planning the projection of a sequence, and so changes or cuts can be very difficult to come to terms with but come to terms with it they must. Responsiveness and flexibility come before, and outweigh, the technical skills and tools needed to be a professional in the field.

Other technicians can support the video artist in realising their contribution to the theatre piece, much like other designers, so that the artist's focus can be directed towards what will benefit the whole production and not just their role in it... to become part of the 'creative ensemble'. Good video design has a synergy with set design: it can help animate it, give form to it, and transform it into a shifting scenography of pictures and surfaces. The use of video imagery relies on its transparency, in other words that it's absorbed into the production without dominating each sequence. Video is a very seductive medium, and its allure can overturn the central work of actors and, incidentally, other designers. The whole creative team has to agree on how video can be specifically used, from theatrical moment to theatrical moment.

> Directors and designers sometimes don't understand
> the power of video design – they know when it's bad
> but they don't know when it's good.
>
> *Douglas O'Connell, video artist*

Video in performance requires two important conditions – trust and time. There is often a degree of anxiety in the creative team when the video designer starts to introduce material into the production, because of its potential for domination, so the director and other designers need to feel comfortable with the theatrical vision of the video artist. It's also simply a consequence of the medium that video can't be just 'slipped in' as lighting or sound can be to, in a sense, underscore the work of the actor. So, time too needs to be set aside to ensure the video content is sympathetic to the *mise-en-scène*. In the worst cases, video designers get frustrated having created material that is not given due time or consideration, and never makes it to the stage, especially when the work has been unambiguously negotiated and agreed in previous detailed meetings. Stage time accorded to video designers can sometimes be squeezed into short periods which have to be shared with sound designers, and as a result they generally have an unsatisfactory time of it all. It's the responsibility of the whole creative and technical team to appreciate the precision with which video must be executed in order to have a possibility of working for the good of a nuanced production. For this to have a fighting chance, the video designer should ideally be part of the process from the very first meetings between design team and director, and not added in as an afterthought. Likewise, video must be budgeted for alongside all the other physical and technical components of the show – if video is under-budgeted, it's very much up there for all to see!

Because video design in its present form is becoming more and more affordable, there is also a temptation for directors and designers to overuse it. A good video designer will, like a set or costume designer, need a director's judgement and use their sensibility to be discriminating about their own contribution to the show: to self-edit. We live in a world hungry for images, and video gives us the opportunity to feed the beast! The images in a video design can be swiftly harvested from the internet, manipulated and projected with comparative (and sometimes alarming) ease. Images can also therefore be cut from a production in a way that the material objects, a costume or a piece of scenery, cannot. There is a much-needed period of reflection on just which images can be absorbed by the audience in relation to the production's culture and concepts, and which will baffle the audience with a frenzy of intercut pictures resembling a sub-liminally manipulative thirty-second TV commercial.

In our modern world, video projection isn't an isolated discipline: it's part of an increasingly diverse digital culture that fuses our daily lives with representations on stage and screen. We are all now 'experts' in visual culture, and we constantly read its meanings, whether subconsciously or consciously. There may soon be a time when video on stage is no longer a talking point for audiences and critics but comes to be accepted as just another cog in the theatre machine, in the same way as integrating sound and light has become second nature to theatre-makers. Douglas O'Connell again:

> Is there too much video in productions? It's moved beyond a 'fashion' to a 'language', and my hope is that, as with all technologies, the future of video is when that question is irrelevant.

10

Crossing the Line:
Theatre vs. TV and Film

On the face of it, what the audience sees as design, whether
in theatre, film or TV, often looks very similar, and in some
respects it is – but to a large degree it's the *process* of design
in each of those working environments that defines their
respective and distinctive discipline. The different
production methods, like most, whether in the
entertainment industry, fashion or other application, take a
good few years to master, so there are only a few designers
who work consistently across both stage and screen.
Theatre-design training still provides a solid foundation for
production design or art direction, although the quick
march of industry-specific technology in, for example, CGI
and post-production software, requires graduates to be
techno-savvy even if they are more interested in 'through
lens' film-making. The National Film School or a similar
screen-based course is therefore more likely to be the
production designer's first choice of training in college, to
build a presentable showreel and be more likely to hook up
with future directors.

Without doubt, the jobbing production and costume
designer for film has to have a taste for either detailed
naturalism or, occasionally, fantasy. The scope for more
overtly conceptual, abstract or minimal work is still firmly in
the non-profit, independent-short category of film-making
and rarely makes an appearance through TV-network
production. The most obvious primary skill that spans both
theatre and film is conveying good visual storytelling and

characterisation. Storyboarding is used as a way of conveying ideas, and costume design still relies on drawings (if the costume is being constructed) or sourcing in shops. Set and costume are also quite separate areas of production. Both set design (real, not virtual) and costume design require an unchanged approach to contributing towards a 'vision' for the project, along with many other design and technical departments. Their work is framed by the cinematographer and, increasingly, added to with special effects. Finally, the editor makes the definitive cut (sometimes leaving a great deal of the designer's work out!), with all this under the director's, but ultimately the producer's, control.

Alongside the deeper hierarchy that a film designer has to fit into, is a wider spread of technical departments to nego-tiate with. Everyone – builders, painters, riggers, electricians, special effects – will express authoritative and critical opinions, whether sought or not, about the choice of location or how the sets have been constructed and dressed, for example. In the costume-design area, wigs, make-up, milliners and even personal assistants will all have their say.

> As a theatre designer your credibility and integrity
> are a given and usually unquestioned; whereas in film
> it's questioned all the time.
>
> *Grant Hicks, theatre and film production designer*

This is largely due to two factors. Firstly, designers, person to person, are a less significant component part of the film-making machine, and secondly the financial stakes are that much higher than most theatre productions. In the main, TV and films are primarily money-making enterprises; the knock-on effect of this is that you may emerge from a proj-ect with a healthier bank balance but having had to endure a physically demanding and artistically challenging process – savoured by some, of course, but not for the faint-hearted, particularly at feature-film level. Budgets are critical, fought over and manipulated above and beyond, often rather than towards, artistic endeavour. The logistics of a production are seldom linear – what, when and how you will design may change at the drop of a hat, as new material is written and circumstances (such as weather, or the availability of an actor or location) change. A life in film design is immersive and involves being there at the point of delivery, every shot; whereas a theatre designer's expertise lies in preparing for the live event, knowing that the show goes on without them.

Theatre design and direction has learned a great deal from TV and film – particularly editing… particularly American editing. Designers now make environments in which gear-changes can happen in the blink of an eye through live performance conventions, as well as scenic engineering. The interplay of digital technologies in light, sound and projection has expanded the design vocabulary – toying with the audience's 'anchor' of real space and time. Perhaps now, more than ever, designers for performance make their choice of medium on the merits of how it's made rather than its impact on an audience.

PART TWO

What Skills Do You Need and How Do You Get Them?

1

The 'Natural', the 'Nurtured' and the 'Convert'

Without doubt, theatre designers are polymaths and, to mis-quote Seamus Heaney, scenography is an angler's art. Designers never know from one moment to another which form, expression or science may be called upon in the pursuit of an idea. With his theatre hat on, here is Grant Hicks's tick list of skills and qualities:

> Researching is really important, and knowing *how* to research perhaps even more so. Draw inspiration and influence from all areas of art, design and music. The more you absorb, the more you can synthesise that into something relating to the project you're working on. You have to be a hard worker – do long hours.

Like many roles in the creative industries, you have to be able to motivate yourself or find within yourself the trigger that will get you out of bed each morning, ready to give, consistently, one hundred per cent of yourself, made up of the clichéd but no less truthful ninety-nine per cent perspiration, one per cent inspiration. Grant continues:

> You also have to be a good listener, good collaborator, leader and man-manager... but not in an ostentatious way. You have to learn the subtleties of how to encourage people to be on your side because there may be people around you that don't quite grasp the madness of a designer's ideas. What you're trying to do is not only explain it to them, but get them 'on board': so be as positive and enthusiastic in achieving those ideas as possible.

How close does this working philosophy echo Hamlet's 'speak the speech' acting masterclass?! The following then is an overview of the qualities of the stage designer – a multi-headed beast!

There is no doubt that life in the theatre is not kind to the shy and retiring, but having said that, many working in the entertainment industry live a paradoxical existence, using their extrovert profession to counterbalance an introverted interior persona. Designers are no exception to this: actors will speak of finding confidence in the roles they play, while designers too create 'second life' environments for perhaps similar reasons. Many will speak of relatively insular childhoods throughout which they constructed, in great detail, alternative realities – sometimes utopian, sometimes darker, Freudian and fantastical. Whatever designers are compensating for or building on, like most artist's roots theirs are inescapable and, ultimately, useful.

Most designers, however experienced, can name a hero or at least a mentor; sometimes they are one and the same. Mine was Ralph Koltai, and although I assisted a number of great designers before going fully freelance, I regret not having the bravery to get in touch and offer assistance to Koltai – mind you, perhaps it's best that at least everyone's heroes are held at arm's length, their 'magic' still enchanting and their tricks a secret! A fascinating area of contemporary research is to spot the traces of a designer's aesthetic that have been absorbed from their predecessor and, perhaps, role model, much like the legacy of a grand-master painter apparent in the work of his atelier. Fledgling designers who have decided to assist other designers as an apprenticeship, rather than, or before, stepping out on their own, have the advantage of having seen how it's done before being in the firing line themselves. Though you need to avoid finding yourself stuck in a senior designer's studio, restricted to model-making, the experience of shadowing a designer 'in the field' is essential to learn how to designers operate holistically. Designer Ashley Martin-Davis is convinced of that:

> At that point in my life I was prepared to be
> penniless, so I was firstly really interested in how to
> put a show on rather than just assisting in the studio.
> I would even turn up to meetings that the designer
> had with his directors. It didn't seem so at the time,
> but he was very generous in that he just let me 'hang
> out' with him. It was about enjoying being in
> workshops helping to work out what we were going
> to actually do. I was lucky – he trusted me.

Being under the wing of a senior designer takes patience for the ambitious, and the trick is recognising when to 'launch'. Assistants may find themselves locked in a pattern of dependence, both financially and creatively, so it's usually best to balance this with some of your own work if you've a mid-term plan to be autonomous.

It's true to say that the theatre is a particularly supportive environment for apprentices, whether directors, designers, performers or technicians. This is largely due to the mutual dependency of each discipline and the fact that it is a fundamentally empathetic and therefore humane art form. Design itself is multi- and trans-disciplinary, which requires a particular brand of empathy. Seniors will make many allowances for their juniors in the knowledge that everyone will probably cross paths with each other frequently over the span of a career, and that 'what goes around, comes around'... As Shakespeare's 'fool' Feste warns us, 'the whirligig of time brings in his revenges'.

Artists and designers have to have an inbuilt drive to succeed. Like many freelance professions, design works on a project-to-project basis and, as the saying goes, 'You're only as good as your last job.' Each success and disappointment colours subsequent projects, and you have to be resilient to the knocks, learn from them, and move on. This capacity can either have been hardwired into you at an early age, or it's armour plating that has built up through layers and layers of experience. A resilient mindset is the most transferable attribute from other art and design disciplines. Therefore, a graphic artist like, for example, Ralph Steadman, can have the confidence to shift from working on the drawing board with a publication as the end product, to a theatre designer's drawing board with a performance as the end product. In fact, coming from outside the theatre-design profession and applying a vision or idea of how a production could be, can have clear advantages over the entrenched conventions that a battle-hardened stage designer might bring to a project.

The following are the broad attributes and sensibilities of a theatre designer that drive or shape the workaday detail.

2

The Artist

Art is the expression of the invisible by means of the visible.

Eugène Fromentin

Artists observe and challenge our modern world. They usually make (but decreasingly so in recent years) visual statements. Contemporary art is, as perhaps all 'true' art has always been, underpinned by philosophical ideas and ideological positions. Whether that makes it good art is neither here nor there. A stage designer's art is to engage with a text, piece of music or other starting point in no less a manner; moreover their work can be given added value by their collaborative partners' ideas and positions to make it not only visible, but visceral. The stage designer's art slips though the fingers: it's less of a commodity than a sculpture, a painting, a video or any other artefact with a signature, but it's intention is the same – to make a difference to someone.

The only important thing about design is how it relates to people.

Victor Papanek, product designer and educationalist

As soon as an object is presented to an audience, it is 'read' as an idea. The audience reads the physical design in the context of the text, movement, music, light and the other components. Often they won't be conscious of the designer's intentions, or for that matter the director's, as they are ninety-nine per cent absorbed in their relationship with the performers and the story. Designers will visually frame that story both with an uber-idea and objects that are at the central to it, but their art is to make a powerful addition to the collective artistic endeavour. The more naturalistic the writing, the more likely it is that the design will need to be transparent, sneaking under the radar of the text: and perhaps arguably therefore, more art-full. Bruegel's paintings are full of domestic detail but are none the poorer for it. However, poetic language will often not sit comfortably with realism on stage: Shakespeare's writing, for example, demands a poetic response from the designer and there is a far greater degree of latitude in the audience's tolerance of a design 'statement' in a poetic play than in a naturalistic one.

Traditionally, fine artists have taken to designing opera and ballet more readily than plays because the music further extends that tolerance: from Picasso and Malevich in the early decades of the twentieth century, to Hockney and Heatherwick more recently. In these forms, the audience can consciously and simultaneously enjoy the interplay of narrative, expressive sound, stylised movement and a designer's artistic interpretation. There is now long history of fine artists working as collaborators with contemporary-dance choreographers: a precedent was set when Antony Gormley's work featured alongside theatre designers at the Prague Quadrennial for scenography in 2011.[17] This work can overlap with fine-art performance and is often characterised by the work exploring abstract concepts, such as the transformation of a space by the body – painting with it, using it as an integral part of a sculpture. The designer in this situation is anticipating how moving bodies will move or use objects: making a tracing of where they have been, and so visually tracking the duration of performance time itself through acceleration, deceleration and repetition. Gravity plays a pivotal part in how both designed objects and dancers create pictures. Likewise, designed objects can be 'played' as well as played with to create a soundscape rather than, for example, the use of music in classical ballet to mask the footfall of the dancer.

Art and film-making has had a healthy relationship since photography blossomed into movie-making. The plasticity of the medium, and its potential to play on the mind and senses, suited Dada and the surrealists particularly: the most notable early example of an artist designing for the established studio system being Salvador Dalí's sequence for Hitchcock's *Spellbound* (1945). However, there is now also a wealth of film recordings of the art/theatre crossover whereby design, whether controlled by director/choreographer or a designer, is intrinsic to the final product. The act of framing, editing and focus are all designed for effect or to serve the conceptual foundation of the piece – even if the film is attempting to objectively document a live happening or a making process.

Theatre design is known to be a 'magpie' art form in that designers borrow any ideas or images and reapply them to performance contexts. There is nothing sinful in this, of course – no artist can deny their influences, whether conscious of them or not. Composers do it all the time: Michael Nyman, Benjamin Britten and even The Who all worked directly with the music of Henry Purcell, who himself appropriated melodies and forms from Continental Europe. The artistry is in the inspiration to make a connection between word or music on the one hand and an image on the other, in order to make a powerful theatrical moment. Recognition of something powerfully unified in a production confirms the assertion that theatre can satisfy a deep human need to bond through the collective consciousness called 'culture', if only from a modernist's perspective. Of course, postmodernism counters this assertion by claiming that all artists are free to reflect our layered and fractured lifestyles and should challenge any audience's visual, musical or spatial comfort zone. As an artist, and designer, you can take your pick!

3

The Architect

Theatre designers have to deal with space and, however challenging that space may be, relish it. Every space is unique – in that sense work in all theatres is, to a greater or lesser degree, *for* the specific site, if not *of* the specific site. If the production will tour and is to all intents and purposes self-contained, designers will ignore the range of spaces it will visit at their peril. One of the joys of set design is taking on the nuances of the building in which it will make its home.

The general public often thinks of architecture as the design of buildings rather than the shaping of the air around people. Architects map out patterns of movement and set the scene for the often repetitious rituals of our everyday dramas. They subdivide spaces, some epic, some intimate, based on the human form, scale and practical ergonomics. They can use materials metaphorically and attempt to uplift our spirits, focusing our attention on each other and what we do, or they can preserve sanctuaries of reflection and thought. Architects are joined at the hip to scenography.

Making your first visit to the space you will be designing for can be either thrilling or disappointing. Whichever it is (and it's often something in between), the designer has to do two things: firstly to step into the shoes of the building's original architect and understand what it was they were trying to achieve, and secondly to find out what the people who use it now think of it. Those two things rarely match up, so the stage designer ends up pitching their ideas into the middle ground. You need to do some detective work – what are the material clues that will 'unlock' the space and what do the witnesses report? The main and simple principle to recognise is the volume around and between the actor and audience, as it's in that air that the production breathes; and a poor design can cut off its supply.

One often overlooked aspect of stage design is how the surfaces, planes and materials that make up the architectural space of scenery can directly affect the actor's voice.[18] There are many apocryphal tales of solid ceilings on sets at just the wrong acoustic angle causing voices to bounce up and down, never leaving the stage! Although this can never be an exact science, a set designer should be aware that reverberations, reflections and echoes of the voice can be the curse of actors and audiences alike.

Theatre is made by a community for a community. The designer therefore has a major role to play in how we commune in a single space. Attention must be paid to the shape and dynamics of the production's architecture and how that connects with the audience, its interface. The foyer they enter, the seats they sit on, the view they have, all contribute to the theatre's social function. Each production is not only a presentation or spectacle, but also a physical journey – the designer can look beyond the stage itself for inspiration and meaning. The scenographer Josef Svoboda asserts that:

> [Architecture is] life, not an abstract discipline – an aspect of life, an organisation of life, the groundplan of life; architecture becomes a kind of puzzle of life that you have to solve.

Theatre designers recalibrate or extend the rules of architecture to provide a context for that same puzzle represented on stage.

4

The Stylist

If, for a moment, we regard a designer as principally doing three things – firstly creating symbolic or metaphorical images, secondly engineering a functioning machine for storytelling, and thirdly enhancing theatricality – then stylisation would belong firmly in the last of these. Stylisation may be considered paper-thin, decorative, referential, and a host of other slights, but it nevertheless helps bind stray parts of a design together and gives the audience a way of reading its visual language. A good stylist stops short of cliché whilst understanding the rules of making a powerful image. Designers cannot break the rules and consciously produce innovative work without being fully aware of the complex visual language used by past artists or contemporary media.

The tools you need for effective stylisation are the ability to use colour for particular effect and to understand the part that light plays in its vibrancy; to use either appropriate or unexpected materials so as to achieve 'a look'; to be responsive to all prevailing, changing conditions and craft what the audience actually sees, rather than you think they *should be* seeing; and to be able to source, apply, manipulate or subvert the vast image bank of both classical and popular culture so as to comfort or shock an audience.

5

The Technician

Theatre designers: are they a 'Renaissance Man' or a 'Jack of All Trades'? Fledgling designers, particularly when graduating from the freedoms of an art-school education, frequently carry a weighty burden of guilt that they don't know nearly enough technical information – there's more about this in the next section. From their own perspective they seem to have spent years on an indulgence and reached the 'end' without any, or at least enough, skills. The honest truth is that the multifaceted and trans-disciplinary nature of the subject means that you *never* can know it all – and that's the joy of its vocation.

Technical knowledge is driven by the work in hand, and so each project presents a fresh batch of challenges. There are two crucial points to remember when designing a show and staring into either a technical abyss ('*I haven't a clue how to do this!*') or a mass of technical possibilities ('*I haven't a clue what's best with which to do this?*'). Firstly that the fear of the unknown should never dictate your ideas, and secondly that there are always other practitioners who have done this before – it's the positive flip side to 'nothing's new under the sun'. The two clueless scenarios above are far better than '*I haven't a clue why we're doing this?*' Don't ask '*How am I going to do this?*', but rather '*How do I clearly explain what I'm trying to achieve?*' The designer's technical problem then becomes one of communication – how do you engineer getting everyone onto your wavelength?

Playing in the theatre is a team sport. Play is an important part of work in that it is the springboard for innovation. No, nothing's new, but perhaps new in the latest circumstances, and it's this unique set of both conceptual and physical conditions that makes each project exciting – it's the drug: the designer's own version of 'Doctor Theatre'. Perhaps the most fulfilling aspect of the technical challenges is that you're never alone solving them. Someone out there, from your past near or far, or in the team you're working with, will have a bright solution if you don't. That network multiplies with every project so, in the long term, patience, endurance and resilience help to close the knowledge gap, and I'm talking in terms of years rather than weeks or even months. This book would have not been possible to write without the support of my own network.

Having let us all off the hook, there's a justifiable reason for our technical insecurities. The theatre takes place in real space and time – it's live, and your designs have to work reliably *every night*. If elements of the design have to move, the need for this reliability multiplies, for the safety and welfare of all involved as much as anything, so each design decision carries with it an undeniable responsibility. Again, this burden is shared, across not only the technical team, but the whole company to a more or less extent – from producer, to production manager, to director and designer; all approaching technical challenges from their own perspective but aiming towards a shared goal: that on every level, the shows '*work*'.

As I've indicated, nothing beats experience – and sometimes repetition – to discover or confirm what the word 'works' means. But there is a world of tried-and-tested techniques in books that stretch back into the nineteenth century – a heyday of craft, invention and illusion. One such fascinating two-volume 'manual' is *British Theatrical Patents*, 1801–1900 and then 1901–1950 (edited by Terence Rees and David Wilmore); it's a wonderland of ingenious ideas which, when coupled to digital technology as theatre artists such as

Robert Lepage have managed to do so convincingly, ensures a healthy twenty-first-century future for the mastery of traditional theatrical practice.

6

The Diplomat

Working in a team is never easy, but when it works mutually, it's probably the most satisfying of professional situations. Theatre-making is a consummate collaborative art form. The collaboration can actually upgrade to collective thinking and doing when the situation and participants are right for it. Good theatre ensembles will often emerge from a commitment to fully negotiated methods, and with no obvious chain of command the global whole can become greater than the sum of its parts.[19] Collectivism is not the ultimate goal of a theatre company, however, and established hierarchies within groups can have tremendous benefits – they often speed up decision-making and, for right or wrong, generate a product with a singular vision or philosophy. In either model of working, designers have to be good diplomats, usually working with more people than any other member of a theatre company. They join the dots of creative team, technical team, performers, front-of-house staff, backstage staff, management and so on – design permeating most corners of the production process. In so doing, they have to empathise with all these groups but also remain focused on their goal.

> Diplomacy is the art of letting somebody else have your way.
>
> *David Frost, journalist and broadcaster*

Theatre is still, even within our culture of communicating through the distancing media of emails and texts, a face-to-face profession. The way a show is produced is through human connections, and it results in a similarly interactive event. In my experience, the more interactive the process has been between participants, the more connected the audience will be to the production: professional life and art in parallel. Meetings are therefore crucial to the bond a designer has with a director. Sometimes they meander, at other times the process could be best dubbed as 'shadow boxing'. It is often the case that such 'creative meetings' represent something else going on underneath or alongside them, and the conversation becomes a metaphor for some other insecurity, indecision or fear. Meetings can't be rushed, impatience undermines rich reflective thought, but time is money and there's work to be done. The designer's timeline (see Part Seven) is often mismatched to that of the director in the pre-rehearsal design phases of the production process. Directors will often have their mind on another show they are working on,[20] or on a future show, or at least on the progress of casting actors for your show, so they can occasionally have a compromised attention span. In these situations, you must make allowances; ask them, for example, how their other projects are going (which is interesting in itself) so that you can move on to the job in hand.

The drawings and models you produce are bargaining chips. They are produced to not only offer an idea, but also, more cynically, to withdraw one in an effort to gain something else. As a designer I understand this because I can recognise the same technique when I'm offered a selection of possibilities to choose from (a prop, for example) by technicians – everyone does it. Made objects initially carry more weight than so-called found objects; they clearly have taken time and thought to produce, so they also carry value – the more material you are prepared to sacrifice through conversation, the more currency you have, whether you choose to spend it or not.[21] For this reason, always go to meetings prepared not only with what you want to gain, but also what you're prepared to lose. After all, this (hopefully) won't be your last production, so you can save the idea for later – park it in your 'bottom drawer'.

In the more complex surroundings of the technical and dress rehearsals, when the opening night is edging towards you and the minute-to-minute working relationships are accelerated, sensibilities (including yours) are heightened. You have an idea or concern that's got to be aired… it's now or never, but at the same time everyone might not thank you for 'sharing'. At this point it is of utmost importance to 'read the room', gauge the temperature and choose an appropriate moment. In these situations, the hierarchy, or at least systems that the profession has in place to get through material efficiently, has to be adhered to. There are lines of communication, usually through the stage manager and director, by which you can change the course of these last rehearsals, so it's best to respect that… As my mother used to remind me, '*Softly, softly, catchy monkey.*'

PART THREE

Education or Training?

The landscape of theatre-design training has undergone remarkable changes over the last three decades. Students of theatre design in the 1970s and early '80s would have had a variety of opportunities to progress from their courses to an apprenticeship in an established theatre company, or to take their fledgling skills into an associated field, such as TV design in a number of departments at the BBC or independent film studios. That route disappeared almost overnight in the mid-1980s with cutbacks to all state-subsidised arts organisations – design was one of the first areas in the entertainment industry to take the hit.

The previous two decades or so of fostering design as a valued and specialised theatre discipline were flushed away and the growing number of theatre-design graduates had to find alternative means of survival. Gone was the design department that had been nurtured in each and every repertory theatre. Gone was its tiered structure of head of design, associate designer, and often a number of young design assistants – learning the ropes with the expectation of succeeding their seniors. That hands-on experience was, from that point, expected to be delivered by degree and post-graduate courses. Henceforward it was now very much a freelance market, and designers too had to earn their place in the cultural economy.

Theatre designers, like directors, have always come from a mix of backgrounds. Some of the most interesting and successful designers have sprung from starting points like literature, architecture or fashion, rather than from a formal specialist theatre-design education. At some point or other, however, most of this brand of theatre designer has had to go through some sort of additional training. The mainstay foundation of the profession is still either taking a validated course or starting in the more lowly ranks of a theatre company and working through the hierarchy. Here are the principal routes to being a rooky professional. Each have pros and cons, and the choice of which is best is often left to personality, needs or circumstances.

It is becoming more the case that the distinctions between design training in an art school as opposed to a drama school are becoming increasingly blurred. Both usually require applicants to submit a folio of artwork and will end the course with the offer of a showcase exhibition. Which route a young designer might take is usually determined by other factors than the academic make-up of a course, such as their sensibility to a particular work environment, whether they want to study in London or elsewhere, and whether they feel it's time to leave the family home, wherever that is.

Entry into higher design education is usually still by folio and interview. Folios are usually best if they tell a visual story. By that I mean that there should be a reason why the work is in a particular order so it can be viewed as a 'journey'. This doesn't have to be literal; it could be no different to the journey in a piece of music. It could have a dynamic shift in colour; it could travel from two-dimensional images to three-dimensional objects. Folios can be themed; having distinctive sections for abstract work, representational work, diagrammatic work, and so on. The main thing is to keep it relatively punchy – between, say, twenty-five and thirty-five pieces. There are time constraints on those who are viewing the work, so think about what they will be seeing without you being there to explain each detail. For example, the selection process for some art schools, and in the early stages of the Linbury Prize competition,[22] folios are submitted prior to, or even instead of, an interview. So provide an introductory sentence or two (no more) of written context for the piece or project. It's also best to show a little of your process work, demonstrating how you think through a problem and have the ability to take risks along the way.

Most colleges, however, will give you the opportunity to attend an interview. The trick here is to try to not let your nerves get the better of you. This is a face-to-face chance for you to find out about the sort of experience you might have over an important two- or three-year period, so consider it a conversation in which both parties can size each other up... dogs circling in the park! Go prepared to ask some questions – that's expected. The sort of question you ask, and how you ask it, says as much about you as do your answers to the interviewer.

1

Training in a Drama School

As part of the 'conservatoire' tradition, there is little to beat this option for hands-on exposure to the practical demands of performers and directors. If your design training runs alongside that for student actors, you will better understand the art and craft of their skill, and therefore you will be coached to design with them in mind. A good drama-school experience will constantly challenge your unflappability, practical resourcefulness and assumptions about 'who does what' to get a show on.

You will see first hand and probably have a real experience of the full range of practical design disciplines, from painting to lighting and sound, to making of all sorts. With that comes the rigour of having to draw designed objects accurately and using a language that is universally understood in the biz. You will also no doubt exercise your powers of diplomacy on a day-to-day basis, something that cannot be underestimated throughout any working life – but, as I've already asserted, even more so in and amongst the complicated and shifting matrix of relationships in a theatre company.

The chances are that the structure of these courses will give you the opportunity to assume sole responsibility for a design and take it through a 'cradle to grave' process. This is invaluable as you will be in an environment safe from the cut and thrust of fully fledged professional projects, where the fear of 'only being as good as your last job' is not inhibiting to your creative spirit and where you may be able to take an artistic risk or two... although you'll probably not feel like that at the time!

A good performance is often reliant on timing. In a drama school you can see this elemental ingredient of theatre being honed again and again. For a designer, too, an attention to timing can be crucial. In farce, for example, the distance between entrances and their relative positions can make or break a comic sequence. In opera and musical theatre there are a number of moments, some quite long, when what the audience sees on stage is design and sound working together in a sequence that is predetermined by the duration, rhythm or tone of a passage of music. I vividly remember a moment of revelation working with the extraordinary choreographer and actor Tim Flavin, who, as we were peering into a model box, gently pointed out that the staircase I had designed for our musical was almost totally redundant because, for dancers, it needed to have a number of steps (for *their* steps) that were strictly divisible by fours and eights.

Networking with your peer group, whatever sort of college you might decide upon is vital. They can be a life-long practical support and a shoulder to cry on in lean or troubled times. Your fellow students can also be a form of extended agency, whereby if they are offered work they can't or won't do, they may pass it over to you, their trusty friend. The camaraderie in a drama school is more apparent than in the alternatives and it is learning how to harness this potential team spirit that will often get you through the darker moments of a production.

2

Learning in an Art School

Art schools have a long association with the theatre. Painters have, from time to time, taken a professional diversion on to the stage to test their ideas and aesthetics behind the alternative picture frame of the proscenium arch – a painting in motion. So when the first theatre-design courses were created, it was in the art school that their various characteristics could evolve. Nearly all these established colleges have since been absorbed by universities and, as such, have thinking rather than doing at their core. There is wide acceptance, however, that artists and designers often as not think by doing and vice versa. The art school is a place for reflection and speculation – for '*What if…?*'

Each institution has its own flavour and ethos, which is often difficult to detect by the casual observer. As with many courses, this ethos is a reflection of the characters and practices of those that originally designed the courses and now run them. Very often a well-established course's philosophy has been passed down through a lengthy daisy chain of tutors and students, so if you're thinking about applying to one of these, it's best to do your homework thoroughly. Treat the hype of a university's website with scepticism, but it can lead you to valuable avenues of detailed information. Research the college's past and find out all you can about what current tutors and students are doing, both professionally and academically. You may then start to piece together at least a sense of what makes any particular college tick and picture yourself there.

What I've outlined as the strengths of the drama-school design course have to be specially imported into the art-school situation. Directors, actors and other collaborators work with design students in 'laboratory' conditions. They often go through the process as if they were mounting a production for the public, but usually, unlike a drama school, without following it through to the actual event. On the other hand, the benefits are that students are encouraged have a distinctive, sometimes innovative vision. Design ambition is the top priority here, free from the nuts-'n'-bolts constraints of servicing a performance course. From this perspective, students in an art school are traditionally encouraged to challenge established ways of doing things rather than work within their norms and protocols. So, for example, drawing is more likely to be used to illustrate how the complete costume or moment of staging might look from the audience's viewpoint *in performance*, often at the expense of using drawing as a way of communicating intricate technical information to creative and backstage teams.

3

Other Backgrounds

If you look at a designer's biography in a show programme you will often see a line or two about what their background has been. There has never been a comprehensive survey of every current designer's stepping-off point (maybe this would make a research project for some PhD student or other), but my guess is that the rank-and-file designer is likely to have been trained in one of the many courses I've already mentioned. However, there are a number of very successful designers that have found their vocation from an unconventional root. Interestingly, it's relatively rare that a stage designer will have developed their interest from starting out as a technician, although most college-trained designers will often begin in the profession by making a buck practising one of the many crafts, such as scene painting, costume-making or prop-building. Some of these folk may eventually stick with making objects rather than designing them – perhaps because they have found it more satisfying or perhaps because they have found a more productive and lucrative niche for themselves – in millinery, for example, or perhaps animatronics. The reality is that there are far more makers employed on a show than designers.

Most designers will acknowledge that the relationships they have with technicians and makers can be rich and creative. Because designers in the UK tend to have an oversight of all the visual components of a production, this means that a technician can feel, through working with ideas close to the conceptual centre, that they have an artistic impact on the production process and on what the audience finally experiences on stage. In that way there may be less of a creative need for a technician to want to design scenery or costumes. Conversely, it may also be that because designers in the UK are busier, rushing from one otherwise specialist area to another, technicians and makers are often proactive interpreters with a good deal of creative responsibility, rather than a more straightforward 'mechanic'.

Lighting and sound design is another matter. Lighting designers, although often also coming from an artistic training of one sort or another, will need to have a fundamental grip on how lighting instruments, lighting boards, computer programming and rudimentary physics fundamentally contribute towards a successful lighting design. In my experience one area that will often bond a design team together is an interest in, or love for, some other medium, such as film or music. Musical backgrounds, whether they are part of designer's formal education or just some sort of hobby, can be hugely useful when knitting together creative ideas for music-based work: dance, music theatre and opera. Music creation and production can serve as a metaphor for other creative processes, such as subtexts being synonymous with a bass line of three movements equating to a three-act drama or three parts of a good joke.

The diversity of backgrounds in the profession can only add to its richness. The enormous range of skills that a designer needs also provides an opportunity for people who discover they may have theatre-design talent to play to those very strengths that a conventional training may not provide. Among these are, for example, storytelling and narratives of all sorts fuelled by a love of literature and poetry. Alongside these are the visual and material arts of graphic design, architecture, interior design and painting or sculpture; all of which are common elements of a designer's skill base or creative impulse. One route that seems to be fairly common amongst both designers and directors is an interest in performing itself. Buried in their histories is often a passion for acting. It may well be that in these instances what develops into a fulfilling career as part of the creative team (rather than the acting ensemble) might stem from a suppressed longing to be centre stage! However, whether the directors and designers are frustrated actors or not, their empathy with performers and their support for them is crucial to the creative and collaborative process of putting on a show. Designers have to appreciate the discipline, energy and at times stomach-churning fear that an actor may need to harness when faced with an audience of anything from fifty people to five thousand.

4

Working Your Way 'Up the Ranks'

I've already mentioned that designers may not have had a technical training, but many designers have found their contribution to technical aspects of theatre-making in their early days to be invaluable. As part of the technical team, they will have understood how all the different component parts of a production fit together. There is, for example, a universally understood order in which a rehearsal and production process has to take shape, and there's certainly a great deal of negotiated demarcation as to who does what.

This common knowledge, as in many professions, cannot be acquired and properly absorbed in an abstract way: it can only be fully appreciated and practised through experience. Reading this book (or any other along similar lines) can never match actually doing it. There is possibly no better way to appreciate what it takes to put on a show every evening than from the perspective of the costume dresser. Dressers are essential to many a production's perfect timing, consistency and smooth running on a nightly basis – they are most obviously the human interface between the actor and their costume, particularly when a quick change is needed, but also between the stage management and the actor's cue that is at the heart of the show's pace and rhythm. Any designer who has found themselves in the dresser's position will have *experienced* the organisation and enthusiasm required to make design tick.

Whether a designer actually needs to know all the technical processes that underpin design realisation is open to debate. Most designers will have missed out on experiencing working hands-on in one technical area or another, and rely on the expertise of others for both the development of their work and the richness of the creative process. Indeed, there's a school of thought that advises a degree of professional detachment from the technical process for two reasons: firstly, that in-depth knowledge of a methodology can sometimes inhibit innovation in the studio when conceptualising, drawing and modelling; and secondly, it's part of the joy of designing that you will continuously learn from experts in other disciplines through realisation.

In any of these eventualities, there are very few vocational designers (I'm excluding those that 'jump ship' from their usual sphere of expertise – such as illustrator and cartoonist Gerald Scarfe, fashion guru Jasper Conran or textile artist Kaffe Fassett), who have not needed at least a short spell as an assistant to an established theatre designer. Many spend years under their wing before launching their own careers – and some stick with assisting for many, many years.

Design assistant or assistant designer?

Being an assistant to an individual designer brings many benefits, often hidden at the time, which will stand you in good stead for years to come. There is a distinction to be made between the job description of assistant designer and design assistant. The latter is usually part of a production team and liaises between designer and the many departments realising his or her ideas. The role isn't so common nowadays as there are very few resident design departments in repertory companies or in the commercial sector that could afford a design assistant – they are largely seen as a luxury and part of a bygone (golden) age when such design departments were part of a producing theatre's infrastructure. What's more, design now being a largely freelance activity, assistant designers, having been employed or otherwise engaged by the designer, have largely superseded design assistants. The closest an aspiring designer might come to the design assistant's position is as some form of internship – you don't have to do a long stint before you begin to see how the factory line of a production process is pieced together and how design feeds the machine. Opportunities for this are rarely formally offered, so the best way of getting into a theatre through this route as a student is to pester people, such as production and technical managers, until you're given a chance or have to give up. You can find their names in the back of show programmes: it may take several letters, emails or rounds of drinks to get your foot in the door – but be reasonably persistent.

Assistant designers are usually the product of theatre-design training. If you're on a course, you may be offered the chance to shadow or assist on some form of work placement. Brief though this usually is, it gives you an insight into how what you're learning relates to practice and, importantly, whether it's a route to being a fully fledged designer that you would favour above or among others… It's not for everyone, but you probably have to try it to know for sure.

As an assistant, you'll have to be a multitasker and multi-disciplinarian. Don't be surprised that when you assist, the designer might not really care about your ideas: they might get interested in what you *really* think when times are particularly hard, but actually it's usually just about being 'a doer'… which is sometimes fine because in that role you'll simply want to be told what to do, or figure out the practical problem in hand.

Assistants may come to a designer's attention as a specialist in one area or another, such as having the skill to use certain software, build a certain sort of model, or follow through visual research, but you have to be prepared to switch gears and tasks as a design evolves and a designer's needs shift focus.

Assistants might work with ten or more designers over a period of five or six years and in a huge range of scales, styles and forms of work. The best assistants, those who stay the distance and are in great demand, understand how and when to listen, when to step back and when to take an initiative. For the designer's part, being clear about how elastic the gap can be between those two positions is key to a mutually confident partnership: particularly on short, punchy projects that need to get off the ground quickly and when both assistant and designer need to be on the same wavelength immediately. There's no formula to a good working relationship, and, like most professional life, it will probably boil down to some form of chemistry. Both designer and assistant will most likely share hours and hours together locked up in the same room, often in the designer's home, so you have to learn to rub along.

> At different times, different skills are appropriate, for example one of the most basic skills is knowing when to make a cup of tea at the right time, when the atmosphere in the room gets a bit sticky, or as simple as knowing where the nearest tape measure is. Mundane things can sometimes be the most helpful.
>
> *David Harris, designer (and associate designer)*

Some assistants just have the knack of knowing how to balance the art of being a good technician, having a 'good eye' and being good company: usually because they genuinely enjoy being in the role and don't feel frustrated by it. Some therefore decide to be part of the established 'circuit' of assistants and secure a good reputation in that niche, soon finding they have to juggle a string of projects that they have to actively break if they have an ambition to design themselves. Being an assistant won't necessarily put you in a position to meet directors – you'll most likely be too busy attending to the studio needs of the designer – so it can become something of a trap for those wishing to move on. Many, however, will realise that it satisfies their situation, both financially and creatively, for at least a short while in their twenties and early thirties and become one of an elite group of specialists. Though I've always found working with these 'professional assistants' fascinating, it seems to me to be something of a twilight existence, not ever seeing your own ideas realised full scale, but I can also appreciate the technical expertise and care of a design that only someone completely focused can give. Speaking, understanding and appreciating the shorthand language of stage design is what gets assistants employed and re-employed – for the most part, I've found the relationship challenging, creative and enjoyable, both as an assistant when I started out and now working with assistants of my own.

Associate designers

Being an associate designer puts your foot on the next rung up the ladder from assistant. This position is a relatively recent phenomenon, and opinions vary as to how to define it and what its merits are in terms of graduating to designer status.

Most associates have had some previous experience as an autonomous designer in their own right before being asked to take on the role. They usually deputise for a designer who has either anticipated being part of a huge project and needs support in any of a variety of areas, or is 'up to their neck' and in need of emergency backup. In either case, the associate will usually go beyond the assistant's duties of researching, model-making or various forms of drawing to the designer's instructions in the studio. Associates will most likely be expected to take on primary decision-making at any point in a process and will often see a production through to its public performances.

Associates, much like assistants, will most likely be asked on to a project having been recommended: usually by another designer. They don't usually come straight from a design course – they need to have had substantial hands-on experience of the knocks and shocks of getting an ambitious show together. This makes the small number of associates quite a tight, crack force in the profession, and busy designers try their damnedest to keep the best ones and engage them for as long as possible until the associate feels the need launch their freelance design career on a permanent basis. Meanwhile, it's not an easy role – often in the firing line and 'taking the bullet' as the designer's front line of defence against an army of pressures from producers, directors and technicians. They are a special breed in that they need saintly patience, the diplomacy of Solomon and the grit of Rocky Balboa... with a bit of extrasensory perception thrown in for good measure.

In the studio of a well-established designer with a team of assistants, as is often the case for a large-scale musical or opera, associates may also steer the studio team in the designer's absence. On site in the theatre, the title means that people should listen to the associate more than they would to an assistant when needs be. If the designer is not around, other creatives and technicians with a concern will go to the associate, who uses their more experienced judgement to gauge if it's something that needs to be checked with the designer or whether they themselves know the answer. Like most aspects of a professional training, often the only way to learn to distinguish between those things over time is by getting it wrong!

In America, being an established associate is a respected and long-term prospect. Its pay usually reflects that. But in the UK, particularly amongst young designers, it's a more temporary condition through which you graduate to be a designer by learning on the job. With today's global inter-connectivity, associates could remotely design from the UK for a Broadway production if, say, the designer had to be in a third country during the design process, so email, Dropbox and Skype are the common cyber-meeting places. This is far less doable for costume designers who have to see the fittings through in a more real-place, real-time process.

Warning: it's not rare for associates in the UK to end up pretty much designing a whole show because the designer's not been present, and yet be given, in the programme and elsewhere, little or even zero credit. Other designers can be a bit more generous, however: not only are they happy to give the associate autonomy, but also have the good grace to tell the world that this is who has been working on the project. Likewise, further down the food chain as an assistant, you may have done just as much work on a project as an associate, but in the end the real credit comes down to not a title so much as what else you can get out of it.

Many associates therefore soon graduate to concentrating exclusively on their own design projects. One can have every sympathy with the view that: *'If I can cope with the rough and tumble of being an associate, why not do my own thing and get the full credit (and full fee) of being the designer?'* Why not indeed?

PART FOUR

What's in a Design?

1

A Designer's Reading of the Script

Designers, like any other theatre artists, need to read a script two or three times before they are in a position to discuss its ideas and an approach to making it a production. Each of those reads will prompt a different response, and after each a designer may have a very different view of the piece. Sometimes even the form in which you will receive a script, whether it's on a screen, printed specially by the theatre company, or in a published volume, may influence a first impression.

In my experience, the fresher the hard copy, the more lively and personal my reaction to it. For example, Shakespeare's plays feel far more like a newly written contemporary piece of writing if it has been reprinted in a modern font and perhaps renumbered or structured by the theatre company who are mounting the work. If I read the same words in a mighty and dusty *Complete Works of Shakespeare*, my initial approach to the words and story is burdened by the baggage of the publisher, the editor, and all the scholarly history that preceded it. Even the illustration on the front cover can have some form of subliminal impact.

That apart, the first reading of any play is likely to engage your sensibilities more than your intellect. The tone of the language, the rhythm of the speech, the structure and length all contribute towards how you and an audience might 'feel' about the play, as opposed to how they might think about its underlying themes and concepts. It's useful, without interrupting the flow of the narrative, to try to record what these initial feelings and thoughts have been. By record, I mean that written notes are probably only half the story: drawings, colour washes, finding associated or obscure objects that resonate with the play, are all equally if not more powerfully relevant to the subsequent days and weeks of the design process – particularly in terms of communicating your reactions to others in the creative team.

I would recommend trying to make a second reading before entering into a dialogue with your director. This second sortie through the play is more likely to engage a slightly deeper intellectual or rational, left-brain analysis of the ideas, forms and logistics of the piece. Coupled with the first reading, this second exercise gives the designer a more rounded view of the play and will help in a more three-hundred-and-sixty-degree discussion of the potential production with the director. This reading is about identifying and gathering evidence. You are as much a detective as an artist: looking for clues and building intellectual arguments. Throughout the second reading it is valuable to note down as much as you can about the following three design-orientated aspects of the author's work.

Firstly, you are looking for clues about the environment in which the author has written the play – its spatial, architectural context… its artistic landscape. Sometimes this evidence is in the stage directions but beware that (in sixteenth- and seventeenth-century plays in particular) these will often have been written or supplemented by editors and are sometimes an amalgamation of directions from the play's previous performances. For that reason these stage directions are to be treated with a good deal of scepticism when it comes to designing a production of your own. They are often superfluous to the essential drama and do not allow for your ideas and instincts to lead the work, although it's tempting to take them on board as a means to understand the possible theatrical 'business' when staging the story. Sometimes those stage directions can extend to describing colours, costumes that are not referred to directly in the dialogue, or perhaps a view through a window with a sky beyond. If taken as 'gospel truth', the implications of these directions can close down any independent thoughts about the theatrical conventions you might want to use to deconstruct the play before reconstructing it in your own terms. There are notable exceptions to this, for example, I would always take note of Tennessee Williams' notes on staging. He describes not only his view of the stage, but his poetic vision for it; that in turn implies, through the qualities of material forms, the conventions and relationships between a performer and their audience. The layout of the stage in the author's mind for farce and other forms of situation comedy must also be treated with respect. An Alan Ayckbourn play will have been very carefully conceived with particular spatial relationships between entrances, exits and objects in mind for the comedy to work fluidly, both in the round and on a proscenium stage – tinker with these at your peril! There are also extreme dramas that rely almost entirely on physical action described in detail by the author for narrative reasons, for instance, Peter Handke's extraordinary *The Hour We Knew Nothing of Each Other*, that has no speaking whatsoever but is, nevertheless, very much a script to be served by the designer.

The second group of clues are concerned with the characters and objects associated with them. Sometimes environment and character inevitably cross over, and that's why in my opinion a production will often have more integrity if a single person designs set, props and costumes. With character clues you have to be watchful for not only the obvious references but also the text's implications. A character may describe a particular aspect of another character's clothing or style, but it's also useful to note down any first impressions you may have of how characters rank against each other, their status in the narrative and how that may relate to contemporary society. For example, if a character comments on another's new shoes, the designer has a number of choices about the design of shoe, but they do have to be new. If a character comments on the fact that they can hear footsteps in the corridor, it's also clearly the designer's remit to imagine the sound these shoes may make on the floor upon which they are scraping, tapping or squeaking. In this second read a designer may also begin to form a clear idea about the need for characters to change clothing for one reason or another: a change of weather, a leap forwards or backwards in time, a change of circumstances, such as getting either wealthier or poorer, and so forth. In this respect the visual narrative will begin to form as the dynamics of each character or group of characters crisscrossing through the story will begin to suggest shapes and change. Inevitably some dramas are written for a particular period in history. Sometimes the author's decision to do this unlocks the story and the audience comfortably transposes the ideas from that era to their own contemporary context. Other dramas that may have been written at a particular but not intrinsically relevant period, and that deal with universal themes, can begin to be transposed into another period by the creative team at an early stage in the design process – of course, an argument always has to be made to do this as the clues in the text may have to be edited in collaboration with the director and sometimes the estate of a deceased author.

The third group of clues is far less well defined but is ultimately perhaps the most powerful – they are concerned with word association: metaphors, symbols and other forms of poetic interpretation. The responses and choices that the creative team makes in relation to this area can colour the previous two and often has the longest lasting impact on the audience. Shakespeare, of course, is packed with them – it's like shooting fish in a barrel! But other more recent playwrights can have tremendous scope for a more intuitive approach to the visual language: Lorca, for example. All these rules are given a different emphasis when designing for opera, in which the music provides a continuous sensational strand to the events that the designer is compelled to respond to in relation to the nuts and bolts of the narrative. I have often found it extremely useful to make note of absolutely *all* the associations that spring to mind, particularly in the first reading. The designer's immediate visceral reaction to a piece can often be their most truthful and can connect directly to an audience's subsequent subliminal receptors – it's the design's subtext.

Finally, some of the best theatre relies on sheer vivid storytelling. So whatever the complexities of each scene, the most important aspect of the read is to retain the thrust of the narrative. The story is what will most likely excite and sustain your work with the creative team and actors, so understanding the narrative drive and how that alone will move and stimulate the theatregoing public is paramount.

Top Tip: *Whatever form the text reaches you in, I reprint it on individual single-sided sheets that I can keep in a flexible ring-bound file. This allows for notes and drawings to be made on the blank reverse of the page opposite and for the possibility of moving scenes around if you do indeed have the freedom to substantially change the narrative of a play out of copyright.*

2

Research and Plotting

Research and plotting are to my mind the equivalent of pleasure and pain. *Researching* in its many forms – from libraries, to the internet, to interviewing, to taking trips and photographs – is perhaps one of the most stimulating aspects of theatre design. Research, whether it's discovering a new material and its qualities or a new philosopher and their ideas, is both an exciting and broadening human activity – by definition it takes you into new territories and reveals the world through free association and the needs of the project. Any of the previous section's clues can lead you along meandering paths with unexpected destinations. In theory, any sustained creative process should always reserve the possibility for research to change its course, but all too often the need to define what you're going to do, and the inevitable fact that some audiences like to see a familiar piece at its recognisable 'best', can often put safety first and close down the more risky aspects of trying new things.

The period of designing between the first read and the first rehearsal is the most fertile research time, still allowing for the possibility of change based on new discoveries before offering the design to the theatre company as a whole and therefore committing to a greater responsibility. Researching theatre history, recent or older, in comparison to researching the social context for a play or opera, varies hugely amongst practitioners. Many directors, designers and actors will look over their shoulder at how a piece was made in the past or how another company may remake that piece now. But, in my experience, referencing another company's work tends to be reductive in that the creative process that motivated their work is usually unknown. Makers should approach each new project with their own thoughts and feelings whilst being completely receptive to the thoughts and feelings of their collaborators, unclouded by the superficial influences of others.

The *plotting* process of a designer is simply a way of analysing a play or libretto that, through sheer meticulous record-keeping, can reveal both the physical needs of a production and the mapping of their entire journey from prologue to epilogue.

There are many forms of plotting and for very many different reasons. The various plots can also be a handy overview or checklist for your collaborators, such as a costume supervisor or stage managers. They can form the agenda for a props meeting or be a really useful aide-memoire in a costume fitting when talking through the permutations of an actor's clothing. Here are some of production's aspects that can be usefully tracked through the story:

- Scenic changes – locations, times of day, weather.

- Principal actors and their characters.

- Exits and entrances.

- Costume changes.

- Chorus activities including musical accompaniment and dances.

- Properties from scene to scene, such as letters or weaponry.

By scrupulously setting out who goes where and when, the exercise has a two-for-one effect. Personally, there's nothing I find more tedious but crucial than keeping track of letters or other missives in Shakespeare's plays, and what they might look like depending on who wrote them and their condition between being written and received… but the properties plot compels me to confront all the realities of the script as written and so develops into a sophisticated to-do list.

Here is an example of an exit and entrance plotting system developed by designer Peter Farley.

Divide each scene in the text (in this instance, for John Webster's *The White Devil*) into entrances and exits:

- Draw a line on the script every time anyone enters or exits.

- The space between one drawn line and the next is called a 'unit'.

- Number each unit 1, 2, 3, etc., until you reach the end of the scene.

- Draw a double line at the end of each scene.

- Repeat until you reach the end of the act.

- Draw a triple line at the end of each act.

- Repeat until you reach the end of the play.

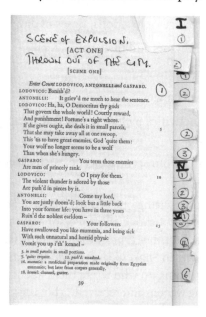

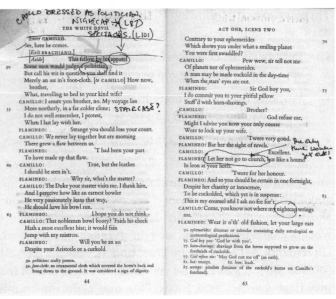

[Handwritten annotations:] CAMILLO DRESSED AS POLITICIAN. NIGHTCAP → (L87) SPECTACLES. (L101)

THE WHITE DEVIL

Enter CAMILLO.
See, here he comes.
　　　[*Exit* BRACHIANO]
50　　[*Aside*]　　　　This fellow by his apparel
　　Some men would judge a politician,
　　But call his wit in question you shall find it
　　Merely an ass in's foot-cloth. [*to* CAMILLO] How now,
　　brother,
　　What, travelling to bed to your kind wife?
　　CAMILLO: I assure you brother, no. My voyage lies
55　　More northerly, in a far colder clime; *STAIRCASE?*
　　I do not well remember, I protest,
　　When I last lay with her.
　　FLAMINEO:　　　　Strange you should lose your count.
　　CAMILLO: We never lay together but ere morning
　　There grew a flaw between us.
　　FLAMINEO:　　　'T had been your part
　　To have made up that flaw.
60　　CAMILLO:　　True, but she loathes
　　I should be seen in't.
　　FLAMINEO:　　Why sir, what's the matter?
　　CAMILLO: The Duke your master visits me. I thank him,
　　And I perceive how like an earnest bowler
　　He very passionately leans that way,
　　He should have his bowl run.
65　　FLAMINEO:　　　I hope you do not think—
　　CAMILLO: That nobleman bowl booty? 'Faith his cheek
　　Hath a most excellent bias; it would fain
　　Jump with my mistress.
　　FLAMINEO:　　　Will you be an ass
　　Despite your Aristotle or a cuckold

50. *politician:* crafty person.
52. *foot-cloth:* an ornamental cloth which covered the horse's back and hung down to the ground. It was considered a sign of dignity.

44

ACT ONE, SCENE TWO

　　Contrary to your ephemerides　　　　　　70
　　Which shows you under what a smiling planet
　　You were first swaddled?
　　CAMILLO:　　　　Pew wew, sir tell not me
　　Of planets nor of ephemerides.
　　A man may be made cuckold in the day-time
　　When the stars' eyes are out.
　　FLAMINEO:　　　Sir God boy you,　　　75
　　I do commit you to your pitiful pillow
　　Stuff'd with horn-shavings.
　　CAMILLO:　　　Brother?
　　FLAMINEO:　　　　God refuse me,
　　Might I advise you now your only course
　　Were to lock up your wife.
　　CAMILLO:　　　'Twere very good. *the only*
　　FLAMINEO: Bar her the sight of revels. *true women*
　　CAMILLO:　　　　Excellent. *yet asde!*
　　FLAMINEO: Let her not go to church, but like a hound
　　In leon at your heels.
　　CAMILLO:　　　'Twere for her honour.
　　FLAMINEO: And so you should be certain in one fortnight,
　　Despite her chastity or innocence,
　　To be cuckolded, which yet is in suspense:　　85
　　This is my counsel and I ask no fee for't,
　　CAMILLO: Come, you know not where my nightcap wrings
　　me.
　　FLAMINEO: Wear it o'th' old fashion, let your large ears

70. *ephemerides:* almanac or calendar containing daily astrological or meteorological predictions.
75. *God boy you:* 'God be with you'.
77. *horn-shavings:* shavings from the horns supposed to grow on the foreheads of cuckolds.
77. *God refuse me:* 'May God cast me off' (an oath).
81. *but:* except.　82. *leon:* leash.
87. *wrings:* pinches (because of the cuckold's horns on Camillo's forehead).

45

[Handwritten:] BRCACHIANO COMES OUT FROM HIDING.

⑥　*Enter* BRACHIANO.
　　Come sister, darkness hides your blush; women are like
　　curs'd dogs, civility keeps them tied all daytime, but they
　　are let loose at midnight; then they do most good or most
200　　mischief. My lord, my lord.
　　BRACHIANO: Give credit: I could wish time would stand
　　still *[CARPET cushions]*
　　And never end this interview, this hour,
　　But all delight doth itself soon'st devour.
⑦　ZANCHE *brings out a carpet, spreads it and lays on it two*
　　fair cushions. Enter CORNELIA [*listening, behind*].
　　Let me into your bosom happy lady,　*CORNELIA*
205　　Pour out instead of eloquence my vows;　*LISTENING*
　　Loose me not madam, for if you forgo me　*HIDDEN*
　　I am lost eternally.
　　VITTORIA:　　Sir in the way of pity
　　I wish you heart-whole.
　　BRACHIANO:　　You are a sweet physician.
　　VITTORIA: Sure it was a loathed cruelty in ladies
210　　Is as to doctors many funerals.
　　It takes away their credit.
　　BRACHIANO:　　Excellent creature.
　　We call the cruel fair, what name for you
　　That are so merciful?
　　ZANCHE:　　See now they close.
　　FLAMINEO: Most happy union.
215　　CORNELIA [*aside*]: My fears are fall'n upon me, O my heart!
　　My son the pander: now I find our house
　　Sinking to ruin. Earthquakes leave behind,
　　Where they have tyrannized, iron or lead, or stone,
　　But, woe to ruin! violent lust leaves none.
　　BRACHIANO: What value is this jewel?

198. *curs'd:* vicious.
220-27. *jewel:* used here with an extended double entendre.

50

ACT ONE, SCENE TWO　　　　*[Handwritten:]* JEWEL

　　VITTORIA:　　　　'Tis the ornament　220
　　Of a weak fortune.
　　BRACHIANO: In sooth I'll have it; nay I will but change
　　My jewel for your jewel.
　　FLAMINEO:　　　Excellent,
　　His jewel for her jewel; well put in Duke.
　　BRACHIANO: Nay let me see you wear it.
　　VITTORIA:　　　　Here sir.　　225
　　BRACHIANO: Nay lower, you shall wear my jewel lower.
　　FLAMINEO: That's better; she must wear his jewel lower.
　　VITTORIA: To pass away the time I'll tell your Grace
　　A dream I had last night.
　　BRACHIANO:　　Most wisedly.
　　VITTORIA: A foolish idle dream:　　　230
　　Methought I walk'd about the mid of night,
　　Into a church-yard, where a goodly yew-tree
　　Spread her large root in ground; under that yew,
　　As I sat sadly leaning on a grave,
　　Checkered with cross-sticks, there came stealing in　235
　　Your Duchess and my husband; one of them
　　A pick-axe bore, th'other a rusty spade,
　　And in rough terms they 'gan to challenge me,
　　About this yew.
　　BRACHIANO:　　That tree.
　　VITTORIA:　　　This harmless yew,
　　They told me my intent was to root up　　240
　　That well-grown yew, and plant i'th' stead of it
　　A withered blackthorn, and for that they vow'd
　　To bury me alive: my husband straight
　　With pick-axe 'gan to dig, and your fell Duchess
　　With shovel, like a fury, voided out　　　245

238. *'gan:* began.　241. *stead of:* in the place of.
243. *straight:* immediately.　244. *fell:* cruel.
245. *voided out:* emptied out.

51

Then, make a chart showing all the entrances and exits by drawing it out in the following way:

- Putting all the characters' names (in order of appearance) along the top of the grid.

- Working from top to bottom, use one line for each unit, dividing the chart into scenes and acts.

- Then shade in the squares to show the units that each character appears in.

You can then nuance the blocks with further information about what happens to certain characters. In the table opposite, for example, the slightly darker squares are moments when a character has to be seen on stage but doesn't speak (Brachiano, Act One, Scene One, unit 3), and the darkest squares, with 'X's in, remind you when someone dies in the play (Isabella, Act Two, Scene Two, unit 2, during Dumb Show 1).

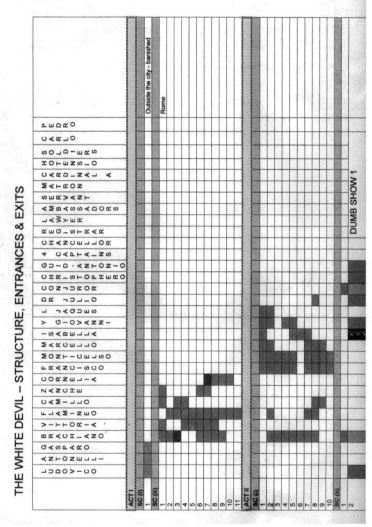

Exit and entrance plotting system developed by designer Peter Farley for John Webster's *The White Devil*.

Depending on your form of graphic representation (and there are many according to taste, from quirky freehand to digital sterility), underlying trends and structures can be revealed that sometimes even the author was not consciously aware of at the time of writing by showing the pattern of contact between characters as a sort of broad choreographic notation. It can also have spatial implications by making a visual statement about the mass of the performer's activity on stage from scene to scene and their arrival or disappearance as a significant element in a shifting scenographic image.

3

The Discipline of Drawing for Designers

Before unpacking the uses of drawing by a theatre designer, it's worth defining first what drawing is or can be. Drawing, as a field of expression and enquiry, is growing rapidly. By that I mean that the way marks are made and applied to contemporary arts, the sciences and production of all sorts is being redefined from minute to minute. The role of drawing as an activity central to how we understand the world around and within us is becoming increasingly acknowledged as a stem subject – much like writing. A classical definition of drawing can simply be, for example, 'the expression of form on a plane surface'; but drawing for a designer is usually more than this. Designers can use drawing to explore dynamics in a space, rhythmic patterns of sound, the construction of a text and the interrelationships between characters, or simply a diagram explaining factual information, such as dimensions, through accurate graphic composition – in other words, the 'technical drawing'. It is because of this range of uses that the designer for the stage has to be prepared to see the graphic world as a multi-headed tool for the exploration and communication of how he or she feels about a subject or object: graphic work also ensuring that the collaborative process of design then functions well through to its construction in full human scale.

The nineteenth-century term 'emotional significance' comes close to describing the underlying thoughts of a designer expressed through the act of drawing. Many of a designer's ideas can be revealed through the analysis of why a line is drawn over here, rather than over there – and the drawing is

nearly always merely the starting point for a discussion preceding yet another stage in the making process. Therefore,
unless you define scenography (remember from Greek
skēnographia) as literally the use of drawing as an illusion of
three-dimensional space (such as in *trompe-l'œil*), the classical skill of drawing forms to depict the world as the artist
sees it is rarely useful because that drawing is likely to be the
start of building an artifact with its own form, mass and
qualities. There's much to be said for the continued practice
of drawing by a designer as a discipline (much like the regular morning's class for a dancer), because whether these
representations are in digital or analogue form, designers
constantly need to draw and it is often the fluidity and confidence in drawing that communicates an idea vividly:
inspiring others.

Having said that, most designer's drawing slips into a personal style or shorthand that is less about the quality of the
finished product and more about the process of thinking
through an idea in an objective medium and in as an economical way as possible. In this respect, the practice of, for
instance, life drawing, is more useful for the designer's
understanding of a graphic language than 'moving' others
by the expression of the figure's form. On the other hand, a
costume drawing can certainly charm and seal the approval
of an actor or director on account of its lightness and empathy with human spirit or frailty. Some of my own most
treasured drawings are those of minor, incidental and often
downtrodden characters who may have only appeared on
stage for a minute or two.

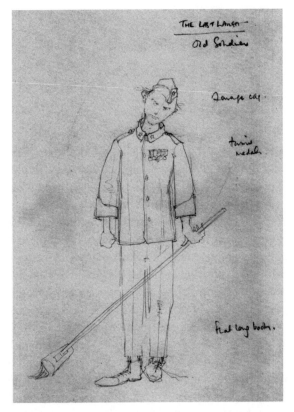

Costume sketch by the author for Richard Harris's adaptation of Kōki Mitani's *The Last Laugh* (Tokyo, 2007), with Martin Freeman and Roger Lloyd-Pack.

Art enables us to experience life at second hand, and theatre art presents and represents a virtual reality live on stage. The art of drawing, in a theatre designer's context, is usually yet another layer deeper (than, say perhaps, a painter's) compacted within the foundations of a final artistic statement.[23]

4

First Sketches

I like the word 'sketch'. It takes the academic curse off the discipline of drawing. Philosophically speaking, and in practice, that word implies that *anyone* can draw: throughout the design process, it's important that it is not only the designer who feels they can express themselves through drawing. To form performance ideas that are central to the designer's role, others in the creative team need to feel they can communicate through a common visual language, and so the sketches of directors, choreographers and others are as valuable as the designer's. In fact, some of the most exciting sketchbooks I've glimpsed have been by people who would probably not profess to being skilled at drawing, but the images are fresh and full of energy because their ultimate intention is what drives them; rather than being clouded by classical tradition. I engineer the design process so that actors feel empowered to sketch out their ideas, rather than endlessly discuss it through the abstract and often misleading medium of words.[24]

The sketch is an immediate brain-to-page superhighway, and the simplicity of its materials – a pencil and a scrap of paper – means that anyone can record a thought split seconds after it occurs. In design meetings sketches are as responsive to the collaborative process, and as malleable, as an actor or dancer's actions in rehearsal. Sketches can instantly morph and twist ideas through one hundred and eighty degrees whilst retaining a linear and visual record of the conversation. Thus, there's a lot to be said for drawing on the back of an envelope, and often the final rendering needs very little development from that initial, instinctive image.

Sketching architectural space – in contrast, for example, to a clothed figure – does require an understanding of the principles of perspective, but that understanding doesn't necessarily need to be of the sort that is calculated on the drawing board: it can be born from simply looking carefully and imagining yourself in the landscape. A sketch of a space can be equally effective if the lines are simply true to what the eyes of the audience might see. In any case, 'accurate' perspective drawing in the tradition of Albrecht Dürer or the Italian Renaissance[25] relies on a single viewpoint, whereas most theatre is now viewed from multiple positions across both the width and height of an auditorium. Not only that, the stage may extend into the auditorium so that the audience's viewpoints are wrapped around the stage, and in this case the designer's drawing must offer an honest and inclusive view not only of what we would see on stage but also of the audience themselves as integral to the image. Including the audience in your sketch, even in an end-on proscenium arch (picture frame) arrangement, is a sobering reminder that the viewing public and their presence, beside or in front, are vital to the live event.

Most sketches are simple line drawings, but the use of tone can be hugely useful in describing early thoughts about the impact of lighting. Shadow is the essence of profiling, and so some sense of where the light source might be immediately engages a lighting designer with your three-dimensional ideas. Likewise, the qualities of clothing and textiles rely completely on the qualities of the light that illuminates them. The weight and transparency of fabric can be described and transformed by the direction and intensity of light, and, of course, the introduction of colour into your drawn ideas will spark a conversation about how the atmospherics of coloured light in the space may affect the impact of the fabrics you plan to use – not only for dance, as previously mentioned, but for any use.

It sounds obvious, but if you regard the blank page as representing your peripheral vision (and you have two eyes), the most sensible format to draw space in is landscape, and you should stick to that so that all drawings can be juxtaposed and valued in the same orientation, even if the distances or focal point in the drawings vary. The vertical-portrait format usually suits drawing the single figure (as above), although you can revert to landscape for groups of figures which will connect more directly with any holistic, and therefore scenographic, spatial sketches in the frame of your paper. In practical terms, I would recommend making early drawings on separate sheets of paper, not fixed in a sketchbook, so that each image can be interleaved with the pages of your script and be repositioned or edited out instantaneously where necessary. This way your sketches will always relate to a particular theatrical moment – this *is* 'applied drawing', after all. The beauty and effectiveness of a sketch is a matter of judging when to stop, as opposed to when it could be defined as 'finished'. That definition is loaded with assumptions about the finesse of the image as a fine artist's product and an artefact in its own right, whereas here, knowing when to stop relies purely on the designer realising that the sketch has done its job in the process of progressing the design. Significantly, though, that in itself can sometimes lay claim to artistic merit.

5

Renderings

A rendering upgrades a sketch of a design to a more lifelike image: putting more information into a line drawing that will give it form and value by evoking the effect of natural or theatrical light. The many types of rendering can be chiefly divided between hand-treated images and those created through computer-aided drafting (CAD) or computer-generated imagery (CGI). In this section I will be concerned with media most applicable to design for live performance rather than the screen.

Traditionally, renderings were most likely to be used for the depiction of backdrops in the theatre. The designer's talent as a classical Beaux-Arts painter, albeit in miniature to be subsequently reproduced full-size by a scenic artist, used to be the foremost criteria for a successful rendering and therefore scenic design. By the early twentieth century, however, advances in lighting and the notion of design relating to the three-dimensional reality of performance meant that these painterly images became more and more integrated with physical objects and bodies in space. Up until quite recently, some theatre-design traditions, such as those in Italy, maintained a belief that the theatre designer's art relied on the transposition of the painted image to the stage. It is now the case that rendering is more likely to be used in and amongst digital media, animation and three-dimensional computer-aided drawings. In the classical form, a designer would paint an image with the intention of the scenic artist 'squaring it up'[26] in order to multiply its scale but otherwise reproduce it authentically. If a fine artist were to design for the stage, they might well contribute towards the final backdrop (Picasso or Hockney, for example), taking the opportunity to make an epic piece of work that would normally not fit into any gallery, let alone their studio, and paradoxically integrate their fictional space with the realities of live performance.

In practical terms, taking my cue from the literal definition of 'render' as 'give', rendering provides a definitive image for technicians to reproduce. The two-dimensional rendering is usually separate from the three-dimensional model in order that a scenic painter can concentrate on its detail and scale. However, with the increasingly sophisticated means by which images of the *whole* stage can be depicted digitally, the need for a finished three-dimensional model can be replaced by visually accurate and atmospheric renderings. The digital rendering generated in programmes such as Photoshop or Illustrator, with their sophisticated application of patinas, hues and textures, can do a better job of communicating what the designer would like the audience to finally see, rather than a three-dimensional architectural model that then needs to be enhanced with lighting at a later point in the production process.

Renderings rather than models are also a more practical (and sometimes more powerful) way of describing a sequence of designed moments. I have found that perhaps the most potent combination of 2D and 3D is the combined use of renderings in all their photographic crispness, with a structurally but neutrally coloured scale 'maquette' (usually just a white or pale-grey sketch model) to describe the sculptural space. Renderings of two-dimensional images can also now be introduced into CAD drawings, making the whole digital process of modelling stage space much like its traditional cardboard, balsa wood and wire predecessor. Digital processes also make the changing of scale, proportion and even perspective an easy job, and there's no reason why both the drawn and painted image cannot be processed and manipulated digitally through the scanner, making today's design process increasingly flexible, and so more responsive to change, than ever before.

Once captured in digital form, images can then be applied to the changing scenarios of performance time and space to form a storyboard in single images or in moving form. A rendering of the set can also often find its way into publications, such as the published text of the play, the production's programme or the theatre's website, or it might feature in an exhibition, as was the image overleaf for *Richard III* at World Stage Design 2013 – and that all adds to your presence as a cutting-edge professional.

Digital collaged rendering by the author for Propeller Theatre's *Richard III* (UK, European and North American tour, 2011).

6

Storyboards

The clue's in the name here: storyboards tell visual stories, and are usually made up of a series of single drawings that give the viewer a sense of how a complete idea is formed of many momentary ideas. Our most familiar experience of a storyboard is probably the strip cartoon in any daily newspaper or magazine. Their art is to communicate, as economically as possible, the arc of a visual narrative.

I use storyboarding to describe not only what could happen on stage but also how the performance might at times extend into the auditorium to connect with the audience at pivotal moments. These moments are also usually captioned with a key line or two from the text to pinpoint what prompts, or even motivates, the action. In this case, I may shift the point of view of the drawing from a fixed seating position and move it to the side, much like a roving camera, to include stage and auditorium. The storyboard then becomes a way of describing how the space is being used, rather than depicting the audience's experience of the show.

Storyboards are not always drawn. When producing a sketch model of a design that is engineered to move, it's often useful to record all its permutations photographically (a 'photomatic'), thereby being able to skip through the scenic plot. These can also be developed into something more rendered, perhaps involving a sequence of proposed lighting states.

An animated film is, of course, a more compact and complex form of storyboard. Its more sparsely spaced cousin, the animatic (which is like a sequence of stills), can be a useful way of presenting a complex project when the scenes or dramatic moments warrant more than twenty or thirty images – an action-packed musical, for instance, that moves from location to location. A prime example of this is the scenic demands of the stage adaptation of Mel Brooks' *The Producers*, which dodges from a variety of interior to exterior locations, or more recently *The Book of Mormon*, that requires the design of an extremely rapid series of filmic jump-cuts as well as transporting us to a theatrical representation of a play within a play.

Here are just a few of the full set of Jocelyn Herbert's storyboard drawings for Brecht and Weill's *The Rise and Fall of the City of Mahagonny* at the Metropolitan Opera, New York, directed by John Dexter.

Jocelyn Herbert's storyboard drawings for *The Rise and Fall of the City of Mahagony*.

Brecht, Weill and their designers Caspar Neher and Karl von Appen used what Brecht called 'Arrangements Skizzen' (plotting sketches) to explore the potential of their work before rehearsals began, as if telling a fable in a picture book – sometimes famously retaining the captions in the performance itself.

The most common use of the storyboard is to show key moments that the director and designer propose as landmarks in their production. However, there are many other sorts of storyboard that show series of objects, sounds, clothes, lighting, and so forth, in a linear sequence. The missing ingredient is therefore time, but a storyboard might also show how rhythms, crescendos or pauses play a part in the design's effect. When storyboards focus on a particular aspect of design, for example, the shoes of the performers, a lot more than just that particular object's plot line can be determined from the drawings. The range of objects, in this case shoes, and the changes and transformations they go through, can be in some way a synonym or metaphor for the production's complete design concept.

In a sense, the first drawing you do on a project can be the start of a storyboard – and subsequent drawings can chart the process and progress you have made, and serve as a concrete reminder of your thoughts as they happened. Usually, though, they are a communication device to others in the creative team, the performers and technicians. When shaded or coloured they can be extremely useful in your early discussions with the lighting designer – they can express as well as describe. One of the greatest exponents of a lighting storyboard is Robert Wilson, whose drawings of contrasting tone and shape verge on the abstract but also clearly communicate the dynamics of light in space and time.

The varied uses of storyboarding can be set against each other in layers, rather like the timeline in film-editing software or perhaps an orchestral score, so that the viewer gets a sense of how the different design strands in a production might combine at given moments of the performance. This can be particularly useful in opera design where the fixed timing of the music provides the structure for everything else – lighting, scenic shifts and transformations, entrances and exits.

Storyboards come into their own in the rehearsal room. Like the model, they can be a vital reference point for director, designer, performers and stage management – a sort of visual roadmap that helps all concerned in the early stages to anticipate the next move in working through the complexity of the production puzzle.

Top Tip: *A designer can get a bit carried away and create unworkable 'jump-cuts' from one image to another, forgetting that they have to be realised in three-dimensional, finite space. Before showing drawn images to a producer and director, check that your trickier proposed transitions are actually realisable – talk it through with a production manager first.*

7

Technical Drawings

I think it's true to say that many designers have a love-hate relationship with technical drawing. Some regard it as a necessary evil and others totally rely on it. On the whole, the majority of theatre-design students approach the subject with a little apprehension, if not outright fear – the sort of irrational fear that I still have of mathematics. This 'block', usually based on the shock-and-awe imagery of unfathomable extreme complexity and exactitude, will evaporate once you have a project which inevitably demands that you simply explore a space in greater detail or which you practically need to know will fit properly. Everyone has had to follow a technical drawing at some point or other, whether it's using an ordnance survey map or following a set of instructions to build flat-pack shelves, so we all have a keen sense of what makes the interpretation of these diagrams a happy experience or sheer frustration and misery.

Tech drawings are 'flattened' top-down and side-on views of the world that we otherwise experience fully in three dimensions, with all the foreshortening and perspective that our eyes' optics bring to our brains' perception. These orthographic projections are the most basic method of representing real dimensional space. To give the reader all the factual information they need to visualise or build an object in three dimensions, they will need two or three views of all its faces, usually set out in line or at right angles (90°) to each other on the page. All the views interrelate, and one view will usually confirm aspects of the others whilst also adding more fundamental information. In my view, the ideal technical drawings are those which include *no more and no less* than is absolutely required – good drawings are measured by their economy of means and effectiveness, not their excess.

In this section I will concentrate more on *why* designers need to do technical drawing (or work with a draftsperson who can), rather than *how* the drawings are made – there are plenty of excellent 'how to' books on generic drafting and many that specialise on scenic drafting for both the drawing board[27] and computer-aided design (CAD).

There are a number of myths surrounding making these drawings. I will now try to identify these one by one, dispel them, and draw up a list of good reasons to cheerfully approach the task in hand.

1. *Technical drawings don't lie.*

One of the first pre- and misconceptions is that a technical drawing, owing to its perceived accuracy, is definitive – it's not. Most applied drawings, and particularly in collaborative industries, are starting points for discussion and negotiation about the next phase of a project. Technical drawings are proposals, not immaculate blueprints.

2. *Technical drawings have merit of their own.*

I must confess that I often do regard a comprehensive technical drawing as a thing of beauty – but that doesn't make it a good technical drawing. As the last point suggests, they are very much a means to an end, so their quality as part of the theatre-design process relies totally on their ability to meet the project's needs.

3. *Technical drawings sum up complete ideas and communicate them clearly.*

In a sense this is partly true, but they are not so much part of a post-concept process as a mid-process aid to thought. I think of them as a more accurate way of sketching: their accuracy being that all the element's relative values are in a consistent language. It's because of this that their prime use is actually an aid to artistic composition. The information that emerges from constantly pushing the lines about on the paper (whether the page is in AutoCAD or Vectorwork's digital-paper space or just a piece of A2 tracing taped to your kitchen table) is merely a snapshot of your thinking at that particular stage in the design process. The chief caveat is that the submitted set of drawings, as described later, will probably be used to cost the production from – so big discrepancies between the designer's drawing and their ultimate intentions can be very costly.

4. *Technical drawings give a true representation of what the audience will see.*

A hundred or more years ago this might have been the case, when scaled renditions of a proscenium stage – involving the use of perspective and *trompe-l'œil* (literally 'eye-deceiving') effects – were drawn up by the scenic decorator. Nowadays, designers rarely make a technical drawing of the whole picture in what could be termed a 'front elevation' view. However, the package of drawings submitted by the designer will usually include scenic components that will show a front-on view, but no perspective is used unless the object needs to be built as a distorted form.

5. *Technical drawings are about measurements.*

These drawings are actually maps. Sometimes they take the long view of the whole world of the project and sometimes they break the world up into regions that require a closer look. Like all plans and diagrams, they are easier to read for the person who drew them than those they are intended for, and it's for this reason that there are some established drawing protocols that help the reader orientate themselves before being able to absorb their content. I hesitate to say they are rules, because that suggests they are fixed – they are not: like any language these conventions change over time and have many variants. So, again, despite their apparent esoteric and somewhat robotic appearance, technical drawings are a product of ordinary human beings!

So what's in the pack of technical drawings that production managers and many others in the creative and production team use on a daily basis? The full set usually comprises of the following:

• Ground plan (of the whole set).

• Side elevation (of the whole set) or section.

• Construction drawings (of scenic components).

There are no rules as to which drawing comes first: they usually evolve together to form a holistic view of the project as it develops and becomes more defined. I would guess that most designers begin with the overall ground plan, since a pre-drawn plan of just the empty theatre space (looking down as if from the grid directly over the stage) is usually given to the designer at the very start of a project. The designer is therefore prompted to start to make even the earliest decisions with the 'footprint' of their design in mind. This would usually be accompanied by a sectional elevation drawing (looking sideways across the stage as if from the wings) – so the heights of objects would also then be considered. Both these views hold vital clues as to what the audience can see of your work when in different positions – the sightlines. Given that theatregoing is a social experience, the plans give the designer a clear sense of how the audience physically bond with each other (or not), and then how the spectators' individual viewpoints either merge or diverge: the audience's dynamic.

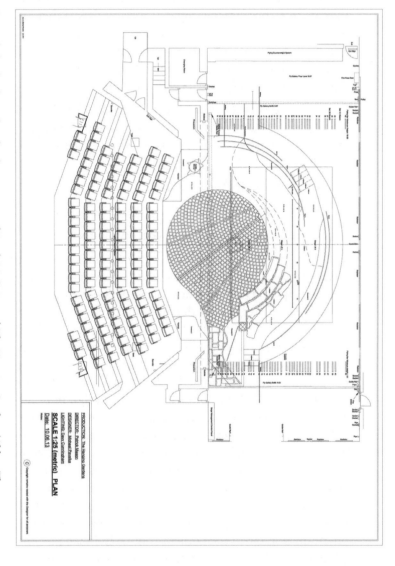

Ground plan by the author for the premiere of Frank McGuinness' *The Hanging Gardens* (Abbey Theatre, Dublin 2013). See the models for this production in Parts Four and Seven.

The ground plan is also probably the most used of these drawings. Stage managers mark out the rehearsal-room floor using it, paying special attention to all those objects that might affect the movement of an actor, such as stairs and ramps. The director then uses it as the designer did to analyse the angles and positions that performers will adopt and the distances they will travel; in this respect the plan represents time and timings as a satnav would when travelling from point A to destination B. The lighting designer uses the ground plan to assess the horizontal angles the lighting instruments will need to be positioned at to avoid certain objects and reach the actors, or the angles through which the lights can draw out particular scenic features such as the texture of a wall or a shadow across a sculpted figure. These positions may also reveal how light might 'bounce' from surface to surface and not always in problematic way – sometimes reflections can create striking and unconventional effects: off a warped mirror, for example, or water. Likewise, a sound designer will also start to gauge where they need to position speakers for the voice to reach the audience, usually using the parameters of the sight line and perhaps also taking reflection into account.

In a touring environment the plan is an essential tool by which a production manager, producer and designer can assess the viability of the design given that it will have to be erected in a number of varied spaces. Often a designer will have to ensure that the plan has a degree of flexibility in its footprint so that the technical team can adjust the scenery to suit both the dimensions and the sight lines of all the theatres on tour.

Having designed in plan what the designer wants the audience to see, there is usually a continual task to ensure the audience doesn't see the rest of the space. On the other hand, Brecht and his collaborators were probably the first to consistently strip the conventional drapery away from theatre spaces, to expose the limits and mechanics of that space, placing the designed essentials for storytelling in the foreground. Even in these situations, however, directors and designers will often want the scenography to include the nuts and bolts of the theatre building[28] but still retain the possibility of actors disappearing and appearing – even Brecht retained his half-curtain! Keeping these areas from the view of the audience is called masking, and whether it's achieved by way of black wool screens and drapes, or with objects on stage providing visual cover for an actor (a large column, for example), the ground plan can quickly reveal who in the audience can see what and from where.

Ground plans usually have more descriptive labelling than numerical information. Measurements of the lengths of scenic walls, for instance, are usually reserved for the construction drawings. There is a balance to be struck between written facts and the at-a-glance clarity of the plan simply as an image. Heights of certain objects are handy, however, such as platforms or ramps.

If the production involves many scenes with the design changing shape throughout the show, it may be necessary to generate a number of separate plans or to devise a graphic way of distinguishing between one scene and another on a single sheet. CAD allows for different scenes to be created on different layers that can be switched on and off for clarity or amalgamated to anticipate any potential incompatibility when moving scenic elements: for instance, winched platforms (called 'trucks') may need crisscrossing tracks in a (raised) floor which might inhibit the movement of other objects.

8

Costume Drawings

Costume drawing, along with storyboarding, is one of the most open of theatre-design processes. It is the visual equivalent of poetry and prose, being a blend of expression and pragmatism: a costume may be beautiful but it must also *fit*! Costume drawing is also an area of theatre-design practice that comes close to the practices of a classical painter, in much the same way as set design is close to the practice of the sculptor and architect. A costume's space has to make allowances for the inner and outer volumes of the body, so in that respect a costume designer needs to appreciate, if not be expert in, the representation of both the human figure in two dimensions and its transformation to a three-dimensional kinetic sculptural form.

These drawings, like scenic maquettes, anticipate collaborations with many others to see it through to realisation on stage. At the time of making them, they are, of course, also a way for the designer to externalise their own ideas in order to engage with them from the distance that an audience will. I like to think of them as a 'visual essay' that proposes a composition of sometimes contradictory ideas, but that reflects or provides a context for the complexity of the character through that character's behaviour in the narrative. The difference here between a costume concept and any written equivalent is that clothes exist in the continually shifting time and space of a live performance, responding almost autonomously to its prevailing conditions.

There can be no doubt that the regular practice of life drawing and other forms of observational drawing of actual people and specific figures, will help in a number of ways. Whatever medium you may choose for a drawing, and this may vary tremendously from project to project, a knowledge of how human beings look, move, gesture – their body language – is vital. Drawing not only helps your fluidity in communicating an idea as economically as possible but also ensures that the mind-to-hand superhighway works to its optimum capability. The shorter the distance between mind and hand, the greater your ability will be to make images instinctively that reflect not only what you think about a character but also how you feel about them.

There are four major methods of revealing characterisation: actions, appearance, dialogue and thoughts. Design arguably focuses on serving the first two of these in the context of the third and fourth. This is a generalisation, and perhaps not wholly appropriate for ballet design, but it's a useful framework. Costume designs contribute to the totality of a performance rather than reproduce it visually or materially – in other words, costume designers will be wary of duplicating other elements in the production and, because of the dominance of vision over the other senses, they will also want to avoid upstaging a performer or anticipating how a narrative will unfold. The drawing should provide a document for a conversation with a performer about how these four areas will intersect, complement each other, and work practically.

Some designers will develop a drawing language of their own over time and stick to it. Others will take the opportunity to experiment with different techniques and media depending on the content of the piece or perhaps the performance style of the theatre, opera or dance company. How 'complete' a drawing needs to be is also subject to a number of conditions, such as the time you have to make it, the particular collaborative process that you intend to follow and whether the clothes are made, hired or sourced. It seems obvious that made clothing requires a faithful image for the costume supervisor and maker to follow, but for bought and hired clothes there might seem less need.

However, thinking through the presentation of your design ideas on the page can begin to elevate bought clothing to a costume, in that by drawing it you will have articulated particular criteria to be used when you and your costume supervisor dive into a vintage shop, a high-street retailer or a hire department.

It's a common but faulty habit to draw a figure from the head down. A costume designer, however, might begin to approach a character from an element of clothing at the other extremities of the body: shoes, gloves, a cane, etc., and so build a visualisation of character in an unorthodox sequence. This is why knowing the visual (and perhaps mechanical) human anatomy helps provide a framework for connecting your emerging ideas.

On a practical level, drawing is an aide-memoire. It need not, as a complete image on the page, give an illusion of how it will be seen in the context of the stage image. Because many productions will involve tens if not hundreds of costumes, it's impossible for a costume designer to cram them all onto the same page and still articulate the level of detail needed to realise them. That's not to say that a costume designer cannot think and draw the *mise-en-scène* – how blocks of performers such as choruses work on stage will rely on a mass of moving textiles, shapes and colours, and that may require the designer to visualise the stage image through some form of costume-based storyboard. It's customary, though, to draw costumes individually or at most in pairs or threesomes with a mere indication of the space they may be in. Indeed, if the costume designer is working with a separate set designer they may not even know the details of the environment, and therefore the visual context in which the costume will be seen, until much later in the production process. Costume drawings are working documents and so can be littered with notes, alternative views, such as from behind, profile or silhouette, and include other references such as photographs. It is important, though, that all of these elements add to an accumulation of complementary information as opposed to conflicting messages about, say, the cut of the clothes. To that end, a written note should clarify the nature of the drawn object, and not be an afterthought that contradicts what we see.

Costume design by Simon Higlett for the RSC's production of *Love's Labour's Lost* (2014).

Theatre designers have to be simply passionate about performance. At the start of a project, when you are sitting in front of that intimidating sheet of paper, pencil poised, it's often a designer's inner performer that will motivate an idea for a character – in fact, it's essential to engage with this facet of your work as it will continually remind you that your work will be subject to the characteristics of a particular actor, how they think, speak and move, as well as their size and shape.[29] When beginning to draw, a designer will usually not know who is cast, so what do they have to fall back on, other than their own performance instincts, to fill the gap? Not knowing who is cast is also the reason why many designers will be tempted to leave a face blank, but then cannot resist completing the image. In any case all clothing, whether constricting or loose, will impact on how the actor will behave, and that will require the designer to anticipate actions.

It may be the case that you either have the luxury, or are determined, to draw after the start of rehearsals. With longer devised projects there may be plenty of leeway so that the design can take shape as organically as the other elements. As outlined in Part One, within contemporary dance this design-rehearsal engagement is almost a prerequisite. Having the designer observing and reflecting what is forming, as it's forming, gives everyone in the process confidence that the design will be integral to the language of the piece.

Sketch by the author produced in the dance studio during the early phases of rehearsal for Stan Won't Dance's multidisciplinary production, *Revelations* (2006).

Textiles, being the materials of costume, need to be considered during the drawing process, although, of course, pencils and paint can only provide a two-dimensional impression of any fabric's materiality; its weight, flexibility, transparency, and so on. By using these media in your drawing you will open up your ideas for discussion and suggestions by your costume supervisor and costume-maker. One of the most enjoyable parts of the process of costume design involves the 'blue skies thinking' of sampling fabrics or putting together materials and processes that create effects under stage light.

However, if you feel confident about the materials in your design, using a collage of magazine scraps of images and parts may be a more vivid way of collecting and communicating your ideas. Of course, software gives you the scope to combine all of these fluidly so that mechanical and more haptic processes interchange and exchange their values and graphic languages – photographs and crayons, scanner and sketch. Collage, because it can give the impression of being a collection of ready-to-hand snips of colour, pattern or compete items of clothing, looks on the face of it an easy option. But don't be fooled – you will soon begin to appreciate how particular your design ideas are when you can't match what you find to your imagination. Sometimes, you may have to abandon a medium to be able to process the idea and you may find that reverting to traditional methods is no bad thing – methods and materials have to meet their match. A drawing in this context is simply a means to an end, and not to be confused with graphic art. Having said that, and not to be underestimated, these images can also, perhaps *must* also, engage and inspire those you work with.

9

Furniture and Prop Research, Reference and Other Drawings

Most of the requirements for costume drawing also apply to drawings for props. Although props and smaller pieces of scenery may look inanimate, they will still be subject to the conditions of a stage environment. That means they will most likely have to move at some point either in perform-ance or when scenery is changed and maintained. Props can be rigid or soft, of course, so your drawing should ideally mirror the found or made object's materials.

One key difference between a costume drawing and a prop drawing is that, because you will be working within a known spatial environment, rather than with a probably unknown cast member, you can stipulate the dimensions of an object with some confidence and accuracy. So, whether you are using traditional media to make the drawing or whether you will be foraging for images from the internet, be sure to write additional information on the picture that confirms the textures of the surfaces and the size of the object.

Prop drawings are also useful to a model-maker. Often there is a fine line between a scenic object and prop. For example, many props may be semi-permanently attached to the scenery: paintings, shelving, objets d'art of all sorts. Your props and set-dressing ideas may well find themselves rep-resented in more than one way – a miniature piece on your model in 3D and a more magnified drawing in 2D. It is important that these two versions confirm, rather than con-flict with, each other.

Even when you are intending to source your props from found objects in the real world, and just as with costume drawings for found clothing, drawings or other references are crucial starting points for a search through retail catalogues and online shopping, antique stalls and other outlets, such as the ubiquitous eBay.

Don't discount the role of the second-hand bookshop in the search for inspiration or clear photographic references – they can be a treasure trove. Furniture and other objects have always been collected, sold at auction and otherwise studied for their intrinsic aesthetic value and their obvious connection with architecture and interior design. Buried in these shops will be auction catalogues, antique guides and directories, along with publications that group furniture and other objects into schools of design within the historic timeline of fashion and style.

Over time, your knowledge bank of decorative-arts movements from, say, *fin de siècle* through art nouveau, deco, utility-ware and retro fads to the present will accumulate (and intersect with artistic movements such as modernism, pop culture and postmodernism) as a resource in your mind as well as on your shelves, to the point where you can draw a Queen Anne chair leg blindfold! Until then, make sure you know where to get your hands on the reference. Museums, such as the V&A, the Museum of London, and the Horniman (fantastic for their array of period musical instruments) and Geffrye museums, give you a terrific opportunity to see the real thing – and draw it.

10

Models: Actual or Virtual?

Although the model of a design is a critical part of the 'design package', in this section I am going to concentrate not on how to make one, but explain why they are important and, crucially, the choices that a designer has between digital and 'analogue', virtual and actual. The skills required to take command of scale model-making could consume a whole book in itself, and there are more than one or two excellent publications on the market that do just that – particularly Keith Orton's *Model Making for the Stage: A Practical Guide* and large chunks of Gary Thorne's *Stage Design: A Practical Guide*. There are also long and short courses dedicated to perfecting the skills that can be transferred to other areas, such as product design and architecture, which, like any applied craft, require a careful step-by-step approach to making. These other disciplines diverge from theatre model-making in one respect: the centrality of live performance.

There are three principal reasons for making maquettes. The first, to discover something for yourself; the second, to discover something with someone else; and the third, to communicate the first two with absolute clarity. It's perfectly reasonable to think that the potential precision and flexibility of the digital environment would be perfect for creating scenic spaces. In some respects it is, but others not. For instance, a virtual model is far more physically stable to manipulate – when you are taking a director through your ideas, bits and pieces don't fall over or get knocked by your shaky hands, but therein also lies a problem. The collaboration between director and designer relies exclusively on the trusting assumption that both can be generous with their ideas and encourage crossover into each other's territories, particularly throughout the speculative phases before rehearsal starts. If a director cannot get their own shaky hands alongside yours in the model box to suggest this and that, the interplay of thoughts and the bench-testing that goes on through taking risks in the model, saying 'What if...?', slows considerably. Another disadvantage of digital is that arranging the building blocks of the design becomes a very one-sided affair. Even if a director has the dexterity to use 3D software, which I doubt, who will have their finger on the mouse or trackpad?

A physical white-card sketch model by the author for Propeller's productions of *Twelfth Night* and *The Taming of the Shrew* at the Old Vic (2006).

The equivalent wire-frame digital model by the author for Propeller's productions of *Twelfth Night* and *The Taming of the Shrew* at the Old Vic (2006).

On the other hand, the distinct advantage of the virtual model in collaborative terms is the ability to 'fly through'. You cannot only get your hands in; you can virtually stand on stage. Models properly function when you and your director really believe you are there in the auditorium. I would always encourage you to make a scale-model representation of yourself and your director to stand in front of your card models so that you can 'be there' in miniature – it sounds a little bizarre, but it works. With the fly-through, you can view *from* the model rather than *into* it. The trick then is to build different sorts of models to achieve particular aims and objectives. In this regard, the word 'model' takes a philosophical shift: you are not only designing the set but also designing the process – being a director of design – and creating a bespoke 'model of best practice' for each project.

Physical models have material properties – textures, surfaces and hues – that change in actual lighting conditions: reflective qualities, transparencies, and so forth. All of these can, with an equal amount of dedicated practice to that of a physical model-maker, be 'built' in software and virtually lit. The distancing and flattening effect of the screen can both arouse suspicions in a director (*'Is this really what we will see in real space and time?'*) and prove tricky to interpret for scenic builders and painters. For the designer or the designer's model-maker who is using software, the nature of a random mark or blob of texture is mediated by a digital process and not directly by hand. This makes sense if the final set-build involves making through digital means, but if the construction and effects are interpreted by eye and executed by hand, it makes better sense that the design methodology is as close to that as possible.

A fully rendered model (1:25 scale) by the author for the Abbey Theatre, Dublin's world-premiere production of Frank McGuinness's *The Hanging Gardens*. The white-card (1:50 scale) prototype can be seen in Part Seven.

Finally, although virtual models have a televisual 'sparkle' about them that may suit some designs that either have their roots in naturalism or razzmatazz, this tonal clarity cannot always best serve more subtle, sensual, 'organic' or lyrical work.

Top Tip: *Drawing, and other work on the screen, is not as physically varied an activity as drawing at the board or cutting and fixing an actual model, but it can be just as compulsive an activity. When working in screen-based media, ensure you take frequent breaks to reduce repetitive stresses that can, in the medium to long term, affect muscles, joints and eyesight.*

11

A Word About Theatre Space

The genus of theatre space, as distinct from, say, exhibition space, is grouped into a number of fairly distinct species, outlined below. These can subsequently be grouped into families, depending largely on the era in which they were built and as each generation responds to its unique set of circumstances. We tend to view the evolution of the stage as sweeping from Greek then Roman amphitheatres and coliseums to the Renaissance's derivatives of these over many centuries. Further developments can then be seen to be compacting into a relatively more rapid series of changes, incorporating increasingly less formalised spectator-performer arrangements, such as the stacked viewpoints of the Inns of Court or the freedoms of the circus's big top, and reflecting society's changing needs throughout Europe's industrial revolutions until today's increasingly compacted cross-cultural urbanisation. Of course, at any one point in history the picture is layered with complexity as one popular form gives way, but still coexists with the next. The current epoch could be characterised by the harnessing of this accumulated diversity and architectural transparency, including the phenomenon of the 'backstage tour': theatre's attempt to re-engage with its increasingly inquisitive and voyeuristic audience through a titillating unmasking of its processes and once-shrouded spaces – from the workshops and dressing rooms to the substage mechanics.

Theatre designers have to not only be equipped to appreci-ate and handle the distinctions between one theatre space and another, they often are responsible for either modifying an established space to another format or inventing the space from scratch in flexible or 'found' environments. There follows a digest of the broad groupings of theatre space you will have to confront, embrace or approach with caution. Each has its advantages and pitfalls, and the success of each depends in turn on so many other factors, such as the creative team's affinity with its proportions and atmosphere or the suitability of the piece. Addressing the audience's relationship to your work is ultimately one of the elementary building blocks of an effective design for performance – here's what to be aware of.

The proscenium's frame

Proscenium theatres, often also called 'Italian' since the frame came to particular prominence during the height of Italian baroque,[30] separate the audience from the action physically, but can, through design, draw them into the space visually. The performer on a proscenium stage, within and beyond the frame, is therefore behind an imagined 'fourth wall', sharing the same dramatic moments as the audience but, potentially, in a totally separate place. The tension between these two existential states is what can make performances in these theatres so powerful. Twentieth-century directors and writers – Brecht, Artaud and countless others since such as Brook and Sellars – have used this duality to fragment the 'realities' of live performance into a succession of changing relationships with the viewer, disrupting their inclination to settle back into a fixed interpretation of what they see. The proscenium's frame, and other arched frames beyond that in the form of masking (screens or carefully composed scenery), allows for the appearance and disappearance of actors and objects. This adds further to the conundrum of what the director and designer are asking both the performer and audience to believe as the 'truth' of the event. Shakespeare wrote much of his epic battlefield imagery in the form of onstage reportage of events off-stage, and its impact is most forceful when the audience understands, through the design, the relationship between what's 'off' and what's 'on'.

Theatre designers now have plenty of technical ammunition with which to exploit both traditional and digital forms of spatial illusion (say, scene painting and projection) to blur the conceptual edges of space and allow, as Walter Benjamin suggests in 'What is Epic Theatre?', an actor to 'reserve for himself the possibility of stepping out of character artistically', thereby having a face-to-face, 'real-time' dialogue with the otherwise passive spectator. Now, one might think command of such issues is the domain of the director, but unless the theatre designer understands, manipulates or frames the space to aid these events to happen, and allow the actor the flexibility to do this on a minute-to-minute basis, the cutting edge of the ideas can be blunted.

Designers also might contemplate extending the world of the stage through the audience on a catwalk, passerelle or hanamichi (a form of borrowed from Japanese kabuki the-atre). Being raised, the actors still have a measure of detachment from the audience in the stalls, but are pre-sented in a dynamic proximity: being physically intimate with the viewer, but tantalisingly 'unavailable' physically.

Many proscenium stages have some form of in-built forestage or apron, extending towards the audience and allowing performers to break the fourth wall. These vary in depth and shape, some deep enough to cover the orchestra pit. They provide a substantial intermediate space that the designer can choose to incorporate into the set (for instance, by continuing the floor) or begin to break from it, allowing for distinct changes in the performer's 'reality'. These stages nudge towards a return to the immediacy of Shakespeare's Globe and hint at what had become a common choice of architects in the late-twentieth and early-twenty-first cen-tury: the 'thrust'.

'Courtyard' spaces

As the name suggests, these spaces that are something of an English phenomenon are a rectangular version of the Euro-pean horseshoe-shaped auditorium. The audience are stacked high and, in the less shallow upper levels (usually only a couple of rows deep), tend to hang over the railing giving the impression (at least!) of being totally engaged with the event. At a glance, courtyard theatres can simply look like a proscenium theatre with a deep apron, but in use, their reliance on the forestage for most of the action, and being served by entrances/exits from doors at the sides of it, mean the space behind both actor and proscenium can be reduced to decorative status if the design cannot cleverly link the two.

The principles of the eighteenth-century courtyard form have been picked up by late-twentieth-century architects and amalgamated with the notion of greater design flexibility to create inherently hybrid spaces, such as the Dorfman (previously the Cottesloe) at the National Theatre. The idea here is to give director and designer the opportunity to design their own auditorium in almost any orientation and audience-actor configuration: using the stacked balconies and an open, clear floor below as a skeletal, structural starting point. The 'upstage' space is given an area finely balanced between being substantial enough to accommodate a conventional 'end-on' staging, but also not being a major sacrifice if used to complete the fourth side of the rectangular balconies for an 'in-the-round' production.

The courtyard's sense of a dynamically engaged audience can easily be reduced to a rudimentary box; a meeting room in which a crowd is organised into an audience, whether on opposing sides as in a traverse arrangement or even dispensing with the seats altogether on the ground floor as in Bill Brydon and designer William Dudley's innovative trilogy, *The Mysteries*, in the Cottesloe in the mid-1980s.

[163]

The theatre designer is key throughout the decision-making processes under these circumstances, from production concept to final realisation; indeed, the whole creative, production and administrative team have to work hand in glove to ensure everyone has the best collective understanding of how the changeable elements of such productions fit together – *nothing* should ever be taken for granted.

Thrusts and no-man's-land

A thrust stage juts deeply out into the auditorium as the name suggests, also causing the architect to wrap the audience one hundred and eighty degrees around it, whilst usually also maintaining some form of proscenium space, however shallow, behind it. The stage platform may be more of an intrusion into the audience's spatial reality than the apron in the proscenium form but that doesn't necessarily interrupt their belief in a theatrical fiction. The thrust's protruding shape makes it the closest form we have to the arenas of Greece and Rome. These theatres were most in vogue in the 1960s and '70s, and were championed by Tyrone Guthrie in the United States and Canada – and to some extent, Laurence Olivier in the UK. They were, and still are, best suited to productions that involve a high degree of movement: epic subjects and musical theatre can work well in them. They were originally thought of as Shakespearean spaces given their similarity to the playhouses of the English Renaissance, although this twentieth-century equivalent also incorporated entrances from the auditorium, usually from 'vomitories' (partially concealed tunnels that help 'spit' the performers onto centre stage), relieving the theatre designer from the responsibility of creating all of the actor's entrances in the upstage scenery.

The depth of the thrust causes a dilemma for the designer. There appears to be a tempting opportunity to fill the upstage space at the back of the thrust through what functions as a picture frame; a proscenium arch. However, many in the audience have such an extremely poor view of it, from each end of the arc of seats, that it cannot be used consistently for major action – but still has to be dealt with in some way by design. Further, actors and directors will, as we know, want to use the 'sweet spot', the position on stage where the performer has optimum command of the audience's attention, as much as possible – and heading for it can be a long journey from the upstage scenery through a 'no-man's-land' of potentially dead space. So, ultimately, much of the scenic design can amount to the floor and furniture on the thrust itself and then, behind that, a large and often costly world that functions simply as a visual framework for the action, rather than being fully integrated into it. In musicals, however, the band or small orchestra can be given a home beyond the 'arch', lending an otherwise problematic 'black hole' purpose, relevance and energy, whilst also visually or physically connecting the musicians to the action.

Of course, scenery can move from upstage to mid- or even downstage and back again in the form of tracked platforms, giving these elements a greater three-dimensional mass and presence – think of them as a carefully lit sculpture on a plinth. Costume too can help the performer's physicality in three dimensions, form and volume being of as much importance to their impact in this context as line and the silhouette does on the proscenium stage. Textures of textiles read, in close proximity, as a tactile sensual layer on the body. The qualities of other objects, such as furnishings, also have their status raised, as they are seen to very much share the same physical space as the actors. Any form of seating has to be positioned very carefully so as not to obscure the view of the audience in first couple of rows – chairs and other pieces of functional furniture have to serve the director's composition and circulation of the actors: they are 'magnets' for the characters, helping to motivate their movement across the stage following lateral, longitudinal or diagonal routes. The designer will try to foresee this, using the ground plan as a mapping tool to chart these 'desire lines' as much as possible before rehearsal, but the open nature of the thrust's floor area usually allows for flexibility throughout rehearsals. The placing of furniture onto and off a thrust, scene after scene, is a perennial problem – often resulting in costumed cast members doing the shifting in choreographed interludes that hopefully appear relevant to the action and as seamless as possible!

Closing the circle

'Theatre-in-the-round' has other names on different continents. In the US it might well also be called 'arena theater', or the less common 'central staging'. The seating, being arranged three hundred and sixty degrees around the acting area, connects the modern audience back to the earliest forms of storytelling, around the campfire. It is the most democratic of forms, and perhaps, like democracy, some 'hopeful' is likely to feel left out! Not unlike site-specific theatre, its emergence comes, in part, from the political climate of mid-1960s, and completing the looping of the audience around the thrust stage's shape.

In staging something centrally, it's more problematic for the audience to be completely 'lost' in a fictional world, such as that we can escape to through a proscenium arch. Everyone in arena theatres – viewer, scenic objects and performer – are essentially in the same space and of equal proximity to each other, so theatre-in-the-round has lent itself more readily to naturalism. It's ironic, then, that naturalistic performance and design is most at home in possibly the two most polar-opposite forms of presentation: arena theatre and television. Perhaps it shouldn't be so surprising, in that both intend to knit people together through various forms of intimacy – TV's screen being the equivalent of both campfire and storyteller rolled into one, in our living rooms.

The largest purpose-built theatre of this kind is the Royal Exchange in Manchester, conceived by a theatre designer, Richard Negri. His aim was to create a (spiritual) space with the actor (representing 'man') at its centre and the audience congregated around the stage. Beyond the auditorium are layers of spaces within spaces, both visual and aural; layers of semi-transparency, half-masked mystery and cathedral-like reverberation. As fresh now as when completed in the mid-1970s, it's a seven-sided jewel of steel and glass anachronistically counterpointing its vast Victorian corn-exchange setting. It has the flexibility to *be* intimate and yet *become* epic, depending on the designer's appreciation of its possibilities and an empathetic approach to its inherent poetics. It cannot be coincidental that the Royal Exchange and, only a few miles away and opened less than a decade earlier, Liverpool's circular Catholic Metropolitan Cathedral, have become not only icons of their age but also enduring architectural landmarks.

In-the-round-theatre presents the theatre designer with opportunities and challenges, although, unlike the thrust, nothing can be 'spare'; every element demands being essential and distilled due to its complete focus on its core. It also presents an opportunity to use volume: the space above and, if there is a substage, below the performer in a vertical spine through the building and, by association, the public. The auditorium binds the audience together around the narrative, and the performers inevitably make entrances from them to tell their story. The limits and qualities of the designed stage floor define the actor's world and, perhaps more so than the thrust, other objects are best kept to a human(e) scale as they will inevitably be intimately connected to people in some way, lightweight and precisely arranged in or around the space. Because most of the audience share the experience of being at close quarters with the stage, any ageing of clothing and objects has to be consistently well executed if not the genuine article – and a blend of the two can be doubly exacting for designers, props technicians and scenic painters.

Going for a walk

Designing for a promenade production is a curious process, in that planning any of the viewpoints is almost entirely reliant on the people who organise the audience, rather than fixed seating configurations. I say 'people' as this function could be carried out by a number of different personnel in a theatre company, from front-of-house staff, to stage management and actors. This immediately has an impact on the costume design – are they integrated into the scheme or not? You should relish the question, however much it may stretch your budget, as it will be a chance to deepen the ensemble and enrich your design world. In terms of storyboarding your ideas, you and your director will have to be prepared to make either subtle or radical changes to your plans after the first performance or two as the public's physical reaction to the performance cannot be totally predictable. Unless the event requires continuous movement of the audience, it's essential to make allowances for those who may need the occasional rest, to design some seating (or at least perching positions) into the spaces along a route, and, of course, wheelchair-friendly access is of paramount importance. A mobile audience is a flexible thing, so getting the balance between the available space and the number of spectators is often the key to everyone being able to adjust their view comfortably. There are exceptions to relying on this, however: any action on the floor, unless you raise that floor, will probably be lost from all but the front row or two of viewers.

Although most audiences are respectful of objects that they could come into direct contact with or even pick up, never assume they won't, and some may be cheeky enough to think they can take a souvenir! Because the shifting environment of a promenade production breaks and re-establishes the 'rules of engagement' with the piece, the creative and stage-management teams will have to make the boundaries of behaviour – and so the show's 'etiquette' – very clear. Alternatively, you may build a tolerance, or even an expectation, of a more anarchic audience's reactions into the piece, although again, your particular boundaries may have to be adjusted once you've opened the show. There is a distinct difference between a dreamthinkspeak and a Punchdrunk production, for example, and indeed each company changes their own rules from show to show in terms of actor-audience proximities.

PART FIVE

Who Do You Work With and How Does Design Affect Them?

1

Producers

Producers, like most theatre practitioners, are multifaceted, multitasking professionals, who traditionally initiated projects in the commercial sector but increasingly have an important role to play in the subsidised regional repertory or smaller scale theatre companies. They are therefore regarded as spearheading the hierarchy of the theatre company, but the best producers have an eye for detail in all areas and will very often have come from a background of more lowly creative or technical levels of the theatre. Though recently there have emerged courses in arts administration, the way that producers reach executive positions is still varied and unpredictable. Producers, like designers, have to be good communicators and excellent team players but know how to influence or lead when necessary.

The theatre designer's first contact with the producer in the commercial sector (say, in London's West End) will usually be at the very start of a project by personal phone call or meeting, or by communication through an agent. They will have set out the context and brief for the project and will then most likely want to arrange a first meeting with the designer alongside other members of the creative team, such as the director, choreographer or lighting designer. If the project is a new dramatic piece, the author might also want or need to be at that first meeting to contribute towards the first collective view of what the production might look like, sound like, or feel like. Those first moments when the creative team and producer meet are crucial in terms of how the different people connect with each other, instinctively, intellectually and practically. The sort of questions that fly around the room could be: *'What inspired the first ideas of the author?' 'Do we have a theatre space yet?' 'What sort of audience is this piece aimed at?' 'How does the structure or conventions of the writing or music impact on the spatial design?' 'How does the piece feel – what is its tone?'*

The designer, and, in fact, all those present, may start to make very early drawings. This, in my experience, is a very powerful way to exchange ideas because it immediately gets to grips with the visual language of the production that might be forming, and in an intuitive, albeit embryonic, way. Very often these early thoughts and images are in some way close to the final outcome, although, of course, they are tested again and again throughout the following days and weeks, allowing for all the other key contributors that the producer puts in place during the design process.

A designer may have to attend one or more of these meetings before the producer has made the formal offer of a contract. This can be a tricky period for both producer and designer, as there is obviously a limit to the amount of brainstorming a producer can expect for free! These early (unpaid) meetings can be a test for all those taking part and the decision to commit to the project on the part of the producer and the designer has to be made at the earliest opportunity, but without either party feeling the pressure of time or other logistics. The designer has to expect these meetings to take place in a variety of surroundings: a café, the producer's office or the foyer of a theatre. It's unlikely that they would be at the designer's studio because that might imply that the designer is on board and already working on the project, so be prepared to talk or show ideas under challenging circumstances! Whilst a show of generosity and creativity is useful to help get the producer on side, exercise some caution, given that your ideas, casually tossed across a table, are still not bound by contract at this point, nor therefore by any protecting copyright clause. There have been instances whereby designers, directors and producers have had exciting and fruitful first meetings but then, for one reason or another, parted company – the designer only later discovering that the final production bears a disturbing similarity to his or her initial vision for the piece.

There has been the odd occasion when a producer has asked me onto a project before the director has been engaged. Although being initially flattering, such a situation usually causes a little unease during early design meetings with the newly appointed director. I was never sure whether at first the director felt that I was an imposition on their usual status in the 'food chain' of casting their creative team, and in these circumstances I've found it's best to (tentatively) bring up the subject early on in an attempt to dispel any worries.

From a designer's perspective, the best producers are those who are open to a number of possibilities for the production, particularly in its early stages, and who give as much time as possible to the director and designer to form a theatrical world for the piece without the inevitable practical and financial pressures that will, all too soon, impose themselves upon the team. Experienced designers and directors will know that these inevitable restrictions nonetheless provide a framework to 'push against' more often than posing a threat to their ideas. So, patience, tact and trust are key assets for the good producer. I've found, however, that the pragmatism of a producer is often a refreshing ingredient in creative discussions, as long as they are as transparent as possible when it comes to talking about how far the money and resources will stretch, as well as filling in any relevant background information (for example, the opinions of influential people behind the scenes, such as sponsors and other financial 'angels', who may harbour their own individual ambitions for the piece).

The stakes are high for all commercial producers, though most, if they are wise, don't invest their own money in a production. They are, though, responsible for OPM (other people's money), and therefore designers who spend some of that cash have to respect the pressure they are under to make the project work. The producer–designer relationship is therefore one in which both parties are mutually supportive and, in the best of circumstances, are working towards the common good and hopefully success of the piece. The designer has, after all, been approved and hired by the producer, so they should have confidence in their own decision. On the designer's part, why bite the hand that feeds you?!

In subsidised theatres, producers will most likely have different, but no less stressful, agendas. They will be working hand in glove with, on the one hand, an artistic director to form a programme for the theatre and, on the other hand, the board of governors, who will have the long-term interests of the organisation at heart. Whilst on the face of it their role may appear more secure than in the commercial world, in today's mixed and turbulent economy, they have to be continually responsive to the rapid change of financial conditions, codes of employment, and broad cultural trends. A designer needs to be sympathetic to these pressures and appreciate that when a company engages him or her, they are contributing towards not only a particular project, but also the lifeblood of a complex organisation. It's always a good idea for a designer to spend a little time talking with the in-house producer they are working with to understand the particular environment in which the theatre is sited and the community it serves. Not only may that feed design ideas, it also connects the production to its specific audience – its community – and often sheds light on a regional visual accent, language and culture. Within London, there's a kaleidoscope of geographic and cultural boundaries to respect and harness – for example, the way the Thames divides the affluent north from the grittier south, or the contrast between the industrial east and the more leafy south-west.

A producer in these 'producing houses' can also be a source of refuge should the component parts of an organisation appear not to be clicking into place as they might. Designers should expect the producer to be, in the first instance at least, a good listener and have empathy with any concern arising from the 'coalface', and to give advice on how situations might be handled to the advantage of the project and/or the company as a whole. Likewise, the designer has to bear in mind the fact that the decisions he or she makes involve the spending of public money, and as such, should be as respectful as those operating in other sectors, such as the National Health Service or state education. Designers in subsidised theatres are, like the producers themselves, public servants.

2

Artistic Directors and Directors

The relationships between designers and directors can be varied and complex, but on many levels it is straightforward. Young designers can often mistake a director as being in some sense their employer, which is usually not the case. The employer, as outlined above, is usually a producer. If the producer in a commercial 'food chain' very often employs the director, in the subsidised sector the artistic director and the producer work more equitably as a team to create a vision for the organisation, but from the director's point of view the engagement of the designer is usually based on artistic merit above all other matters.

During the mid- to late 1960s, 1970s and early 1980s, a 'golden age' of public philanthropy, many repertory theatres had a resident design team, and the artistic director would work very closely with the designers-in-residence over a number of projects, sometimes spanning many years. Nowadays an artistic director has the freedom to pick and choose a design team bespoke to the individual project. In that sense, the artistic director of the regional rep and the director of a commercial project have a very similar starting point when casting their eye over the landscape of theatre design. Occasionally, directors will think out-of-the-box and invite artists from other disciplines in an attempt to create a fresh and original onstage world for the production, and this is their prerogative. Directors should know that they are taking some risks when going down this route, in that artists who are not familiar with the visual language or common theatrical protocols of the profession may jeopardise their vision because they lack the standard industrial skills. But in their turn, the jobbing theatre designer must keep their eyes and ears open for influences from outside the theatre world, thereby broadening their own possibilities, as well as the potential in any one project and the scope of the profession at large.

Some designers feel that the best directors to work with are those that they can sit down and have a pint with. Others prefer a more detached and businesslike relationship. It often depends on the nature or scale of the project, and no doubt that's just the same from a director's point of view. Likewise, some of the best creative meetings happen in coffee bars, but for many that would be a disaster and the more focused environment of the studio is the only place to work.

On the whole, directors will work with a compact 'stable' of designers with whom they have built up a relationship over a number of projects. This situation can be frustrating for those designers who would like to work with a director but who know the director's close circle of familiar faces will be difficult to crack. On the other hand, if you have established an interesting and exciting partnership with a director over a number of productions, it's understandable that you would be protective, or even possessive, of that relationship. A long-lasting working relationship with a director can, however, contain contradictions. Sharing a mutual language and, over time, forming shortcuts in communication can progress ideas at speed and cement a bond by which both director and designer can explore their material through common experiences of what works and what doesn't work. But the flip side of this kind of 'marriage' is that there is an increasing danger of complacency or simply that one or other of the parties automatically assumes their ideas have been taken on board. Each has to be attuned to the pros and cons.

Directors have to be pragmatic in that they can only make choices about what the actually see, hear or feel. Much as in the rehearsal room where an actor will physically and verbally demonstrate their ideas to the director, designer must similarly use everything at his or her disposal to make their ideas both clear and powerful in design meetings. Drawings and models are the 'field of engagement' on which battle lines are drawn, conflicts resolved and agreed ground discovered.

There's a paradox in that the work of the director is seen by most, both inside and outside the production process, to be of paramount importance to a project – but their material is essentially mediated by the effort and product of everyone else in the company. The director's stamp on a production (or rather, more often its perceived absence) can be the making or downfall of a successful theatrical experience.

It is a common frustration for designers that the director will be credited with conceiving the stage design, the designer having merely carried out his or her instructions, but this is born of the mystique surrounding the status of the director: that direction per se cannot be taught, and that they rise to their position by way of their intellect and charisma. The director, like all theatre practitioners, balances ideas and skills, and the nature of both these drivers should be appreciated by the designer if they are both to receive mutual respect and recognition. Likewise, a designer must realise that the artistry in a drawing, and the mystique that may surround it, can be a misleading or distracting element in making shared work. In order to make strong artistic decisions you often have to be vulnerable: which is impossible with somebody you don't trust. Collaboration is a craft.

As I've said already, once established, directors will very often work with a small number of designers whom they have faith in and whom they regard as creative contributors to a project. The frequency with which a director will work with a favoured designer can change according to the pattern of the director's projects and the nature of the work. Sometimes projects will run back to back, and sometimes there will be gaps of perhaps months or even years between opportunities to work together. If you have worked with a particular director for some time it's quite easy to get a little paranoid about the occasions on which that director chooses not to work with you. But these situations are often governed by a variety of stresses, checks and balances that have nothing to do with the director's preferences and opinion of you. These can range from timing and availability, the genre of the piece (for example, opera, drama, musicals), and other logistics, such as outside commitments for both of you which preclude regular meetings during what can be a lengthy process. It is strange that designers, however eclectic their work, will sometimes be pigeonholed into a particular form of theatre. For instance, my tutor when I was a student, the designer Malcolm Pride, remarked that Laurence Olivier always phoned him up when he needed a designer for a Shakespeare play that included twins! It seemed that because Malcolm had once successfully designed a production with twins, he would from that moment onwards always be associated with twins in the director's psyche. At the time of writing, I seem to be going through a phase of being associated with courtroom dramas: *Twelve Angry Men, A Few Good Men, The Merchant of Venice*, and so on.

Sometimes the reason a director contacts you is more instinctive. It may be that you begin to get a reputation for a particular colour palette, or sense of composition, or some other niche such as puppetry or spaces that demand complex physical structures, mechanics or other engineering. The trick is to recognise these as strengths rather than handicaps or straitjackets, and either seek out directors who you know will enjoy working with your particular talents, or actively seek directors who may challenge you to work in unfamiliar ways. At the bottom line, a job is a job, so once you have had the skill or good fortune to land it, the director-designer process will most likely take you on an unpredictable journey to a surprising result.

On the whole, directors enjoy working with designers for both the camaraderie and the challenge. Both should enjoy the cut and thrust of debating and editing their ideas. Some of my most creative and enjoyable experiences have been in the studio during the early stages of the design process with the director. The world is, at that point, your mutual oyster. With your director, you walk through a labyrinth of rooms, each with a world of possibilities behind each door, and the more doors you dare open together, the richer the outcome – each being a '*Why not...?*' space for thought and play. The latter phases of the process will then most likely involve closing some of the doors so as to better define the pathway towards a framework for a production that you can then share clearly with other contributors in the company: the management teams, the technicians and, importantly, the performers.

3

Choreographers

There are many sorts of choreographers. They all share a common understanding of body mechanics, expression and aesthetics, but most carry with them a personal attitude towards dance. They will most likely have been dancers themselves, formally trained in one of the many excellent specialist dance academies across the country, and this can have shaped their choreographic futures. There are now an increasing number of choreographic courses, both at undergraduate and postgraduate levels, and these courses often make a connection with designers on a parallel trajectory. This isn't always the case, though: choreographers may also come with other skills and passions in tow – perhaps drawing, sculpture or performance art.

The nature of the project will reveal their flexibility or niche. Much of this will also be determined by their position in the creative team's hierarchy. A very experienced choreographer may find themselves involved in only a very small element of a project, the 'knees-up' at the end of an RSC production, for example; or, conversely, they may find the scale of their involvement changing throughout a rehearsal process so that, though they thought they were being brought in for a short section of physicality without words, the production might have evolved into something bordering on what could be described as a physical-theatre piece.

There is a pretty clear dividing line between choreography that enhances the movement of an acting company and the necessary rigour of music theatre. For a designer, understanding the choreographer-director relationship in a musical such as *Top Hat*, which requires a number of choreographic sequences, can be more a more complex and crucial factor in developing the design. This is primarily because the dance in this context develops the narrative, so the design should dovetail with, and support, the choreography seamlessly as it would with dialogue. Sometimes an object, either singly or many of the same thing, can be at the centre of the dance sequence (for example, umbrellas, canes, a hat stand, flags), while extravagant costumes clearly contribute to the choreographic patterns and shapes.

There is also a clear division between dance in the theatre and in the established dance companies, which are themselves split between what is loosely recognised as classical ballet and contemporary dance. What audiences now see, however, is an increasing blurring of the two traditions. These specialisms tend to be mirrored by groups of designers who in turn have strengths in one or two, but not usually all, these forms.

Some designers will see no special differences between the process of designing for theatre or dance: just starting from a script in one and evolving it in the other. A designer of musicals that happened to have a strong choreographic content would usually not necessarily be considered for a ballet. Likewise, a designer noted for their work with a contemporary dance company, Rambert, for example, is less likely to be asked to design a dramatic piece even if there is a strong element of choreographic movement involved. There are, thankfully, always exceptions to this – Lez Brotherston is notably one of these. For designers, there is probably a stronger connection between opera and ballet design, than ballet and drama – its sheer scale, musical pulse and visual storytelling are key factors here. But, again, there are obvious exceptions: designers such as Anthony Ward, Mark Thompson and Richard Hudson have titanically straddled them all.

In the dance world, a project would usually be led by the choreographer, who would then engage a designer of their choice. In the world of theatre, albeit in West End musicals where direction, sound and vision are coordinated to within an inch of their lives, it is the director who will most likely suggest the engagement of the designer alongside the choreographer, so they will have to be sure that the chemistry will be right.

Designers for dance have to have what can only be described as a symbiotic as well as practical relationship with their choreographer. Essentially, the work is devised and, although it may have a narrative-driven or musical structure, is flung open to a myriad of instinctive and intuitive choices to express its conceptual foundation. Like the director, the choreographer is not always responsible for initiating or editing ideas, and some of the most outstanding choreographer-designer relationships have been built on a long-term working relationship where perception of each other's work, rather than verbalisation, is needed, so that a mutual understanding of the work grows as it physically develops in rehearsal. The best choreographers (and drama directors, for that matter) have a gift for being able to take a design idea, absorb it, and integrate it so well into a production that you can't tell from whom it originated.

Ballet has unique rules for choreographers and designers alike. When both can foresee and agree the challenges of a piece, the rules are a useful stepping-off point – a key one mentioned earlier, for example, being that the floor space must be kept free whilst at the same time creating a location or other environment. Ballet being a highly stylised form of performance, the more realistic the environment, the greater the challenge. Within that, what you can bring to the table with a choreographer can focus on the tactile use of materials in performance.

There are always some unrealised ideas in the back of
your mind you'd like to try out, and dance is one of
the few areas where there is an opportunity to
experiment.

Liz Da Costa[31]

The dialogue between choreographer and designer is usually longer than its theatre counterpart, unless you're
collectively devising a drama: witness the lengthy research,
development and rehearsal process of writer-director Mike
Leigh and designer Alison Chitty. The evolution of ballet
and dance ideas can take months, but the timeline is sum-
marily defined by the budget or by the availability of the
dancers and/or the studio space.

4

Other Designers

Theatre design in the United Kingdom is unique in that it's the only country that celebrates the fact that its designers for the stage cope with both scenery and costume. In most other countries, those two areas of design are handled by a specialist set designer, prop designer and costume designer. However, on the continent of Europe a set designer may also incorporate lighting design into their range of disciplines and so may well be asked to design both.

Having said that, there is a growing tendency in the UK to divide the discipline of stage design between the two main specialist areas of costume and set, particularly on productions such as musicals and operas which, in terms of scale and logistics, cannot be easily undertaken by a single designer.

The emergence of an increase in audio-visual and other additions to scenography over recent years has seen the inclusion of a number of other designers in the creative team. Sound design was the first of these to take a prominent role, not only enhancing the sound for musicals but also providing a soundscape for drama. Digital sound, in advance of digital imagery, meant that sound designers became an integral part of the creative and production team in the mid-1990s. Lately, video design and its applications have become increasingly useful and, as in some productions, crucial to the storytelling and aesthetics of the show.

In the US, if you look at a billboard on Broadway, for example, you will see other designers alongside that of set and costume. These could include prop design, make-up design and hair design.

If you find yourself part of a larger design team it goes without saying that you will have to be super-sensitive to the work of the others. In these situations, being able and willing to produce drawings, references and other objects becomes more important than ever. Without these being shared regularly at design meetings, there is a very real danger that the cohesion of the production will rest solely with the director, and their ability (or not) to hold the show together will only become apparent when you're actually on stage and, perhaps, too far down the line to salvage it. The design team must be generous with each other's ideas, and, although there has to be a practical demarcation between the disciplines, the exchange of ideas has to be fluid for as long as possible, right up to press night, with any luck. The matrix of possibilities – once you multiply this extended group of designers with a large group of specialist directors, such as fight director, choreographer, stager, as well as producers – goes on and on to infinity, it would seem, much like the endless credits in the movies... It's what makes large-scale musical and opera productions such a challenging, exciting but exhausting experience for everyone. You certainly earn your money!

On the other hand, as a result of working on one element rather than all (in my case this has either been set design or lighting design), the process has revealed a great deal about the mystery of design. Working with another designer is like talking to yourself but having no idea where the conversation is going to take you – an out-of-body, out-of-mind experience. There are a couple of other advantages too: there's something very satisfying about concentrating in detail on one area of the visual world you're trying to create, at times in ignorance of all the others, holding your breath before putting it all together. The revelation of an unexpected combination of final design ideas, under designed light, wrapped in designed sound, nearly always makes the wait worthwhile. Also, if you do have a close working relationship with the other designers, you have the comparatively rare experience of talking with someone who shares the common language of pure design.

5

Production Managers

The production manager is the designer's lifeline – they provide your scenic 'oxygen supply'. Not only are they vital, in that without them you'd most likely never get your set built unless you built it yourself, they are also a support to the shaping of the design itself. Other than talking with an assistant, there is no one on the technical team as close to the design as the production manager, and as such they provide a terrific reservoir of knowledge and a sounding board at any point in the process.

PMs have usually had technical experience in either construction or lighting and, like designers, need to have worked in a number of areas to appreciate how the whole production team fits together – in order to help you. They've gained this experience from working on show after show, and although certain elements of what they know can be taught formally, most battle-hardened production managers have accumulated their knowledge from a range of companies, situations, and scales of production.

An experienced production manager will have found a coping strategy for the pressures that come with the role. Those pressures are, at times, immense. Along with having to take the initiative in realising a design as soon as it starts to take shape, they will also be fielding the technical crossfire from every other part of the team. Each PM has a different style, which is probably because so much of their work depends on personal temperament and the unique combination of projects that they have worked on. Some take the lead and feel they can be of most help in a proactive position, and some take on a more executive role, if they feel other members of the technical team can fill in. Some take a pragmatic approach, very hands-on, and whether they like it or not, feel compelled to have a physical connection with how set is built, installed or maintained. The everyday intensity of being a production manager takes its toll. I'm sure it's not a coincidence that many of the early deaths that I have come across in the profession are most often those of production managers. These fatalities are usually not accidents and nor are they accidental – they simply result from a build-up of stress upon stress.

Designers really appreciate the benefits of a good production manager, and the joys of a great one. The designer will probably not be asked by a producer if they would like to make a choice of production managers. Very often the producer will engage a production manager as a first line of insurance against a production process running away with itself in its first days – particularly financially. Production manager Nick Ferguson's definition of his job:

> I manage time and money. I always consider myself
> as working *for* a producer and *with* a designer. It's
> useful to make that distinction clear. Alongside that, I
> realise a designer's idea – it's my job to get it from
> paper to floor.

The first meeting, on the first project, is crucial. Like all collaborations, both parties need to feel that they can trust each other completely. The production manager is directly responsible for the production budget and very often for a number of technicians who are there to realise the work, so, in the early days of the process, design can quickly start to determine the lives of others. The ideal situation is when both designer and production manager realise they are totally dependent upon each other, and so honesty and transparency are key to a successful and supportive relationship.

For example, it's common practice for a production manager to reserve at least a ten-per-cent contingency in the budget, and it's a good idea at the start of a project to be open about this and discuss its use. A designer may feel, with their knowledge of the project's progress, and their knowledge of the way the director works, that this proportion may not be enough in reserve during the coming weeks of trial and error. Alternatively, if the designer feels there's a watertight case for reserving a smaller proportion, then the production manager will be very clear as to whether that's possible not, or whether it's simply unwise.

The connection between the producer and the production manager in terms of the design timeline is also a contractual one. Designers will have deadlines built in to their agreement, and it's the production manager who makes sure the designer is up to speed. Most deadlines, other than the first public performance, of course, are open to a degree of flexibility and negotiation. It's very often the case that the designer's contract will state that targets for the delivery of designs are movable if revised dates are agreed with the producer, director and production manager. So another important discussion to be had at the start of a project is just how your design process will marry up with the dates in the diary.

A production manager in the commercial sector will have a quite distinct and different life from one in the subsidised sector. Their bonds with designers are just as crucial in either, but their connections with the other teams, how they are managed and their impact on the budget, are worlds apart. A commercial project will demand that a production manager seek out the best people for the job of realising the design, and that requires both quality control and a firm grip on the purse strings. A subsidised project, say in a regional repertory theatre, will involve the production manager in the deployment and care of an in-house established technical team and, perhaps, a number of fully functioning workshops.

It's important for you as the designer to realise that the PM is on your side, and so you must also be prepared to meet them halfway when there are no obvious solutions to a problem. I can think of no greater need for clear drawings or models than in a conversation with a production manager. It's only by both of you understanding the scale and qualities of the design that the best way of achieving it can be found.

For example, a chair is never just 'a chair'. That chair can represent the whole design or a very small component in a big picture. That chair might warrant a great deal of money spent on it, or very little – even nothing. Thus producing that chair may mean a skilled craftsman spending a considerable amount of time and money to realise it, a trip to the charity shop or finding it in the theatre's prop store. Without a reference image, drawing, or model, the chair's future is uncertain, and possibly therefore a whole bunch of other elements further down the line. So, knowledge is power, and a production manager has to be empowered through design to be able to fight for what you want... they are not mind readers! Nick Ferguson makes this very clear:

> As soon as I see a white-card model I know how the journey is going be. You can look at the sketch model and instinctively tell whether you're going to be able to deal with it: and to afford it or not.

Wise PMs are also discreet when tempted to make value judgements about the artistic merits of a design. If the work looks feasible, both financially and technically, they are usually encouraging no matter what they might think of the aesthetics or the overall visual impact it might have in performance. Having said that, it is always your job as designer to give an artistic reason for what any particular element of design is doing for the production – by engaging collaborators in your ideas, as well as in the raw technicalities, your colleagues will more likely be enthused, make better choices when they need to take the initiative, and sometimes may have *really* good suggestions to make. An instance of this was trying to solve the moment in my production of *The Comedy of Errors* when Dromio and Antipholus of Ephesus are locked in a 'dark and dankish vault' and then tortured. I explained to the PM and scenic builder why I wanted to cram them into the boot of a car, though this looked like being both costly and tricky. Deadlock. Then someone suggested, 'Well, if we were going to hide someone, we'd stuff them into the Wheelie bins at the back of the workshop...' – inspired, and far wittier. Two bins it was: ready-made, flexible in performance, actor-controlled and more practical on a number of levels – you can imagine the fun we had with them in rehearsals!

As scenic workshops up and down the country are broken up and their skills dispersed, production managers in subsidised repertory theatres are now having to acquire a deep working knowledge of all the commercial builders across the UK and, in some cases, abroad. This working knowledge includes knowing who is expensive and why, and who is cheaper and why, along with all the specialisms that each workshop is capable of. For example, some commercial workshops have the skill base and equipment for metalwork or engineering, whilst others are far more at home using timber. Some workshops have sprung from making props and others from mechanics – whoever started the company will most likely have more of a passion for a particular process or product. An up-to-the-minute company will now be most likely investing as much money as it can in machines that respond to CAD (computer-aided design) drawings. The CNC cutter (a computer-controlled cutting machine) has also revolutionised some areas of production. With increasingly large-scale 3D printing on the horizon, the production manager of the future will be on the lookout for the shortest lines of communication between the designer's studio and the workshop's finished object.

Producing a design in a regional rep is a more intense experience for a designer than one might at first imagine. You will find you have to fit into an established institutionalised team and the in-house production manager is your compass around the building. They should be able to tell you the strengths of each department, the inevitable oddballs and idiosyncrasies of the organisation, where you will find enthusiasm and where perhaps just a little more caution. You will most likely have to spend part of a day travelling to the theatre, so, unless you stay overnight, the working day is packed with getting around to see everyone, not forgetting that you will probably need to put some time aside to look in on rehearsals and remind yourself what your director looks like! Your production manager should organise your days so that you have maximum contact and maximum effect. They will be aware that a resident team is more likely to stick to daytime working hours (to preserve some semblance of a work-life balance over a long season) and not necessarily be able to hang around until well into the evening. They will also need to be sensitive to the needs of the costume department, as you will most likely be designing clothes as well. If this is the case, the production manager will be pulling on one arm and the costume supervisor pulling on the other, but I would rather be kept busy throughout the day than regretting that I could have spent my time more usefully, when I step back on the train for that reflective journey home.

6

Costume Supervisors

A costume supervisor is the costume equivalent of a production manager. They work closely with the costume designer to realise their designs, which means dealing with the logistics and budgeting as well as organising the making of all aspects of the costume design. But crucially they also have to engage fully with the intention behind the ideas and with the designer's concepts and aesthetic. For example, the design might be set in a particular historical period or have a very tight colour palette. The supervisor's role is firstly to gauge whether the idea is feasible given the resources, and then to have a 'design eye' with which to judge which makers would be best to construct the designs or, in the case of a more contemporary design, which retail or trade outlets, contemporary or vintage, would be the best places to source clothing as close as possible in spirit, cut and colour to the drawn designs.

The supervisor is also a consummate tactician; bridging the gaps between the designer's imagination and the costume-maker's, and between the designer and the actors. The fittings are usually when the supervisor's skill is most evident and crucial, as she or he shapes ideas on the actor's body and weighs up in minutes what are the most practical and creative solutions to progress the design, whilst anticipating how the costume will be seen and used on stage in performance and if it will be durable enough to sustain a run of shows. There is, incidentally, a distinction to be made here between the costume supervisor and wardrobe manager, who is more closely allied to the theatre company in performance and ensures that the show's costumes are maintained during the run of the production, and who is probably also in charge of a team of dressers.

Costume supervisors have sometimes moved into their role from being a dresser or from a making background – there are now courses that prepare graduates for supervision, but it is a senior position and relies on a wealth of knowledge and experience, no matter how modest the scale of show. Costume designers, particularly in the UK where the designer is likely to do both set and costume, obviously need to trust the supervisor to make the show happen smoothly and ensure the best possible quality. The designer will often have the choice of supervisor, so the transition from maker or wardrobe staff to supervisor can be a big leap for both parties. Often a less experienced designer will have a more experienced supervisor recommended by the theatre company, and it would be my advice as a designer to go along with this – you will learn a great deal throughout the intensity of a project, and the more experienced supervisors can also help afterwards with recommendations for up-and-coming supervisors to team up with on smaller future projects.

The practicalities of any project should always be viewed by the designer as a useful framework to help shape design ideas. The supervisor is a valuable part of that frame: pushing, pulling and testing both the concepts and sometimes your resolve!

> The most important thing about my job is persuasion: persuading designers that they're making the right decision, persuading costume-makers that they can make it and persuading actors that they want to wear it.

> *Jan Bench, costume supervisor*

Discussing an idea with your costume supervisor and getting to grips with its realisation will give you an armoury of possibilities, probabilities and certainties that will carry forward into negotiations with the director or choreographer, performers and, of course, costume-makers. When a costume is being made, the process of choosing between the myriad of fabrics offered by the supervisor is very much a part of this preparation – it's when ideas actually *materialise* and are tested against the meanings of texture, pattern and colour, or pliability and movement. The cultural contexts of fabrics also play a part. For example, what signifiers do tweed, or silk, or rubber even, communicate consciously or subconsciously to the audience in relation to an actor's character in action? The fabric can transform a costume's conceptual meaning, but the clothes must also be wearable and durable night after sweaty night.

Supervisors 'cast' the costume-makers. The experienced ones have a directory of makers who all have slight or more pronounced specialisms. For instance, it's probably a waste of time to ask a dressmaker to tailor a men's suit, or makers of period soft tailoring to produce faux haute couture. Supervisors are also tuned to temperaments, both of the maker and designer. If, from their experience of each, the supervisor feels that a maker is not going to be on the same wavelength as the designer, or, when it comes to the fitting, that a particular actor/designer combination might require particular diplomatic prowess or saintly patience, then they'll bear that in mind, along with targeting their special-ist making skills.

As with most close working partnerships, the best strategy is to discuss openly how you have worked with supervisors in the past (or not at all), and how you anticipate the current project shaping up. There can be either considerable, or very little, crossover in 'who does what' throughout the process, so agreeing principles early on in the relationship is wise. For example, some designers try to go on all shopping expe-ditions for clothes and fabrics, some expect the supervisor to do the legwork and bring back samples for approval, and some may even leave the whole process to the supervisor, demanding more of the supervisor's and maker's interpretation of their drawings or other reference material. If this is the case, and to be fair to everyone, then the design on paper has to be impeccable – detailed front view, back view and full notation.

Occasionally the opposite is true and the designer may have fittings without the supervisor being present. This is fine as long as the supervisor is then kept up to date with what information has been passed on, because invariably there will be further questions down the line which they need to know about – a good tip is to always take a snapshot of the dressed actor for future reference. You want to avoid situations where false assumptions have been made about what the design looks or behaves like, so keep lines of communication open constantly, always referring back to drawn images when possible and being clear about the priorities in making that image 3D.

On large-scale drama and opera, supervisors may well take on greater design responsibilities when costuming a chorus or supernumeraries. Again, it's best for the designer and supervisor to be clear about the extent of these decisions, and it's important that the designer can offer at least sketches of the shapes or unity of colour that suits the production. Quite often, photographic references from photojournalists are a good solution – they are usually clear and genuinely of a period.

During the production week, when actors are wearing the complete costumes (often for the first time) and both you and the supervisor see how the complete ensemble is shaping up under stage light, the partnership is at its most dynamic. You will both be adjusting this and that until the to-do list reduces in length and the level of exactitude reaches a threshold of what's sensibly noticeable by the audience at a variety of distances. I tend to leap on stage quite a bit to talk to actors about sometimes the smallest detail – how their tie is knotted or whether they need to wear the hat further back on their head to keep shadow off their faces. This is partly to reassure them and partly to be seen to be keeping in touch with the ensemble; the costume supervisor will often be doing the same. They are your link to what's happening offstage too, which is often too far to keep visiting in the hurly-burly of a technical rehearsal – particularly if you also have the set and props to attend to.

An 'aftershock' of costuming a show comes with the arrangements for understudies, covers, 'swings' and walking understudies. An assistant director may well be responsible for overseeing how actors may understudy other roles in the company and the logistical knock-on effect as actors rotate roles. Emergencies happen – an illness or an accident – and so a company has to be prepared for all eventualities at very short notice, and that includes having fitted alternative costumes on standby. Often actors won't have knowledge of who they will understudy until well into the rehearsal process – so knowledge of who's playing what as early as possible is vital to the supervisor. Sometimes the replacements are radically different in size and shape, so a supervisor will usually consult with the costume designer about the pros and cons of the design on the body of another actor – particularly tricky on occasions when the budget has been stretched to its limits so that duplicating certain items of carefully (and perhaps fortunately) sourced vintage clothes is financially impossible.

Finally, the supervisor is responsible for keeping an accurate record of each costume in a show in the form of a carefully annotated folder – it's grandly called a 'bible' – and without it, the decisions that are made can be lost for ever in the frenzy of delivering the production. The bible has the measuring sheet of the actor, their picture, the design, fabric samples of the final costume and other sources of found articles, such as shoes and jewellery. The bible usually stays with the production after both the designer and supervisor have ended their formal contracted employment with the theatre or production company, so if it's needed again, for instance if the show extends its run and there's a change of cast, or the production is revived after a period of time, the details can be recalled. These are precious documents that have also found their way into theatre archives and have become a valuable academic resource for historians. Nobody can be sure if a show is dead and buried after its initial run, so the bible, production photographs and video recordings are vital for a production's further life.

7

Stage Management

Stage managers are the engine room and navigation system for a theatre company. They form a close-knit and well-trained support to the creative team, actors and theatre company. The stage-management team usually comprises three or four people who have distinct roles and in a chain of command from top down, as follows:

Company stage manager: At the top of the stage-management tree, the CSM's role varies a little depending on whether the show is commercial or subsidised. In the commercial world, they would have the responsibility for seeing a touring show installed at a venue, looking after the company of actors to make sure their travel arrangements and accommodation are supported as much as possible, and overseeing some of the finances for the show, such as petty cash and, sometimes, actors' subsidies and wages. The CSM might also put together the rest of the stage-management team for a project. In the subsidised sector, the stage-management team would probably be resident in the theatre company along with the CSM and so they would probably have fewer financial responsibilities. The CSM may write and email the 'show report': the record of facts (such as audience figures), difficulties and anomalies for each performance, although this task is sometimes the deputy stage manager's (below).

Stage manager: Next in line, the SM will often organise the day-to-day business of the rest of the stage-management team. Whilst in rehearsal, that would probably entail organising or communicating the day-to-day schedule of rehearsals in close collaboration with the director and deputy stage manager. The SM could also be responsible for finding and buying props. In the production week, the SM runs the technical rehearsals ('techs') and makes sure that everything backstage runs smoothly and safely. To do this they are part of the technical team that is linked by the internal communication system of headphones and microphones ('cans'). In performance, the SM is backstage ensuring that the movement of performers and technicians runs according to plan and in safety.

Deputy stage manager: The DSM's title sounds like they are in reserve for the stage manager, and that's probably true in emergencies, but their chief role is to constantly be in rehearsals alongside the director, making notes of the actors' motivations or moves as they develop, and formally entering these notes into what will become the 'prompt copy'. They have to keep their eye on the ball as they are continually prompting the actors whilst learning their lines (when they are still 'on the book', as opposed to 'off the book'), and making notes for the rest of the creative team who can't always be in rehearsal, such as what new props might be added or costume queries – these all make their way into a daily emailed rehearsal report. Throughout the production week and on into performance the DSM will be cueing the show (calling, on cans, when lighting, sound, flying or other mechanics are actioned), using the cue points that were established during the last days of rehearsal in the rehearsal room and during the tech in the theatre. As they have their finger on the show's pulse, it is often the DSM's job to complete the show report. It's important to add that the DSM has to have an acute sense of timing in performance. They are, in effect, an unseen performer, in that they operate the cue lights for actors' entrances should they need them and generally have to tune in to the rhythm of each live performance

– particularly if something unusual happens; anticipating the 'lag' between calling the cue and the action taking effect.

Assistant stage manager: The ASM, and on larger productions there may be two, supports, particularly, the stage manager. They may be responsible for sourcing and making smaller props – they will often find themselves scouring the net for hours to find the best and most economical solutions for sometimes the most bizarre objects! In production, the ASM is usually backstage, although occasionally they may also have to go on stage to help with scene changes. The ASM makes sure that all the small props are organised clearly on props tables for the actors so they can be easily found at speed and usually in very dim lighting. Incidentally, designers need to be aware of the backstage space needed for these props stations, where furniture might be 'struck' to, and other service areas such as quick-change booths. ASMs may also be involved in these costume changes and operating smaller, often low-tech, effects such as pulling lengths of string to trigger something or fastening windows and doors. On tour, the ASM is often responsible, alongside others in the stage-management team, to 'dress' a detailed set with the set-dressing paraphernalia. Finally, ASMs are occasionally asked to appear on stage in small, non-speaking parts.

So, the stage-management team is vitally important to the designer's relationship with the director and performance in rehearsal, and later, with the smooth running of the show. One of the designer's first points of contact with stage management is when, at the start of rehearsals, they will be given the designer's ground plan of the set to 'mark up' on the floor of the rehearsal room. This is an opportunity for the designer to stress the importance of particular aspects of the physical design. There may well be a discussion between stage management, designer and director about the orientation of the mark-up in relation to the rehearsal room, which is often smaller than the stage and incidentally is also usually flooded with natural light (although I've known director Roger Haines to frequently insist, but 'lovingly', as he'd say, on rehearsing with a few theatre floodlights, which gives each rehearsal a focus and intensity). There may have to be quick decisions made with stage management about the temporary construction of, for example, platforms and doors.

The DSM will often be the one to schedule costume fittings, so the liaison between DSM and costume supervisor is vital. The DSM will often be caught between the director's need for an actor in rehearsal and the designer's need for a fitting – sometimes not easy! It always works out in the end, but the crucial thing is to give as much advance warning as possible to the DSM through the costume supervisor of an imminent need for a fitting.

Perhaps the trickiest situations for a designer and the stage-management team are in the area of prop sourcing and making. Sometimes the show will engage a props buyer and, in the more complicated and larger scale productions with larger budgets, specialist prop-makers of all sorts will be brought on board, usually by the production manager. Sometimes a required object will be in the grey area between costume and props, what is known as a 'costume prop' – I once had to design a prosthetic metal hand for Roger Lloyd-Pack, for example, which involved a costume-prop team effort. A stage manager's level of making skills can vary wildly. Some are naturals, can turn their hand to anything and, importantly, know the limitations of their prop-making prowess. Others, however game, can produce alarming results and can spend a great deal of time and effort on an object that has to be diplomatically rejected. Many ASMs have been put in the position of having to make something owing to an insufficient budget, and in this case the designer has to open up negotiations with others to insist on a change of strategy and a sensible reallocation of funds!

As with most elements of design, one of the best forms of insurance is a drawing, or at least some visual reference with measurements, for the maker. If something is amiss or just plain wrong, the drawing can be brought back to the table for further discussion and, hopefully, a successful outcome.

Top Tip: *Always try to read the DSM's daily rehearsal notes as soon as possible after receiving them. They sometimes need clarification as to which character is using what prop or costume accessory and at which moment in the scene, but often the questions will be more about 'why?' – what is the motivation for that prop and how might it fit into your design's conceptual framework?*

8

Scenic and Costume Technicians

Makers of sets and costumes are usually introduced to you by the production manager and costume supervisor respectfully. Carpenters, metalworkers, scenic artists, prop-makers, costume-makers, milliners – none would survive unless they were pretty good at it (like designers or any specialist professional), so working with this group of talented interpreters and craftspeople is usually an absolute joy. They are making your ideas come to life, and, much like actors cast in the right role, they are doing something that they are particularly expert at. Any doubt and worry on your part will be understandable, but usually needless.

When meeting a maker there are usually two things going on in a designer's head, firstly: *'Have I given them enough of the right information and visuals?'* and secondly, *'When and what can I comment on and, if so, are words enough or is another drawing required?'* The two are related but the second is the most poignant. The maker is looking for clear directions and leadership, although they will be anxious to tell you that the job is only half-completed and 'you'll have to use your imagination' to fill in the rest as designed. The poignancy is that experience tells designers to hold their tongue and listen to what the maker has to say – their craft and creativity overlap as does the designer's, so they may well have thought through your ideas more thoroughly in the handling of materials and may come up with interesting ideas to develop the work. Having said that, you may only get one or two chances to see work as it's being made, whether in a costume fitting or at a scenic builders, before it hits the stage, so it's best in the end to pull no punches and say everything you have to say at the time, as there's nothing worse than wishing you had when it's too late or too costly to put right.

Top tip: *If you are in the position of assisting a designer, usually as a model-maker in their studio, ask if you can shadow them when they visit a workshop or attend a costume fitting so that you can observe how they handle a variety of situations. You won't be paid for it, but it's a priceless part of an apprenticeship.*

9

Box Office and Front-of-House Managers

A quick word about how designers connect with the people who interface with the public before the start of a performance. At the presentation of the design before the start of rehearsals, the box-office manager and front-of-house (FOH) manager may well be present. Personally, I applaud this as I know that they will have very practical comments about what the audience sees and therefore their perception of your work. Box-office staff, ushers and others who deal directly with the audience usually bear the brunt of complaints, so it's no wonder they like to get an early look at what are likely to be the challenges for the audience, and therefore for them, in the weeks of preparation ahead. After all, it's they that have to make sure the event is safe for the theatregoing public, your customers, and ensure that disabled viewers and listeners have as vivid a time as possible. It's usually sightline issues, and sometimes audibility, that are their main concern, but there are cleaners to be considered too if you plan to do messy stuff in the auditorium, and refreshments' revenue threatened if you and the director plan not to have an interval.

Of course, nowadays designers and directors like to challenge conventional theatre spaces and might propose a modest or radical restructuring of the stage-auditorium relationship. Indeed, many auditoria are designed by the architect to be flexible, offering alternative seating arrangements, and sometimes allowing for the possibility of the audience being unseated and promenading. In these situations, the box-office and FOH managers, in collaboration with the theatre's administrators or the producer, will count the cost of lost seats over the run of the show. On the other hand, seats, and therefore revenue, can often be augmented by reducing the stage space to an intimate and focused area, as in a three-hundred-and-sixty-degree, in-the-round configuration.

The central question always revolves around the actors' proximity to the audience and whether that relationship should be as equal and democratic for all the visiting public or whether those relationships will vary depending on ticket price. In the final analysis, these discussions will all have the audience's experience of the event as paramount, which is as it should be.

10

Publicity and Marketing

It's pretty obvious, but you do need an audience to come to your work, so respect for how they might find out about it and then be attracted enough to part with hard-earned money to see it is only sensible. How the show is marketed and how you market yourself as a freelance designer are closely entwined, so before we move on to the next section about finding work, let's consider the common goals and where they diverge.

Design is perceived as visual, so the still photographic image remains an important shop window for your and the production's success. Video trailers offer a cropped and edited view of design in action, although obviously without the sensations of a live event – these too loom large in your shop window. Designers are increasingly asked for visual material in advance of the production hitting the stage – publicists clamour for it, so, for example, you may be asked for costume designs or storyboard images accompanied by a question-and-answer interview about what you're doing or how you're doing it. My advice is to be cautiously generous – which sounds paradoxical, but it's actually a matter of viewing the issues in both the short and long term. In the short term, the show's, and (assuming you'll be proud of it) your own associated, success is vital: help all you can – designers have enough gripes about not having their contribution recognised so we can't complain when it's handed to us on a plate! In the longer term, however, we know that all our words and images, when published digitally on the web, will linger a long, long time and probably outlive us –

so be cautious by keeping editorial control: proofread copy and make sure you have power of veto over the final destination of your visual work before you part company with any of it.

One might think that copyright of images is a concern to theatre designers – I believe that not to be the case. Firstly, because the theatre biz is a small world and direct copies of other people's ideas would devalue a designer's professional credentials overnight. Secondly, images themselves are not what are crucial about our work: it's how the image is applied to a particular theatrical moment. Thirdly, theatre design has always been recognised by designers themselves to be a 'magpie' profession, borrowing this and morphing that and using it in the other, until it no longer really resembles the original, such are the particularities of the new context. We all do it, so it's a case of 'let he who is not guilty cast the first stone'. Theatre's and theatre design's humiliation as a 'bastard art form' was supposedly exposed by critic and art historian Michael Fried when he declared that, 'Art degenerates as it approaches the condition of theatre.' The point is missed: it's precisely the impurity, the inappropriateness, the human mess, that give theatre and its designers their artistic status.[32]

Production companies will invariably hire a photographer and film-maker to make the most of the visual impact of your work. It is usually a contractual right of the company to use still images with which to market the show and to make a short promotional trailer without seeking your permission. My advice is to secure as much access to this material as possible – it's of a professional standard, so use it when you can in your folio or on your website. It's common courtesy and sometimes a legal requirement to credit the photographer in a caption under the image, as you'd expect others to credit you. It's copyright 'horse-trading': the photographers and film-makers have copyright concerns too, but this is a situation where mutual trading usually leaves everyone happy.

Top tip: *Make sure you're there for any scheduled photo calls: costumes out of place and your set in disarray caught for posterity can be maddening! Still photos are usually taken at the first dress rehearsal, which is a great incentive to get everything right first time. Befriend the photographer – they will be most interested in taking exciting close-ups of the actors, so I advise that you kindly request the odd long or wide shot that you can use for your own purposes later. There's more on this topic in Part Nine (2. In the Theatre: A Survival Kit).*

PART SIX

How Do You Land Your
First Production?

1

Theatregoing

Knowing the context in which we all work is key to 'making it'. Theatre, like many professions, relies on a common specialist language that is shared by all those making work, as well as all those that comment upon it and judge it, such as academics and critics. Theatre culture in England has been forming and subtly shifting over the last five hundred years. Many of its historical reference points are unique, such as the cluster of theatres and theatre producers that have contributed towards the success of London's West End 'Theatreland'. However, much of its basic terminology is universally shared across the United Kingdom and, through the work of directors such as Peter Brook and Yukio Ninagawa, or producers such as Thelma Holt, across the whole *world* of theatre-making.

To learn the grammar, syntax and vocabulary of theatre-speak there's nothing quite like going to as much of it as you can. You will begin to form strong opinions about how directors and designers create interesting and entertaining work that will add to your personal lexicon and give a potential richness to conversations you will have with your collaborators when making work. There is obviously (and this is also true of any profession) an ongoing requirement to stay up to date with your industry so that you remain aware of what your contribution towards it is.

In London, access to world-class theatre just gets better and better. Well-established organisations and festivals, such as the London International Festival of Theatre (LIFT), the artistic programme at the Barbican, and co-productions such as the Bridge Project between the Old Vic Theatre and Brooklyn Academy of Music, have made it possible to see a wide range of work, which employs an eclectic array of theatrical conventions from companies that frequently, within themselves, are composed as a multicultural ensemble. Often the creative teams are multinational which, although regularly producing interesting work, makes it difficult for the lay-theatregoer to recognise a particular national or cultural characteristic. The danger here is that universality can sometimes lead to a bland, generic, predictable outcome. It's just as likely that the sharpest and most powerful theatregoing experience comes from a company steeped in its own traditions and practice. I think back to such landmark productions as those toured by the Berliner Ensemble or the Rustaveli National Theatre from Georgia, which offered a life-changing experience by which we can see our own society and its dramas through the lens of another.

Paradoxically, even though the UK has a reputation for liberal support of the performing arts, many British practitioners with a flair for more eclectic forms of theatre-making have found more success in mainland Continental Europe than in the UK. Peter Brook found the need to establish his own ensemble at Les Bouffes du Nord theatre in Paris, for example, and directors such as Simon McBurney of Complicite will make as much work in the drama and opera houses of Europe or Japan, as in their equivalents in the UK. In this day and age, though, much of this top-end material can be seen, if only perhaps as excerpts, on the internet – or as full productions on DVD.

Different regional centres in the UK have also contributed towards the kaleidoscope of international theatre work. Some regional theatres in the past have tried to form a more internationalist artistic policy, such as Leicester Haymarket Theatre some twenty-five years ago. The Edinburgh Festival, over a period of more than thirty years, has been the most obvious example of an explosion of interest in (not always world-class, but nevertheless) global theatre. It remains the most vibrant, diverse and still affordable of festival experiences. Many cities across Europe have festivals that go a long way to matching the pre-eminence of Edinburgh's combined International and Fringe festivals, such as those in Dublin, Brighton or Avignon. Grant Hicks talks about the value of his early work at the Edinburgh Festival:

> What I carried forward was resourcefulness and determination – the ability to forage for something that will spark your imagination and then give you a lead to something else. I could be a problem-solver and think on my feet. I was watching, listening, asking and learning – it was my apprenticeship.

What's important about these opportunities to see and make new work is that to a large degree it's made by the upcoming generation of theatre-makers who thrive on a support and (hopefully) acclaim from their own generation of young theatregoers. If you are lucky when browsing through hundreds of performances in any one year, you can see an early snapshot of theatre's future movers and shakers. Much of what is produced is often dismissed by seasoned critics as poor-quality, 'student-level' work, but for both those that take part or go as spectators, that's the point! Without a national subsidised infrastructure where else can this work form, take place and reach a wider audience? For those wanting to make a start or change in their careers, a festival is a great way to meet new faces from across planet theatre.

Theatre festivals also offer the chance to see and get involved with exciting work in alternative spaces. All manner of buildings are commandeered into service, from churches, to factories, to schoolrooms to telephone boxes – all testing a designer's assumptions about what a theatre space can be, and sometimes lending a production a powerful metaphorical context as well as a technical challenge. If you see something that is interesting and you have the time, there's no harm in offering to help out.

Closer to home, and usually closer to the young designer's price range, are productions in small independent venues such as the now well-established range of pub and club theatres. Although very often starting out as a personal project of an aspiring producer or director, some of these small theatres now have a strong and rich history behind them and have established themselves as part of a city's cultural life. Every week there is seemingly a new kid on the block, and by keeping up to date with where they are, whom they are run by, and the sort of work they produce, you may find a seedbed for your own first productions. Many a reputation has been made by creative teams that build a consistent body of innovative work from modest beginnings. It has to be said, however, that director-designer partnerships formed in this way will very often drift apart when an ambitious director gets an opportunity to work in more established or varied company. If this happens, it's important for the designer to also move on with his or her confidence and experience intact. You too will have a production or two under your belt, and hopefully a few good shots for your website!

2

Networking

Don't write to anyone you wouldn't want to work
with – you may just get the job!

Alison Chitty, designer

But first things first: meeting directors, and striking up a
relationship with them, is quite frequently a daunting mystery for theatre-design students. However, there are a
number of ways to make your first steps on a journey that
can last a good deal of your professional life.

Due to the networking possibilities of the internet, designers and directors have a great many ways of familiarising
themselves with each other's work. Social networking
greatly helps what was already largely a 'word-of-mouth'
industry. Directors can instantly access the visual work of a
designer, and, likewise, a designer can get feel for the tone
or subject matter of a director's work – that being said, there
is no substitute for seeing another's work live. Sometimes a
website can do you an injustice. Websites can often merely
reaffirm the kind of work that you have already done with
the result that you can get pigeonholed.

The most fruitful meeting place is at previews and press
night of a production when the director is most likely to be in
attendance. A casual meeting in the bar, followed up by a
meeting at a safer distance from that particular production,
will test out the possibilities for a future working relationship.

Established directors, like designers, will very often have an
agent. If you can't contrive an 'accidental' meeting, face to
face, there is no harm in contacting a director's agent, who

can then fix up a meeting either formally or informally. Quite often, agents will represent groups of both directors and designers, so if you are looking for an agency to represent you for the first time, it's also worth looking at those that have a balance of clients across the disciplines of the creative team. In the early phase of being represented by an agent, one of the first things they can do to help launch your career is to introduce you to the directors and choreographers that they may already represent.

There are a number of organisations that promote opportunities for designers and directors, starting out in their professional life, to meet and make work together. Amongst the most established of these are the Linbury Prize for Stage Design, the Jerwood Young Designers scheme and the Young Vic's Director/Designer Network.[33] The success of these initiatives has given rise to a growing awareness of their benefits in the regional repertory theatres as well as in London. Many theatres take on young directors as assistants from courses such as Birkbeck's Directing MFA, offering them the chance to make experimental small-scale works. This is obviously an excellent opportunity for a designer to forge a working relationship.

Universities and colleges themselves have their part to play in matchmaking. In many other countries, directors, designers and other creatives, along with performers, will very often learn their discipline in the same conservatoire. The obvious advantage to this is that early working relationships can be formed with the benefit of an institutional 'safety net'. The flip side is that assumptions may get firmly established and entrenched concerning the hierarchies of conventional theatre-making – a pyramid, with the director very much at its apex, and the remainder of the company forming an ever-broadening support to the director's opinions and wants. In the UK, student directors and designers tend to study in very different institutions: the directors at university or drama school, and the designers in an art school, for example. This situation is healthy in the respect that each discipline maintains an integrity through specialism and autonomy, but, of course, the drawback is that both parties will be less likely to form patterns of work together and share either established or newly found theatre languages and protocols. The picture has improved in recent years, owing partly to the fact that cooperation between drama schools, art schools and universities makes economic sense for much the same reason as cooperation between theatres themselves is on the increase.

3

Subsidy

If you are aiming to make work in alternative and smaller independent fringe venues, what is almost certain is that you will be working with your director for little or no financial reward. In fact, along with others involved in a project, you may well be using your own money to get a show off the ground by underwriting some of the costs to secure a venue. The shows you make together will also have little or no financial support for the physical production, and these trying but exacting experiences will make or break the two of you – in that sense, you will have a bond! The good news is that your ideas will always need to be as precise and cost-effective as possible – an economical aesthetic, in all senses, often makes for stronger, more direct design and allows both actual and conceptual space for performance.

You may think about applying for more formal funding. Not often the domain of the designer and more of the producer/director, making these applications can nevertheless be a big eye-opener to the perplexing maze of governmental policies and bureaucratic systems. If nothing else, even if you only dip into it, the experience will ensure you appreciate the time-consuming frustrations that producers have to endure to support productions and ultimately, therefore, your practice.

There are various small grants that are available through the Arts Council of England (ACE). The best place to start is to download their criteria and check if your project broadly fits the profile they are looking for. This exercise sharpens up a creative and producing team's thinking about a project even

PART SEVEN

A Theatre Designer's Production Timeline

1

Contracts and Letters of Agreement: How Design Triggers Payment

It's a cliché, I know, but time definitely *is* money. Here's why. The busy and diverse working life of a designer pushes and pulls your commitment between a responsibility to yourself and to others. Much of the day is preoccupied with making decisions about priorities, knowing that whatever activity that moment demands, you'll probably be feeling twinges of guilt about all the other things that should be simultaneously happening. It's for this reason that a designer has to be very sure of their working partnerships including, if needed, assistants. How a designer gets to the starting point of the project is covered in other chapters of this book – whether you have secured the work through an agent or whether through some other contact of your own – so for the purposes of this timeline let's assume that you are 'on board' and ready to tackle the design.

Also, let's assume that this example of a design timeline follows a fairly conventional schedule for drama productions that begin with an existing text, whether new writing or a classic – in other words, not an opera that could have a gestation period of years or a devised piece that may have a less orthodox regime. In this more conventional situation, the lead-in time from first ideas and discussions to the production week of rehearsals, previews and press night can vary hugely, but will usually be something in the region of twelve weeks. Designers and directors may know well before the twelve-week mark that they are going to tackle a project together and they'll keep the project simmering away for a great deal of time, but still may not really focus their energies until a couple of months before the start of rehearsal.

What's included in the contract?

Designer's contracts are usually structured with a number of standard conditions of employment that are agreed between a producer and designer or designer's agent. These contracts have evolved through a period when designers were chiefly protecting their own freelance work, and then latterly, when designers could be represented by agents and supported by their union Equity, the contracts had a more consistent and legally binding integrity. Every designer should now expect to negotiate, agree and sign either a formal contract or a letter of agreement that covers the following areas:

1. What the production is, where it is to take place, and sometimes who the director is.

2. What your design responsibilities are (set, costume, etc.).

3. The important dates – when rehearsal starts, the production week and opening night.

4. What the production budget is and who you will be responsible to in agreeing how it's spent (usually the production manager).

5. What your fee will be and how it will be paid in relation to the schedule.

6. Your attendance at particular points in the process.

7. Any expenses that may be covered by the producer (travel, accommodation, etc.).

8. Any budget available to you for assistance, such as model-makers, and any materials needed for the model.

9. Future use of your design – extending the agreed number of performances, taking the production on tour, or transferring to, say, a commercial venue.

10. Any further payments that these extensions may trigger, i.e. a royalty agreed at a set amount or a percentage of profits (recommended).

11. Billing – where your name will appear on publicity material, websites or on the front of the theatre building.

12. Copyright – linked to the future-use clauses, this can also include filmed recordings or selling the production on.

13. Signatures of both parties and dates.

It is, of course, most important that all parties involved sort out a mutually agreed contract as soon as possible, and ideally before any work on the production is undertaken. However, it's more important to get the contract right than to rush it through, even if that means that initial work on the project will begin before the agreement is actually signed off.

In some larger, building-based, theatre companies you may well be given a supplementary design brief, which tends to outline how the designer and their design weave through that specific organisation's human resources infrastructure and chains of command. The brief can also include technical information, such as a list of stock items or the fact that they have a basic architectural theatre model box you can reuse, or how the building's various technical departments support design and how they may be positioned in relation to the shape of the building or a complex of different buildings across a site or even city. It may also remind you that you are temporarily part of the theatre programme's fabric and need to be mindful of the demands of their season of productions in repertory – how your production fits in with others that may be parked in the wings, dock area or flies.

Occasionally these supplementary documents will also nuance the lead-in times to design deadlines, so check them carefully as they may not always synchronise with what you believe to be your formal contractual obligations.

Payment 1

The first trigger for receiving a proportion of the fee, usually one third, is your signature, so there is a strong incentive for the designer to agree to terms without quibbling, but there are many contracts signed in haste that designers have regretted further down the line, wishing they had been a little more vigilant or patient – particularly with regards to 'further use'. Sometimes designers, along with directors and others in the creative team, may be offered alternative arrangements for the further use of their work such as a buy-out clause and fee rather than a regular royalty, and the situation becomes not unlike that in a casino. My advice would be to resist the temptation of the upfront fee and trust in the longevity of the project: you could be far better off financially by taking the long view and modest amounts of cash, but taking them every week.

Payment 2

The next trigger for the second third of designer's fee, outlined in the contract, is usually the submission and approval of the design. Approval will usually come after the costing exercises that follow submission of technical drawings and models – or, in the case of the costume design, often the completion of the initial drawings – and usually therefore before full creative consultation with the performers. Quite often, if the design has been agreed subject to revisions, you may well receive this second portion of money before you actually deliver a changed set of drawings or model, but strictly speaking this constitutes a 'gentleman's agreement' and depends on the level of trust between all concerned. The designer just has to make sure that the production manager and producer are talking together so that the process of approving final designs is as efficient as possible. Of course, the director may then also be involved in this approval process if drastic changes have to be made in order to keep to budget, but, again, keeping the lines of communication as open and short as possible through a series of meetings will ensure that you are not out of pocket for an extended period.

If you do have a budget for a model-maker and for model-making materials, it's important that you sort out whom that assistant will invoice: you the designer, or the producer. There is a choice to be made as to whether you are given that budget to use as you need (and often exceed!) or whether you feel more comfortable with your assistant being financially independent from you. The model-making budget can be viewed as a supplement to your design fee, but you will inevitably pay for that process one way or another, whether it's your own time or the time of your assistant. If changes need to be made to the design, you may need to negotiate an extension to the assistant's budget, in both labour and material terms, in order to complete the revised work.

Payment 3

The trigger for the final third of the design fee is the press-night performance. This landmark event is usually fairly straightforward in financial terms – the play is on and you're paid. I have occasionally been in a situation when either the director or producer requests or even insists on further changes to the design in response to developments in performance. Your professional integrity, coupled with an instinct to support a director, may dictate whether or not you continue with the work. Also, if your ongoing association with the project and possible future use is valuable to you, you may choose to invest time for the sake of a later reward.

Royalties

Royalty payments secure the *use* of your design, not your time or presence – in other words, it rewards your *intellectual* contribution to the production. So a royalty payment should never secure any further commitment to the work beyond the extent of the fee, but sometimes on a long-term project everyone in the creative and producing team realises the benefits of the project's evolution and possible greater success or longevity. For example, a production might extend a tour to unusual or awkward venues that weren't anticipated when designing to the original brief, and in these cases a designer is not only eager to make the production work but also keen to ensure their work looks and works the best it can.

Occasionally, the designer solely negotiating payment for that use and nothing more resolves future or further use of a production's design that can't be overseen by the designer. Also, if not having faith in the production company's ability to use the design as intended or maintain it to the required standard, the designer may wish to remove their name from the billing of the show. This sounds like a drastic measure which would only result from a dispute, but that's not always the case. Sometimes the decision is made mutually between designer and producer, both taking a pragmatic and professional position. I've also had to make a similar but more straightforward decision such as this when a company wished to reuse the structure of a set, but redecorate it themselves – clearly I didn't want my name associated with something well beyond my control but nevertheless thought it only reasonable that I should be 'bought out' of the set's second life.

A trickier grey area is when items that have been stored after the lifespan of one show and are then used by the theatre company in another show – sometimes years later without the designer's knowledge. This is often the case in a subsidised repertory theatre and applies more to costumes than large scenic items due to the relative costs of storage space. My belief is that most designers accept this situation for a number of very good reasons:

- Public money should be put to good use.

- You may also want to use stock items left over from a previous production.

- It will probably be used in a totally different context and so it's not an infringement of intellectual property.

- Sustainability issues demand as much upcycling as possible (see the more detailed later section on Sustainability).

Theatre designers are largely an open-minded, pragmatic, thick-skinned and generous bunch that realise 'what goes around comes around', so on the whole they tolerate and understand a fellow professional's need to just get the show on.

2

How Do You Need to Prepare for
Your First Design Meeting?

Assuming that you are on board with the project, there are a couple of crucial things you will need to do before your first design meeting with your director. If you have been sent a script then obviously you need to read it! Likewise with a piece of music, listen, and listen again. I would recommend at least three readings of a script before meeting your director. The first would be to get a sense of the story, trying to ignore any stage directions that might have been included, and fundamentally reading the narrative for enjoyment. Although as professionals we can enjoy our work, when we realise we are responsible for its production, it's easy to lose sight of why an audience might enjoy it or at least be interested in it. So in this first reading try to approach the text as the audience would. If possible, try to read it at the speed of a performance, that is, about one to two minutes per page – I often find myself acting it out in my head or, sometimes and embarrassingly, giving in to the urge to speak it out loud in public places. Again, although difficult to resist, it's best to refrain from jumping to immediate conclusions about imagery, getting distracted and, as a result, literally 'losing the plot'. Of course, as a visual artist your mind will be racing, but it is crucial that those images are informed by the collaborative process. If you approach your first design meeting with your head crammed with pictures, you may compromise the first discussions as well as the open relationship you will need in order to trade ideas freely.

> I am interested in making work that is less literal and
> more politically or theatrically radical. I need
> designers that have an appetite to interrogate both the
> script itself and how the script is talking to the
> audience.
>
> *Christopher Haydon, director*

In some acting editions of plays that have already been
produced, the stage directions are often a verbal description
of how the first performance was staged, but they are not
necessarily useful in subsequent productions of the play.
These additions to the play itself, such as in those published
by Samuel French and some which are produced in the US,
unfortunately reinforce the outward impression that some
still powerful plays are outmoded and a little quaint: whereas
the content could be ripe for rediscovery. Each creative team
should therefore approach the staging, the footprint of the
set's ground plan and the ideas that inform it, from a fresh
start. You may even find a ground plan of one of the original
sets at the back of the book. This is very often the case where
the play is printed with an eye to amateur theatre companies
who need a short cut to the design. Again, restrain yourself
from looking at this drawing unless you are prepared to
analyse in every detail why those decisions were made so
that you can free yourself sufficiently from these ideas in
order to be completely original. In my experience, these
plans are most useful for any production that could be
classed as 'farce' – Joe Orton or Ray Cooney, for example –
but even then they can be worth a radical overhaul. Farce's
reliance on comic timing, surprise and speed requires an
extremely precise spatial relationship between the entrances,
the playing space and the exits. Knowing that the text of one
of these productions has probably been published because of
its success on stage gives you a reliable roadmap to follow: a
spatial skeleton structure on which to hang your own
aesthetic. But even in this case I would recommend you
think through the drama for yourself, it plays out on the

page, because this published design is only a snapshot in the life history of the play, and you can add to that with the significance of your own production.

After reading for the first time, make some notes about what you both think and feel. For example, it's quite reasonable to assume that you won't understand everything in the play in terms of either narrative logic or the author's deeper intentions, philosophies or ideals. It's a good idea to draw up a list of questions that you can hope to address either through your own subsequent readings, research, or through discussions with your director. In the case of a poetic classical text such as Marlowe, Molière, Lorca or Shakespeare, this list may be lengthy, and there are a number of other reference points that you might want to take in before any serious reading. Again, this is as much to do with approaching the text with the knowledge and expectation of an audience. Some of these texts may be well-known because they have found their way into our culture through other media and through the schooling.

If you're having difficulty, don't be a victim of your pride: just pick up a children's adaptation of the play, listen to an audio recording or watch a film of it to get an instant narrative 'hit'. The only word of caution here is again to avoid being influenced by any visual material, such as illustrations in a book or the seductive cinematography in a film. For this reason it is probably wisest to listen to an audio production, such as those put out by the BBC. Of course, as I mentioned earlier, opera can be designed from the very earliest stages with previous recordings rattling around in your head with no danger of intruding on your work but only to inspire it. Notes about feelings can be verbal but may conjure visual material as well. Try to keep these responses open-ended and holistic, such as noting down (in either words or sketch form) a range of colours or tones, or the sense of a material that might have metaphorical as well as sensual attributes.

You may feel, for example, that a particular tragedy has a cold atmosphere that might be underpinned by an impervious substance such as concrete, glass or raw steel. These 'design notes' can include things that are indescribable through words or even images: you might find particular objects, or paint or draw particular hues which will help to remind you of these instinctive reactions and interpretations at your first meeting with a director.

The second and third readings are principally about detective work. You will be looking for clues in three categories:

- Location, objects, time and space.

- Character and costume.

- Poetics and ideas.

These are in no particular order of priority, but you will probably want to have three different sets of notes, one set for each category, which will crisscross over each other, one detail not only confirming the other but also possibly unlocking the doors that surround your *'What if...?'* room – and which just may be the beginnings of a complete production concept.

Let's take, for instance, Viola's (in contrast to Iago's!) declaration 'I am not what I am' (*Twelfth Night*, Act Three, Scene One). Given that the character is a girl in disguise as a boy (but that might also be being played by a male actor), the designer and director's approach to how the audience perceive all these layers of reality and representation is crucial to the language of your production. So how will the costume allow the audience 'in' to Shakespeare's toying with what the other characters see? How do you portray twins on stage visually, given that the two performers are unlikely to actually be twins (male or female)? When we see Viola off-guard in the 'privacy' of only the audience's company, how does she behave? The questions are endless, but all can be enriched or answered in production terms by what actors do and how they use your designed objects. This moment combines three key questions:

1. A question of space: *How is she/he placed in relation to the audience – e.g. behind some notion of a 'fourth wall', crossing the stage's edge, or in the round?*

2. A question of character and costume: *How does she get away with her 'cross-dressing' disguise?*

3. A question of ideas: *Does anyone's appearance truly represent who they are, and if not, how might you expand that notion in terms of motifs in the production's design?*

All of this preparation should result not in a narrowing down of your territory but in opening up the vista of your ideas landscape. At this point *be patient*: there will be plenty of opportunities to be motivated by the pressures of deadlines later in the process! Your first creative meeting with the director or choreographer can be defined by prefacing all topics with the simple, '*What if…?*' Your early readings of the play along with those of the director will draw up vital criteria with which you can test your '*What if…?*' flights of fancy in order to methodically reclassify possibilities into probabilities and then into certainties. This gestation period can be frustratingly slow, engagingly reflective, or lightning fast – the important factor here is not to pre-empt an action or assume a thought, but to create a framework that sits comfortably with you and your director's outlook on theatre-making and, crucially, that serves the piece. This, whether you like it or not, will become your 'brand'.

3

Pace, Intensity and Rhythm

The notes you make of your findings and thoughts will all contribute to the previously outlined 'research and plotting' process, but it will also, by providing an agenda for your meetings with others in the creative team, start to characterise the nature of your collaborative relationship and therefore, to some degree, the pace and rhythm of it.

One early but significant decision for both you and your director is where and how you're going to meet. In the interests of an un-skewed discussion and in the best diplomatic traditions, it's sometimes a very good idea to find a location for your first meeting that is neither at the director's home or working place nor in your design studio/workroom. Very often this will mean a public place such as a bar, café or, I suggest, the front-of-house foyer of a large theatre. The only problem about this is that you may just bump into people in the profession that could interrupt your meeting, but otherwise it tends to be a good blend of concentrating one's mind on the production while yielding a good supply of coffee and an airy atmosphere. There are usually time constraints that will dictate the length of meetings, but towards the end, try to recap what's been discussed, what each of you will do or think about before the next meeting, and, as meetings stack up, how the progress of your work fits in to the production timeline as a whole.

If you've not worked with this director before, and sometimes even if you have, the first discussion takes on the characteristics of two dogs in the park, circling each other, assessing each other's compatibility, and making moves towards some form of partnership. Designers have to gauge how they are going to respond to the words of a director, for words are often all they have. Increasingly these days, however, directors come armed with visual material, albeit references to movies that need to be scrutinised for a precise motive – *'What precisely is it about this reference that is relevant to our production?'* The best strategy is to listen patiently to what they have to say, recount your early thoughts by all means, but concentrate on extracting what you as an artist feel you can work with in your own way. In this sense, you are still looking for clues. Most designers will not take on face value the director's description of the stage space they imagine, but rather try to work out why the director is motivated to envisage the space. Designers will also be on the lookout for an interesting philosophical, contextual or dramaturgical idea that they can engage with through visual or spatial equivalents. This is where theatre reveals itself to be truly multidisciplinary: sensitive to the crossovers but respectful of each discipline working as economically and dynamically as possible.

It's realistic to assume that if all parties are available, meeting every two to three weeks keeps the ideas alive but gives each a useful pause for reflection and, most importantly for a designer, time for 'making'. It is through making, showing and further discussion that designers and directors shape their ideas. For a director this is not unlike the process of rehearsals, in that they will motivate ideas as much as initiate them, work with the material, edit the material, and move on. This next phase of the production process will most likely be located in the designer's workroom or studio: partly for practical reasons, in that models in an unstable and sketch form are difficult to transport and repeatedly piece together whilst adding fresh material, and partly because it keeps the meeting focused on the piece itself, not unlike a rehearsal room.

Directors may be frustrated that a designer hasn't made enough work – or equally frustrated that a designer has made too much – at a particular point in the process. It is for this reason that you should take pains to explain why you have made these particular drawings or why you've advanced the model to a particular stage before proceeding to discuss the content of the work. This will not only eliminate your guilt about what should have been done but also focus on what you have done. Explaining your methodology as it unfolds will help your director partner appreciate the cycles and rhythms of (your) design and how this pulse might continue through the rehearsal process and onto the stage – possibly even onto another project. I am always in awe of how generous most directors are throughout the rehearsal process in the interests of interdisciplinary inclusion and engagement. They are usually perfectly happy to invite other people from the production or creative team to see them working 'in the moment'. I have a similar respect for lighting designers for the same reason, in that they paint and sculpt with light on stage in a very open, public and consciously observed critical environment. Of course, inclusion is not a new phenomenon: Brecht certainly endorsed interdisciplinarity's virtues through his working design partnerships with Neher, Otto and von Appen, as did Harley Granville-Barker with Robert Edmond Jones[34] earlier in the twentieth century or, more recently, director Declan Donellan and designer Nick Ormerod: each director striving to embrace and define a genuine ensemble ethos but, paradoxically, from the inevitable position of leadership.

> Time is important – time for blue-skies thinking, time to let thoughts percolate – because inevitably you are going to have to throw out a few ideas by meeting number three or four. Good thinking time means you're more likely to create a filter through which you both can see everything clearly.
>
> *Edward Hall, director*

Before meeting, make sure you are prepared to say every-thing you want to say and show everything you want to show. Sometimes circumstances mean that meetings are skipped and assumptions are made about how ideas are developing, so make the most of these face-to-face occasions – they should be some of the most fascinating experiences of mak-ing theatre work: the wonder of a dream and the promise of a plan in the safety and relative privacy of the studio.

4

When Do Your Ideas Start to 'Go Public'?

I consider 'public' in this context to mean the many colleagues beyond the creative team. I might give a special dispensation here to producers who, given that they are responsible for funding the project, may well want a sneak preview or two before anyone else outside of that team. Producers, though, are usually wise enough to steer clear of making an inappropriately early enquiry into the progress of a project that is still in its early stages of evolution. There will be, without doubt, questions that a producer can answer which will in turn inform creative decision-making, such as the seating capacity that the project's finances are founded on, but on the whole a director and designer will know when it's best to open out their ideas for their producer's input.

Beyond that, the first opportunity that the creative team have to share their ideas is usually with a production manager. The designer often has to have that meeting without the director's support, so he or she usually has to give an overview of the conceptual foundation stones as well as the prospective technical challenges. Depending on the scale of the production, this could either be some weeks or many months into the design process, but using our twelve-week preparation time span, this first meeting would probably be about six or seven weeks in. For the production manager's view of what's expected, please refer to the earlier chapter on their role, but from the designer's perspective this first meeting is generally very useful on a number of levels, can be lengthy, and should be frank and open. What is needed here is a snapshot of where you and the director are at this point in time, outlining the few knowns but importantly describing the parameters of the great unknowns. It is most likely that the production manager will then use common sense in judging the level of detail needed for their subsequent meetings with the producer and workshop managers or prospective scenic builders.

Unless the project is completely unfeasible from a financial or technical point of view, or it's apparent that the project has reached an impasse, this early meeting with the production manager will support, if not add to, the designer's creative context. Sometimes, even a complete rethink is what fuels a new and better idea – necessity often being the mother of a stage designer's invention. The production manager's logistical framework for a design functions much as the building does for a designer's space or the text does for a designer's subject matter – indeed, all designers need the prevailing conditions of a project to push against and help define their vision.

My experience of working as a specialist designer, tackling only the set or costume, tells me that there are very few rules as to when or how the design team and the director meet. It's obvious, though, that for a dynamic and self-motivated creative team to be feasible, that team should not be continually reliant on the director as the sole conduit for the thinking behind a production: the designers themselves simply must meet as many times as possible. If the venue and audience is the set designer's chief context, then the costume designer needs an understanding of the production's scale (distance), audience and, most importantly, casting.

Designers who usually design both set and costume but find themselves designing just one of these, have to be attuned to their potential schizophrenic artistic tendencies, acknowledge the sensitivities of their fellow designer's territory, to not blunder into it, but also be open to discussion about the collective vision. The main topic for conversation as the design blossoms is often its aesthetic language, including the surfaces, colours and tones that I previously mentioned as arising from the designer's instinctive responses to the text or music. Other important early but changeable considerations are: the period (fashions) in which the drama was originally conceived or which might now have been revised to an alternative time and place; conceptual ideas concerning what theatrical or other performance principles the team will experiment with, such as exposing or declaring transformations of character and location to the audience. Equally, whether this show will look and feel, or indeed *is*, modernist, postmodernist, constructivist or any other '-ist' hybrid, should be discussed and revisited so that everyone is aware of how the ideas can either complement or counterpoint each other – ultimately reaching an understood 'school of thought' that will permeate the whole production's values and, again, contribute towards your collective 'brand'.

5

What Do You Need for the
'White-Card Model' Stage?

This landmark in the design process is crucial in that what you offer to the project should be clear enough to indicate whether your ideas are technically viable and financially affordable. The meetings you have at this stage are perhaps the first that will allow the production manager to catch sight of what you are really planning. As I mentioned earlier in the production-management section, the structurally accurate white-card maquette and its accompanying drawings are what a production manager, and subsequently the workshops, will use to cost the design from.

It is usual for the model to have been generated from the technical drawings, whether drawn on the drawing board or printed from a CAD programme, so there should be very little discrepancy between the two. Be prepared for a lengthy meeting and a lot of questions – you will probably be able to answer most of them, but many will also prove to be, in your view, premature or tricky, and the outcomes a reality check. The director may not be there for this meeting – depending on whether you both decide it will be a relatively straightforward affair and therefore can be left to the designer alone, or whether the director is looking for a more participatory discussion that will move the production's thinking onward significantly.

White-card model (1:50 scale) by the author for the Abbey Theatre, Dublin's production of Frank McGuinness's *The Hanging Gardens*.

The point of a model and drawings is that there is something concrete on the table to pick over and negotiate. These are now the objects of the production and not entirely your possessions. They invite collective thought and will only be progressed into more definitive work if everyone understands the work's intentions and owns a stake in its future. The tone of the discussion should be open and frank, and by the end of it all parties should be happy to at least take these ideas forward for further consultation with a scenic and/or props builder for costing purposes. As you can see from the model above, this is also an opportunity to invest the stage image with the beginnings of a lighting idea, particularly (as was true in this case) where some of the materials rely on light from a particular direction to enhance the set's qualities and sense of distance – translucency, for example. The structure of the scenic forms also gives the lighting designer the first real idea about the set's sculptural possibilities, and the set designer will then enter into a dialogue about how to accommodate lighting positions to maximise an effect or just simply how to light the performers.

It is usual for the white-card model and working drawings to be left with the workshop manager if in a repertory theatre, or with three different workshops in turn if in a commercial situation, to enable each to return with costings (see next section) and a building strategy. The outcome of this process will then determine how or whether you push ahead with the final model for presentation at a full production meeting before the start of rehearsal. Essentially the aim is for everybody in the team to start rehearsals confident in the knowledge that the design is doable and for everyone to fully commit to it. These earlier products of the design may also be useful as working 'bench' drawings should any prototype elements need to be built for rehearsal purposes.

6

Costing Your Design

There are two vital things to hang on to when you're thinking about the funds that bring your ideas to life:

- Design defines and drives costs.
- You are (probably) using other people's money.

Both of these are sobering considerations and focus the mind at whatever scale of work you're involved in, from the most modest Edinburgh Fringe project to the Royal Opera House. In fact, the smaller the scale, the more possible it is that you may be using some of your own money, and that *is* sobering!

Both money and other resources needed to realise your production will be both a curse and a blessing. No one likes limitations, but in practice there's no other way of proceeding – all professional designers need to push against something, whether it's an awkward space, a challenging actor or a budget. You will have had a figure for the budget in your contract, but its breakdown into set, costume, props and any other area is always negotiable after the design's detail is revealed. Each area has to be assessed and you, as the designer, have to have an idea about how the areas balance so that you can prioritise one item over another across the whole production. This is more problematic if you are designing only set or only costume, in which case, designers tend to be a little less generous in giving over funds to the other!

For the costume supervisor and designer, the task of putting together a rough estimate of costs is somewhat simpler than it is for the production manager and designer with the set.

The costume supervisor, working from the cast list and breakdown of characters, creates a costume plot, and a simple division of these against the budget will reveal the funds available for each costume, or part-costume. Priorities can then be established when all this is applied to the drawings.

With sets it can be a more complicated business because the individual parts are always different depending on the director and designer's approach, and the costing depends not only on the materials required for their making but also on their size or if mechanics are involved.

The other crucial factor for both set and costume is whether the set will be built in a resident workshop, with the labour costs of makers 'absorbed' by the producing theatre company, or whether the budget also has to accommodate a commercial workshop with all their inherent overheads and profit margins. The costing period will differ in length and will be a very different experience in each of these eventualities.

If it is crucial that the production manager and costume supervisor are as transparent as possible to the designer about costs and how they are prioritising available funds, it follows that both need to be transparent to each other – the team is triangular. The bottom line is that the creative and production team need to know that the show is achievable before the start of rehearsal. There are few things more unsettling for a director and designer on day one of rehearsals, when the design is presented, than facing a company of actors and others without the confidence that their ideas might have a chance purely on financial grounds... There are enough variables along the way without that!

7

What Do You Need for Your
First Major Production Meeting?

Reaching this stage with any confidence that the design is viable relies to a massive degree on whether the costing exercises have proved to be positive, and everyone has agreed that the design process can progress as planned.

The main difference between the items you submit earlier for costing and those needed now in order for everyone to start work is 'quality'. The details should have been added or confirmed; the surfaces and materials indicated on technical drawings should be present in the model; props references or drawings should be completed and costume drawings should be in at least a late stage of readiness before starting rehearsals.

There is often not a single grand meeting, but rather a series of smaller ones aimed at the various aspects of production, principally set, props and costume. This is understandable because, however seemingly simple a design is, the level of detailed discussion required at this stage would render much of a single meeting irrelevant to those not engaged with one or other of the elements. That said, you will find yourself repeating your overview of the design concept again and again to give each specialist a notion of the context in which her or his work will sit.

The progress of your costume designs will be helped along if you can attach some fabric samples to the drawings, although this has a danger of closing down the costume supervisor's interpretation of your drawings in a way that can sometimes give you a fresh view of your work, particularly if you have a more fluid style of drawing, painting or collaging. Include them if you think it will enrich this first creative conversation about style, themes, period accuracy and importantly, feelings, movement and textures – how you want textiles to behave on the body.

Prop information can be communicated in a number of ways, depending chiefly on whether you anticipate they will be made, found, borrowed or hired. It's frankly a waste of time to make a detailed drawing of an object, complete with rendering and measurements, if you're pretty convinced it will be found and not made. In this case, a picture reference will suffice, with some sizes to give a sense of the dimensional parameters needed, and, of course, you should feel free to add notes as they spring to mind. Indeed, think of both costume and prop designs as working documents rather than art works – they should contain every idea you're convinced about regarding the clothes and character, or period style and material.

I would recommend making a plot sheet (opposite page) of everything you and the director have talked about intending to use, much of which might be discarded or added to through rehearsal, but at least this will form an aide-memoire and a definitive design to-do list for you, as well as preparing the stage-management team for the stand-in rehearsal props they will have to amass early on.

'*Edmond*' Scenic/Character/Property Plot National Theatre

Scene	'Location'	Character	Item
1	The Fortune Teller	Edmond Fortune-Teller	Chairs x 2
2	At Home	Edmond Edmond's Wife	Chairs as Sc1 Dining table + dressing
3	A Bar	Edmond Man	Bar as designed Drinks
4	The Allegro	Edmond B-Girl Bartender Manager	Bar as Sc3 Table Chair Drinks
5	A Peep Show	Edmond Girl	Booth screen Curtain Number infills
6	On the Street, Three-Card Monte	Sharper (a cardsharp) Bystander Shill Shill Edmond	Upturned boxes or crates Cards Money Steaming manhole cover
7	Passing Out Leaflets	Edmond Leafleteer	Leaflets
8	The Whorehouse	Edmond Manager A Woman	Credit card machine + plinth Light Stool
9	Upstairs at the Whorehouse	Edmond Whore	Massage table Trolley with oils etc.?
10	Three-Card Monte	Edmond Sharper Shill	Upturned boxes Cards Money
11	A Hotel	Edmond Desk Clerk	Reception desk as designed Grille and public phone
12	The Pawnshop	Owner Customer Edmond Man (in the back)	Display counter as Sc11 Gold objects Wedding ring Grille Knife
13	The Subway	Edmond Woman (in a hat)	Light in floor Knife
14	On the Street, outside Peepshow	Pimp Edmond	Wallet and money Knife Lit doorway
15	The Coffeehouse	Edmond Glenna (a waitress)	Table Benches Dressing
16	Glenna's Apartment	Edmond Glenna	Settee Chair Carpet Knife from Sc 12 Bottle of pills Table + Telephone + light
16a	On the Street	Edmond Hobo	?
16b	On the bridge	Edmond	Above the doors Steps for access
17	The Mission	Edmond Mission Preacher Woman (from subway) Policeman	Mission doors Flown cross + harness Handcuffs
18	The Interrogation	Edmond Interrogator	Table Chairs x 2
19	Jail	Edmond Edmond's Wife	Table Chairs
20	The New Cell	Edmond Prisoner	Bunk beds + lights Table + Chair + light
21	The Chaplain	Edmond Prison Chaplain	
22	Alone in the Cell	Edmond Guard	Bunk beds + lights Table + Chair + light Writing paper + pen/pencil Newspaper Flown Window
23	In the Prison Cell	Edmond Prisoner	Bunk beds + lights Table + Chair + light Flown Window

Scenic, character and props list for the start of rehearsal for David Mamet's *Edmond* at the National Theatre, designed by the author.

[255]

8

What Do You Need for the
Start of Rehearsals?

The start of rehearsals is an opportunity to put your ideas across to the whole company, and you may well not get a chance to do this at any other point in the rehearsal process. Presenting your model and drawings can become a minor production in itself! Without doubt, the thing you need most when presenting your work is organisation; and this will help you keep your cool.

Setting up for the design presentation

You will often not know the space that you are using for the event until the day itself, but if you can, try to find out what it's like beforehand from the producer, company stage manager or stage manager. The things to check out are how big it is, whether you can reduce the light levels or even black it out, whether there are power sockets around the room and what furniture is available for seating and to put your work on. These all sound elementary, but you would be surprised at how often the situation doesn't meet your needs and expectations – take nothing for granted.

Day one of rehearsals is when everybody is excited to start the project and eye everybody else up – just who will you be working with for the next few weeks? Once you have some shows under your belt you may well come across people with whom you have worked before, and usually the rekindling of friendships is the jollier aspect of the first day. But you will have to concentrate on preparing your work for the presentation, so this first session ends up being a mix of excitement, curiosity and frustration at not being able to relax into the social aspect of getting to know everyone informally before the hard work begins. For that reason it's best to try to get to the rehearsal room as early as possible so that you can have some quiet time to get properly set up – and, of course, this always takes longer than you think; usually twice as long, however well prepared you are. It is also safe to assume that, because these rehearsals often take place out of the theatre's own building (such as a church hall or community centre), there will be no facilities for presentation other than those you bring yourself. So, if you are projecting images, storyboards, costume designs, etc., it'll probably be you that has to source and bring a (powerful) projector that's compatible with your laptop. There won't be a screen in the venue, so ask yourself: '*Where's the most pale wall in the shadiest position?*' '*Where will I put my projector: on a box, on a table?*' '*How will I light my model?*' You won't have all the answers, but be armed with the questions.

Presenting your ideas – what do you want to say and show?

When you're presenting, think about where you'll be most comfortable speaking from – from the 'audience' just using your words, or beside the work, with freedom to move about and make eye contact with all these people whom you'll be trying to convince you're on the right track with your ideas? In many respects this *is* a performance, and while I'd advise against any whiff of hype, you are attempting to engage and enthuse these strangers who are now suddenly your colleagues and collaborators.

Your presentation will no doubt be part of a double act with your director. It's rather important therefore to work out beforehand which elements of the design and of the production at large will be presented by the director and which by you, the designer. This will vary hugely from project to project and according to the nature of your working relationship. My recommendation, though, is that a fifty-fifty split, balancing ideas and practicalities, is best. There should be no assumption that the ideas are the domain of the director and the practicalities that of the designer. Directors will have the whole of the rehearsal process to explain their ideas, as they develop, to the whole company. The designer, however, will probably only have this one occasion, and so, in the interests of balance and respect for the thinking that you've put in up to this point, it's now that you seize your opportunity to explain your part in the evolving concept for the production. Some directors will give every opportunity to the designer to do this, and others will tend to dominate the proceedings – not out of mean-spiritedness, but more from force of habit, in that their leadership gene surfaces irresistibly. Likewise, designers may well be perfectly happy to retreat into the shadows, behind the work, and observe.

This turn of events is perfectly understandable, given that designers, who are visual people after all, are often not overly confident with verbalising their ideas in public. They tend to be 'backstage' characters. There are also some of us who would rather people-watch in these situations, preferring to project an air of 'inscrutability'. Whichever of these you feel you are – and most of us have impulses both ways depending on the chemistry of the situation and how you 'read to the room' – make the decision as to how you are going to play the event with your director and stick to it. The company of actors and stage managers who are your principal audience on this day will not appreciate you both floundering around. It's also then a good idea to agree and declare which areas of the production are still part of 'the great unknown' for the creative team, consigning these to the category of 'a voyage of discovery', and in so doing, giving others in the ensemble an opportunity to make their mark on the production and have an equal stake in its ownership.

Keep faith in your work, pictures do tell thousands of words and everyone there will be sophisticated readers of them, not only as scenery and costumes, but as images, with signs and meanings in relation to what they already know of the piece. Give your 'audience' the time to absorb them and don't feel you have to justify their significance – give everyone time to ask questions and that will be your opportunity to realise what might not have been clear enough, both visually and verbally.

The length of the presentation can vary hugely, again depending on the project and how verbose you and your director are inclined to be. As a rule, be economical. Although the assembled company are interested in what you've been hatching – the actors in particular are going to have to live in your set and wear your costumes for many hours of their life – there's a limit to how much abstract material anyone can retain or simply be interested in. For that reason, stick to a three-pronged strategy, addressing the *Why?*, *What?* and *How?* of the project:

1. *Why* you have approached the play/opera in a certain way?

2. *What* are the results of that approach?

3. *How* are you going to achieve them?

If you stick roughly to this formula and in that order, you will be explaining your process as a narrative in itself, mindful that you should also balance these areas, i.e. not dwelling too much on decisions you made along the way that have now been ditched or changed, but emphasising the conclusions you came to and why you hope they will contribute towards a rich and fruitful rehearsal process.

On the first day, everyone will probably want a piece of you. You will most likely be fending off many requests for meetings with the stage-management team, costume supervisor, production manager, and many others (including the odd actor who could be already questioning the wisdom of your costume ideas!). Keep calm, your head clear, and your diary to hand! Establish with everybody what your work pattern is likely to be in the following weeks, including days that you are not available, and agree with all parties when the regular production meetings will be. These, usually weekly, meetings are when all the company other than the actors get together to discuss the progress of all technical aspects of the show and another opportunity for you to show leadership in the group, ensuring its cohesion from the design point of view.

How does your design relate to the rehearsal room?

One crucial task for the designer on the first day is to check, with the production manager, stage manager and, hopefully, the director, how the set is 'marked up' on the rehearsal-room floor. The mark-up is usually taken from the map of your design on the ground plan you drew, so you will need to check that all the lines on the floor – usually marked out with plastic electrical tape in different colours representing different objects or different positions of moving elements – are as they should be. As I mentioned earlier, the room is, more often than not, smaller than the stage you've designed for. The director will probably have a very clear idea of the orientation of the set to the rehearsal room's shape so that the best use of the room's dimensions in relation to your design is agreed. Sometimes directors will want more depth than width in the room because, for example, there may be important aspects of the production that happen upstage centre; on the other hand, the movement of actors from left to right may be more important, and so the director will want an emphasis on the width. Other factors may include the light in the room or the door to the rest of the building. The director, actors and stage-management team may also request that the set model spends some time in rehearsal so that everyone can refer to it – decide where this might be in the room so that it is both accessible but also safe!

9

What is a Designer's Relationship to the Rehearsal Process?

Designers could spend an awfully long time in rehearsal, and some do, but your commitment to contributing towards the performance, as well as your responsibilities for design, will vary depending on whether you are designing for a previously performed play, a new play or a devised piece, such as dance or physical or improvised theatre (a verbatim text, for example). Your attendance will probably be governed by other people's needs – to discuss newly invented props, to check that the use of a piece of scenery is possible, or to be at production meetings. In that respect it is often easy to lose sight of what *you* yourself want or need to do in relation to the director and actor's work.

Generally, it's fairly safe to assume that you should be spending at least half a day in rehearsals every week, but sometimes the demands of the design and the scale of the piece can mean that your contact with the rehearsal room will be far less than that. When designing both set and costumes, as is customary in the UK, there will be a million things to attend to away from rehearsals. Directors and others understand this on the whole, but they will also be sensitive to periods of time when your presence could either be practically or diplomatically useful. In some situations, costume fittings may be carried out in the same building or very close to rehearsals. This is usually a cost-effective use of space but also means the actors will miss the minimum of time with the director in the rehearsal room – particularly if the piece requires every actor to be engaged with every moment of the performance's creation, in other words, an ensemble production.

Designers, unlike directors, can work on more than one production that is in rehearsal at any one time, and that's also often a practical necessity given the variability of the profession's financial rewards. There are limits, however, and I would say, as a rule, it is unwise to tackle more than two shows in parallel. Lighting designers are past masters at this; they have to be because their fees are significantly lower than a set or costume designer's, so they may have three, four or more shows cooking at the same time. If the show is devised or is a new play, you will need and want to be in rehearsal considerably more, perhaps two days a week. This will put pressure on the other practical tasks you have to perform outside the rehearsal room, but devised shows usually have a longer gestation period, and new work will most likely be a slippery, shifting thing, no matter how long you have – and that's the fun of it.

There is usually a formal structure to the rehearsal period in that the opening couple of weeks are usually dedicated to text analysis, the last week is usually peppered with complete runs of the play, with the intervening period, however long that is, given over to experiment and detailed interpretation of the subject matter. Each week there is likely to be a production meeting to which all the creative-team members, stage management, production and costume management, plus anyone else beyond that immediate circle, such as producers, are invited. They are usually very useful events and shouldn't be missed. On occasion your absence may be unavoidable, but there is now the possibility of 'being there' via Skype or FaceTime, which, although tricky to manage in a group situation, is far better than missing out completely.

Each day, the business of rehearsal is recorded by the deputy stage manager (DSM), in the form of a rehearsal report.

These will be circulated on a daily basis and include mainly design-orientated matters in the form of questions, clarifications and requests from the director and actors. These emailed reports have to be read and digested as soon as possible to keep track of what can be rapid and far-reaching changes to the initial design, and is evidence that designers do indeed come into direct working contact with more contributors than most in a company, needing an octopus-like grip on proceedings. Here is an example:

PR❂PELLER

THE WINTER'S TALE

REHEARSAL NOTES

SHEET NO: 3
DATE : Wednesday 14th December 2011

GENERAL
– The interval is between scenes 6 and 7

DESIGN
– A candle is needed for Mamillius during the prologue. Is this the wee willy style one?

PRODUCTION
– The candlesticks will be brought on to the stage lit during the prologue.

PROPS
– Robert Hands as Leontes will use a wheel chair and walking stick in Scene 11
– The Clown and Old Shepherd will need a number of shopping bags from posh shops for Scene 12.
– Nick Asbury and Robert Hands will light and smoke cigars during Scene 1.
– 12 brandy glasses are being used in the prologue/Scene 1.
– Mamillius lights a candle on stage during the prologue, see design note.
– 2 brandy decanters are needed for Scene 1.
– 13 wooden mannequins are being used.

WARDROBE
– In Scene 11 Gunnar Cauthry will play Dion not John Dougall. John will still play Dion in Part 1.
– Karl Davies as Clown will need a showy gold watch for Scene 12. Tony Bell as Autolycus will steal it.
– Robert Hands as Leontes will need a handkerchief.
– Ed has asked for Dickie Dempsey to have pregnancy padding in rehearsals please and for rehearsal skirts for the girls.

STAGE MANAGEMENT
– No notes today, thank you.

LIGHTING
– Ed would like to use the mini-mist inside the tent in Scene 10 for Tony Bell's entrance. He would also like to highlight the tent for this.

SOUND
– Ed would like a crack of thunder and some wind for the reporting of the death of Mamillius
– Scene 6 should be stormy with spot thunder effects.
– A bell is needed for a 'ting' in scene 8

Thank you, Ellie Randall, DSM

Rehearsal notes from Propeller Theatre's DSM, Ellie Randall for the production of *The Winter's Tale*.

The rehearsal report is usually also accompanied by information about the next day's activities – the 'rehearsal call' – so you should be able to plan your days at least a little in advance to, for example, arrange costume fittings around an actor's availability and in collaboration with your costume supervisor. The rehearsal call for the following day will also warn you if a scene is being tackled that requires your input or is something you are concerned about. It's usually a great pleasure to sit for just a little while in the company of performers trying things out, and on a good production you can be easily seduced into spending too long with what can become a displacement activity for those other 999,999 things you have to do. What I appreciate, however, are the risks that actors take in experimenting, sometimes creatively making a fool of themselves and looking for improvement, in the company of others. The time you spend there will pay off later, though, when you will need to have a rapport with everybody in the theatre during the production week.

In relation to costuming, there is a broad skeletal structure that mirrors that of a standard five-week period of rehearsal from when the actors are just getting to grips with the fundamentals of their role, through to the final run:

Start of rehearsals	⇔	Present designs
End of week 1/ Start of week 2	⇔	One-to-one discussions about character
End of week 2/week 3	⇔	First costume fittings
Week 4	⇔	Second costume fittings
End of week 5	⇔	'Costume parade'?

It is absolutely vital that you watch at least one complete run of the show in the rehearsal room. This will usually be towards the end, if not the actual end, of the rehearsal process, just before the production hits the stage. It is only through seeing a complete sequence of scenes that you will begin to know whether particularly the transitional moments of your design will work, and if not, you still have time to change it. This is also an opportunity to come together again with your director and (hopefully) enjoy the closing stages of a design process which started when you sat in front of the model in your studio before rehearsals began – full of expectation, then and now, and both also streaked with a few nerves. Support your director in the same way as they supported you at the moment when a great deal of your design work went public.

You can also then elect to orchestrate the 'costume parade' listed in the table on the previous page. This is a more informal event than the term suggests and comes at the end of the rehearsal period when all the clothes for the show can be worn by the actors. It used to be a sort of catwalk affair for the benefit and approval of the director, so that they could see what you've been up to and that you haven't deviated from the original drawn ideas. Thankfully that's changed over recent years to be a far more pragmatic opportunity for you and your supervisor to check everything over before the pressure of the forthcoming production week, when the costumes will be worn all day and therefore not easy to access for any adjustments. Designers and supervisors will have mixed views about the merits of the costume parade, even without the director's axe hovering over proceedings, but I've become more and more of an advocate for them as it's a chance for you to see the clothes off the costume rail, worn all together and in movement. You can check that the colour pallet still works and view the clothes for the first time at some distance. It reminds you about decisions you may have made weeks back and refreshes the actor's memory of a fitting that might seem like a lifetime ago. If quick changes are anticipated in show conditions, the actors, director and stage management will have a much clearer picture of the realities at this point, so there can be some very useful swapping of notes before having to sort much of it out in the heat of a technical rehearsal, often in cramped and dark conditions backstage. All in all it's usually a little time invested well, so that the production week has one of its many potentially volatile elements rendered a little more manageable.

Top tip: *Make sure a Dropbox account or similar is set up so that as many people as possible can access your designs and other information you may have generated, such as plot sheets. Schedules and contact information can also then be easily updated and shared with you and the rest of the team.*

10

Production Week: How Do Designers
Approach Technical and Dress Rehearsals?

The production week is the first period of time that the show is on stage. It is often shorter than a week in that the first public performance for most plays in a small or medium-sized theatre will probably be on the fourth or fifth day, but for some commercial work, and particularly musicals, this production period can continue for many more days – even weeks. For designers, as for most of the production team and the actors, it's a time of mixed thoughts and feelings in that everyone is excited by the prospect of the show but also nervous of how it will be received by the public and then later by the critics. For this reason everyone has to keep their cool and focus on what the audience will experience.

Here is a typical schedule for a 'production week' for drama productions:

Day 1 (Sunday)
- Rig lighting (overhead only).
- Get in and fit up scenery.
- Rig lighting (onstage) and sound.

Day 2 (Monday)
- Continue fit-up details. Distribute costumes to dressing rooms.

- Focus lighting on stage and front of house ⇨ plot states for lighting.
- Sound check.
- Actors dress into costume/wigs/make-up and onstage for an 'orientation' session.
- Technical rehearsal ('tech') session 1 and technical notes to finish.

Day 3 (Tuesday)

- Technical rehearsal session 2.
- Technical rehearsal session 3.
- Technical rehearsal session 4 and technical notes to finish.
- Paint call (overnight).

Day 4 (Wednesday)

- Technical work onstage including lighting/sound or technical rehearsal 5.
- Dress rehearsal 1 (production photographs taken) and technical notes to finish.

Day 5 (Thursday)

- Technical work onstage including lighting/sound. Actors' notes offstage.
- Actors' rehearsal onstage and/or dress rehearsal 2.
- Preview performance 1 and note session afterwards.

Day 6 (Friday)

- Technical work onstage including lighting/sound (can include a last paint call).
- Actors' rehearsal onstage and/or filming video trailer/press photo call.
- Preview performance 2 and note session afterwards.

Day 7 (Saturday)

- Technical work onstage including lighting/sound.
- Preview performance 3 (matinee) and note session afterwards.
- Preview performance 4.

Day 8 (Sunday)

- Rest day.

Day 9 (Monday)

- Actors' rehearsal onstage.
- Preview performance 5.

Day 10 (Tuesday)

- Press performance.

'Getting in' and setting up camp

As described earlier, the week usually starts with the scenic 'get-in' on a Sunday morning. This is a time for the production manager and stage crew to get to grips with the set, so they are largely focused on making it stand up and stand up safely, you may also be needed at any moment to answer vital questions. The important aspect of your input at this foundation stage is that these early decisions can sometimes affect fundamental principles of your design, such as the exact position of the most downstage edge of the show floor: get this wrong, and there's a good chance there will never be another opportunity to adjust it later.

So, although much of the first couple of days could be spent with lengthy pauses in between moments of frenetic activity or decision-making, you have to keep your concentration levels up. It does take a bit of experience to appreciate when, and when not, to make a point or observation to your production manager, knowing that its implications could mean delays or changes that can subsequently affect the rest of the week. I would therefore err on the side of patience, but ensure you leave no thoughts unspoken even if you might feel foolish or ignorant – sometimes the simplest questions can reveal a gap in everyone's understanding of the show's priorities.

It is also sometimes the case that you will have knowledge of what will be happening in performance, a Plan B, which has lately come into being as the consequence of final rehearsals, but the production manager may not be fully aware of this and is still busy executing Plan A. The main points to remember are that any collaborative process relies on respect for the integrity and craftsmanship of all other partners in the team, that you don't always know best, but that you are clear about your priorities as others will be clear about theirs. Make notes (as suggested earlier) and find or arrange the earliest appropriate pause in a work session to have that conversation. It is also important to appreciate that the production manager and head of stage crew are responsible for everyone's safety, so your interruptions must not compromise this in any way.

Lighting-wise, these early stages can be a good opportunity to check in with the production electrician and lighting designer about what the latest developments of their plans are. At this point they are also adjusting the design on paper to the realities of the theatre space and the set-design elements that are now in it. As you begin to see your work forming in real space and at full scale, thoughts might strike you about how it might be enhanced by light beyond those which both you and the lighting designer had when peering into the model box or perhaps discussing lighting possibilities in the somewhat abstract circumstances of the rehearsal room. Chew it over with them while remaining sensitive to the fact that the physical elements of the design are often being created by using lighting equipment and stage facilities that they are only seeing for the first time, and so are having to also deal with a multitude of variables in the pursuit of their original design ideas – and they haven't even turned on a light yet to see what effect these conditions may have in the context of a performance!

Costume-wise, assuming that you have had some form of review, such as the 'costume parade', perhaps only hours before on the last day of rehearsal, preparations to bring the clothes into the theatre and distribute them amongst the dressing rooms will be underway, and you probably won't have that much to do on that front until the technical rehearsal (see production-week timeline above). Find out where the wardrobe department is in the theatre – it can sometimes be a welcome refuge for designers given their somewhat nomadic status during production week. Older theatres such as those in the West End tend to locate the wardrobe department high up in the building and the many flights of stairs can certainly help your cardiovascular condition, but you need to know where this hub of costume activity will be throughout the week and you will probably pay it many a visit along with your costume supervisor. This may be one of the first opportunities to be acquainted with the wardrobe mistress or master (also sometimes called wardrobe manager) who will be looking after your show throughout its run. This linchpin of the day-to-day running of the production will also therefore be organising costume-maintenance staff and other crucial personnel, such as dressers. For most drama productions this may amount to a team of only two or three people, but on a major musical or opera can extend to a small army who are precision-drilled and also very much part of that production week and the success of a performance, given that their skill is to assess the minute-to-minute liveness of performance and support the costuming of actors, as designed, in between split-second exits and entrances.

As you will see from the schedule, lighting designers may or may not set some lighting states into the memory of the lighting board before the tech starts. This is sometimes due to personal preference and practice or simply because they've run out of time for any number of reasons. In any case, I'd advise that you arrange to have even just a few minutes with the LD to take a look at some lighting ideas and agree some principles that might start to form the production's 'language' of the light – its tone, colour, mood. During the tech, the LD will be preoccupied with establishing lighting states, often amounting to hundreds of carefully timed cues, while you will be concerned with your own fine-tuning – both of you split between ensuring the quality of your specialist area whilst also objectively 'stepping back' with the director to contribute to the *mise-en-scène* and the production as a complete event – so grab some quality time when you can.

Technical rehearsals

The technical rehearsals are generally understood to give time in the schedule that's dedicated to (among many other things) knitting together and establishing:

- The timing of actors' entrances and exits.
- The testing of the scenery, especially moving components.
- The practicalities of costume, especially quick changes or changes in view of the audience.
- Lighting the performers in their costumes (and lighting scenic elements), giving each lighting state levels of strength and focus.
- Sound levels (live or pre-recorded) and direction (audibility) – in synchronisation with lighting.
- Video projection – balanced with the timing and intensity of lighting.
- Cue points for all these elements as recorded by the DSM.

To the casual observer and novice, the complexity of all of this can be perplexing, daunting and thrilling. At times, that can be true for the seasoned professional too – *that's why we keep doing it!* The reality of the experience, however, is that for the designer, concentration levels ebb and flow, hectic or surprising one moment and frustratingly repetitive the next – I liken it to the goalkeeper's role, in that whatever you assume about how the team in front of you is doing, you cannot allow yourself to take your eye off the artistic ball. Changes are constantly happening, often undetected, unless you somehow keep your finger on the show's pulse.

The directors I've worked with all have wildly varied approaches to the tech. These veer from rigorously executing their 'route-one' plan to seemingly complete indifference (and even periodical non-attendance), and range from obsessions with particular objects, lighting or costume through to laid-back confidence in all things mechanical; electing to dedicate themselves to extending the freedoms of the rehearsal room. The best are a blend of all these, the trick being knowing when to be which.

Patience is undoubtedly the principal virtue en route, and although everyone (not least the actors) want to get a straight crack at the play, everyone buys into the fact that ultimately any theatre, let alone good theatre, is a complex business and that wisely used time in the tech is likely to be the foundation both for a confident dress rehearsal and for a show that's at least fit for public consumption and perhaps even 'a hit'.

At some point, usually during the tech period, the designer will be offered a 'paint call' by the production manager, when the scenic artist from the original builder, or a resident or local scenic artist, is called in to make what should be only adjustments, not major changes, to the colours, shading and detailing of the paintwork. It's often scheduled for after an evening session so that the stage is quiet and their work has time to dry before the next day – particularly any floor work. Save up your notes and be prepared to spend as long as it takes to describe what you need them to do. If they are working overnight, there will usually be two scene painters for safety reasons, so the work can often be completed in one call; if not, and when you return in the morning to unfinished business, impress upon the production manager the importance of seeing it through. Paint effects can impact everything from the grip of a floor to the reflection of lighting, so it's pretty vital to make these adjustments as early as possible.

Dress rehearsals

Each dress rehearsal is preceded by a resetting of props and costumes that usually takes an hour or so, depending on the complexity of the production. There are, of course, statutory[35] lunch and dinner breaks of at least an hour in between sessions, so it's best to get as many running notes communicated, if not dealt with, during the sessions themselves if possible. For example, in principle, actors should not have their breaks intruded upon, so having flash in-session costume fittings is advised, although many actors will be generous with a bit of their downtime and usually realise that it's to everyone's benefit that problems are sorted out as soon as humanly possible.

Unwritten rules include the need to resist giving technical notes that would involve changing performance conditions just before a dress rehearsal or show, and there is a formally recognised (although still unwritten) rule that absolutely no design changes should take place between the last preview performance and the press performance. This is all based on sound common sense, of course, in that actors will have enough to remember without a designer throwing spanners in the works at the last minute, which could be anything from just bothersome to downright dangerous.[36]

> Finally, only one or two voices can be heard, because the closer you get to performance, the more nervous actors become and so the more important it is for them to hear one choice, one decision. This has to come through the director to an extent and the designer has to step back a little sometimes: knowing when to speak as well as what you're going to say. It's all about reading the room.
>
> *Ellen Havard, director*

The dress is the first time that everyone will be a part of something like the complete performance – sometimes it can go very smoothly and the show can 'settle in' quickly, and at other times, particularly for musicals, the first couple of dress runs just illuminate how much work there is still to do. You are all working against the clock, and no show, like any creative act, is truly one hundred per cent 'perfection' – whatever you imagine that to be. It is the fact that it is live, and therefore prone to the 'imperfections' that gives theatre its edge over cinema. That's not to excuse sloppy thinking or poor production values, but just to emphasise why theatre is both so challenging to make and thrilling or thought-provoking to experience.

Practical considerations at this point include varying your viewing position in the auditorium. Try moving back a little from your close proximity to the stage (besides, you can't leap up there to change something on the dress rehearsal!) and find out what the worse seats in the house are. Will you need to make any adjustments that you simply hadn't noticed up until that point? I try, at least once, to get to the balconies in a high proscenium theatre, or the wide positions in an arena – there are often more people up in the circle and 'gods' than in the stalls, and I think you owe it to them, whatever the seat price, to make the show as technically 'clean' as possible. From there, you can also be the eyes and ears of the others in the creative team. Also: sit with your production manager and costume supervisor as much as possible – there will no doubt be a stream of observations you need to make. Tempting though it may be to reacquaint yourself with your director as your joint vision comes to life, resist; you can check in with them after the run, they will have their own house to put in order during the dress. Go for a drink and do it then.

Top tip: *A basic necessity, as well as a simple courtesy, is to try to quickly learn everyone's (or as many as possible) names on the stage crew, lighting and wardrobe teams. Of course, you'll only be working with them for a few days, but from a practical point of view it saves time in the long run and also makes the whole experience more inclusive – you'd hope that they would learn yours, after all. Resorting to the ubiquitous 'darling' is nowadays not recommended, but you'll still hear it from time to time!*

First Performances and Press Night

The first public performance of any theatre project, and it's probably the same for a first preview of a film, is a curious mix of sensations for those that make the work. Performers have to be completely engaged in the event, of course, as do those behind the scenes, and most are simply trying to survive the terrors of getting through it. For the creative team, however, the first preview is a cocktail of nerves, curiosity and what can only be described as something akin to an out-of-body experience; floating above your work, semi-detached and seeing it as if for the first time through the lens of both the telescope and microscope of complete strangers.

This is a natural and healthy state to be in, as it gives you more of a true perspective on your work and refreshes your to-do list – sometimes radically. It might be at this point that your director has some seismic shifts to make as well, so be prepared for them to make some bold editorial decisions. There is a litany of anecdotal evidence from many a designer confirming that directors and choreographers can be ruthless at this critical moment when their instincts chime with the audience and time is not on their side to do something about it. Not unlike any crisis in the studio phase of a project, when a great deal of a designer's time and effort can be consigned to the bin of 'experience', talk is of making sacrifices for 'the good of the production', sometimes major, but preferably agreed first.

Over the course of the previews, you have a choice of which colleagues to sit with, depending on who you feel you might need to nudge or be nudged by, who might get fidgety or what new viewpoint you may need from the auditorium. You are there to do a job, have a dispassionate view and improve what you see, but there are many productions during which I have been transfixed and transported by the skill and, dare I say, magic of those on stage, proud to be associated with the work and thankful just to have played my part.

The end of the press performance is when you will most likely be parting company with the production – at least for the time being. As such it can be a mix of sadness, celebration and relief, but usually you also will be already thinking about another project that you're only partway through. It's a cliché perhaps, but designers, like most freelance practitioners, are most interested in what they're doing now, rather than indulgently reflecting on even the most recent past. Hindsight requires long vision. For the rest, we have the critics.

Critics are not expert makers of theatre:[37] if they're any good at their job, they are experts in criticism.

> Design is phenomenally important – far more important than it's usually given credit for; by critics, for instance. Design shapes the context in which everything else is understood. You could produce a conventional play and it's the design that makes the critics think that it's an astonishingly radical piece of theatre – the critic might not realise that it's the design that framed it in a particular way.
>
> *Christopher Haydon, director*

The press used to be constrained by the column inches in their broadsheet, or, more so, in their tabloid, but professional critics online have the opportunity to expand their critique to those other than the actors, director and author. The American press have always been more generous in this regard than in the UK, but with the proliferation of social media, everyone across the planet is now a self-appointed expert, critic or, at least, commentator. What this has opened up space for is a greater interest in, and exposure of, design. Audiences of all ages are now far more aware that design is not a fluke, but a deliberate act, and that someone is responsible for the statement it makes itself or contributes to. It's still sometimes hard to weather what at times can seem harsh criticism, but the good news is that design is now on the theatregoers' radar and that can only help sharpen up your work. Any wounded ego usually heals without the trace of a scar, and Doctor Theatre provides the drug of your next project – besides which, there will always now be plenty of choice superlatives you can use on your website… stage designers now have to peek out from behind their proscenium and self-promote as never before.

12

Touring and Commercial Projects

Whether the show was originally set up as a commercial venture or was publicly subsidised in a regional or smaller repertory theatre, your production may be fortunate enough to have a lifespan beyond that which you planned for or were contracted to. Contractually speaking, extending the pay and conditions is usually fairly straightforward, in that you would go back to the producer and renegotiate terms from the confident position of knowing that they need you as much as you need them. If an otherwise modest show develops into something more ambitious with extra financial rewards attached, this may be the first prompt you need to seek out an agent who will advise you and be your advocate. An agent will also probably be more likely to take you on, even if it's only for a short provisional period, if you have a project in the pipeline and something for you both to get your teeth into.

The important technicality to get to grips with is *where* the production will be mounted, and therefore what changes will be required in the design. Changes, and ongoing change in the form of a flexible design that would accommodate a number of varied venues on a tour, can sometimes mean a radical reworking of scenic elements, especially if you hadn't seen this eventuality being likely beforehand. Your first port of call will be the original show's production manager, presuming they themselves are continuing with the project. If so, they are likely to know what the producer's intentions are with regard to the scale and nature of the new proposal. It is likely that all the plans of the show's afterlife will not be known and confirmed by the time you have to go 'back to the drawing board'.

A one-stop transfer to, say, a West End theatre may well be a near certainty based on sales, but precisely which theatre it will transfer to could still be in doubt a long way down the redesign process. In this situation you will be working within a set of spatial parameters that are essentially guessed dimensions based on the size of theatre that is both financially viable and possibly available. In any event, the technical support that you might have enjoyed at even a small venue will not be forthcoming in a commercial West End venue, unless the management buys it in. Sometimes even parts of the infrastructure of a theatre that anyone would reasonably take for granted, such as elements of the flying equipment, may be missing from the theatre's original specification. Plans and elevations too might be outdated, previous productions having made modifications to the stage that were never taken account of in the drawings. You will have to work very closely and vigilantly with your PM to assess what your theatre's condition is likely to be.

Commercial venues also very carefully count the cost of each performance sacrificed to the get-in and re-rehearsal of the show, so the pressure will be on all concerned to make the transfer both economical and artistically viable. There are essentially two types of commercial run in a fixed venue: limited or open-ended. If the show has a predetermined lifespan of, say, twelve weeks, then you and your PM will need to assess whether the original set, and indeed costumes, will last the duration. Props too may have a limited lifespan in that they may have been borrowed for a specific amount of time and been returned, or they may have been hired, in which case they will definitely have returned to their source: a theatre store or a hire company. The lending/hiring company, on a 'promise', can sometimes put costumes and props that have been hired aside for a short period of time, but that won't last indefinitely, so the originally agreed terms will have to be renegotiated.

The element of the set that usually gets the most punishment throughout a run is the floor. Again, you and your PM will have to gauge whether a refurbishment or perhaps even a rebuild is required to get you through particularly an open-ended commercial run. It's counter-intuitive, I know, but your first transferable show into the big world of West End theatre may actually mean reducing its size – many of these late Victorian buildings were designed for a totally different form of presentational show, framed by slim, painted scenic screens, 'legs' and 'borders', and backed with lightweight elements such as canvas cloths, gauzes, scrims and other soft drapery – so they are narrow and shallow internally, and may have originally been crammed by the architect onto an awkward site's footprint. Furthermore, they may have a preservation order preventing modernisations, such as the dock door through which all that skinny scenery originally entered and left the space… unlike your twenty-first-century 'monster'!

If your production is heading for a tour, the designer's landscape can be equally misty. New demands on your original ideas kick in, such as how much kit the PM can fit into the truck. The size or number of the trucks is governed by the producer's budget, and it's not usual for the designer to have to 'design' exactly how the show will be packed in the trailer, but in any case sooner or later you are likely be consulted about transport. There is more than just the scenery, prop skips and travelling wardrobe of costumes to fit in: sound equipment and lighting equipment can take up an enormous amount of space and, although economically contained in equipment cases on wheels that stack somewhat like containers on a ship, what was once a seemingly huge trailer can become surprisingly cramped – and, if deemed unsafe or unstable, can become a liability for the crews that have to load and unload it each week.

If your scenery was designed to give the illusion of complete solidarity, such as continuous walls, this may have to be rethought to provide an opportunity for splits to be built in to it, and you may well have to design extra sections to accommodate greater depth or wider width. A bugbear of all touring productions is a raked stage. The slope will probably vary from one raked floor to another, so walls have to be adjusted and any moving parts on wheels have to be firmly braked to stop them heading for the orchestra pit or landing in a spectator's lap. A seemingly innocuous article like a bottle, when placed on its side on a gentle 1-in-24 rake and rolling uncontrollably, can become an actor's nightmare.

If you have designed traps in the floor through which actors or objects make appearances, unless you redesign the whole of your travelling stage with depth enough to accommodate this, you can forget it on tour: they will just have to surprise the audience by other means. Likewise, from the top down, any flying pieces, and particularly flying performers, will have to be repositioned depending on variations from venue to venue in the counterweight systems. As with a West End show, your ambition should be to be as self-contained as possible while knowing that, when needs be, crews and technicians can be immensely flexible within professional tolerances.

So whether you enjoy these largely technical challenges or not, it can also be a chance to adjust all those niggly little things that you yourself didn't get quite right first time around. There are rare occasions with drama productions when a production might go into storage and come back out for another run, in which case correcting your own faults is usually the only reason to be in involved, moving on as we do. Designing Shakespeare for the Propeller Theatre Company has given me that opportunity repeatedly as we revisited productions in new combinations and with different casts going on a new sequence of tour dates. This is the closest equivalent to being a painter that I can think of in theatre-design terms, repeatedly but fondly revisiting a theme.

13

Aftercare and Further Uses of a Design

There is no reason why, after the show has had its press night, you should ever see it on stage again. But it is the nature of the business that we care about a project as a living, breathing, developing 'work'.[38] So the chances are that you will be self-compelled to at least keep in touch with it.

In one respect you have little choice as, after each performance, the DSM or CSM generates and sends out a show report, and you will be copied into the emails along with the producers and others in the creative team. The report records factual information, such as performance timings (of each act, for example) and audience figures, but there is also a brief commentary on the strengths and weaknesses of that particular performance, including any technical difficulties or anomalies that might have occurred – stressing whether the glitch was due to human or technical error. The bulk of these reports are only of passing interest to the designer (although many can be very entertaining and could form the basis for an amusing, if potentially libellous, book), but as sure as eggs are eggs, if you don't read one of them you will miss an item that is relevant to how your work is being used or perceived. If you are receiving some form of royalty for each of the performances, it is also handy to track how well the show is selling as this can determine the size of your weekly payment, although that information should also be formally declared by the producers when these payments come through to either you or your agent.

Over the span of a long run, illness, injury or some other fate might affect one or two of the cast. Of course, you will, as a responsible professional, be concerned that any injury wasn't due to some aspect of the design, which can be anything from the heel of a shoe to the collapse of a platform, but in the main, it's petty acts of God, such as a touch of laryngitis, that mean understudies have to take over. In these instances your part in the reshuffle should be covered by the fact that you and your costume supervisor will have prepared for all eventualities during the rehearsal period and production week. Understudies and 'swings' are usually part of the permanent acting company and will have costumes on standby, so you will not be called upon in person to make any extra provision, but it's wise to monitor the situation so that at least you can picture the extent of the change should anything develop beyond the company's immediate control.

An extreme example of this was an international tour of mine that relied on the set being shipped to Tokyo from the West Coast of America. The vessel, for one reason or another, bypassed Japan and headed for mainland Asia. You can imagine the ensuing predicament! The situation was exacerbated by the fact that our show was opening a new season of work at the theatre, but the pressure of time and consummate professionalism all round resulted in a splendidly improvised welded construction of my hastily sketched design – the crew and all concerned were magnificent, the production was a success as the audience were none the wiser, and our ultimate victory against the odds was nothing short of exhilarating!

14

Sustainability

Theatre-making has always been described as an ephemeral art form, but in this day and age we are increasingly aware that what we leave behind after the show is anything but. As we move towards a more sustainable society, we recognise that we must reuse and recycle more, and landfill less. With increasing landfill taxes, landfill-operator and haulage costs, and more stringent waste regulations, the recycling of materials, including wood, assumes an increasing importance.

As with most industrial sustainability concerns, theatre production is having to grapple with how it can reconcile the needs of the planet with the logistics and finance of a business. The cycle of making a programme of work, or individual productions, has not always had a bad track record of wastefulness. Repertory theatres and commercial producers alike have a well-established culture of storage and reuse of props and costumes. Traditionally, however, it has been more problematic to reuse bespoke scenery that has been designed for a specific production by a specific creative team, although structural modular elements behind the scenes, such as platforms, trussing and other types of bracing, will be used again and again. Back- and floor cloths often had multiple lives, being repainted for successive shows, but since their decreasing use in favour of more structured surfaces and shapes, opportunities for reuse have all but dried up.

Likewise, the more traditional construction methods once met environmentally friendly criteria. Glues, textiles, such as canvas or flax, and paints were essentially made from natural biodegradable ingredients, although very often coupled with a less palatable use of animal products – rabbit-skin glue size, for example. With the cost of steel becoming more competitive in relation to timber products, it has been possible to deconstruct and reconstruct some forms of seemingly non-eco-friendly monolithic steel-built scenery, although the labour costs incurred to do this have often militated against any moral obligation to recycle.

Those days are over, and there is now a legal requirement as well as an economic argument for more sustainable theatre production. The Arts Council of England now requires organisations to complete an environmental policy and action plan, and report their carbon footprint. Every aspect of a theatre company's operations now contributes towards a measurement of their green credentials, particularly forms of transport if their productions are built at a distance from the theatre or they tour their shows. The enigmatically named Julie's Bicycle organisation is at the forefront of defining criteria for sustainability in collaboration with both producers and authorities, giving organisations a star rating for achievement, raising awareness of practical solutions to what were thought to be insurmountable problems and generally doing a superb job of sharing good practice across the globe.

Until recently, the vast proportion of theatre designers paid little or no interest to the green legacy of their work. There is a quiet revolution going on in the profession, however, and some designers, such as Brooklyn-based Donyale Werle, fully embrace recycling methods, not only in the generation of material objects but also the ideas that underpin them: giving their designs subtly submerged layers of richness and meaning. Others may not integrate sustainability into their thinking but at least ask questions about the design's material afterlife, which is usually the responsibility of the production manager. It will not be long, I'm sure, before sustainability clauses will be written into designers' contracts so that these discussions take place at the outset of a design process; not necessarily impacting on a design's conceptual framework, but certainly interrogating previously held assumptions about how scenery, props and costumes are made and what happens to them when the last curtain falls. Designers may also need to modify some of their definitions of further use, or loosen their grip on copyright regulation, for the cause.

There are now companies that specialise in the storage, re- and upcycling a whole set or just its separate elements. For example: timber is chipped and becomes chipboard, animal bedding, insulation products or mulch, etc.; plastics are made into pellets and reused for manufacturing any number of items; metal is crushed and sent for smelting to become raw product; and polystyrene is sorted, compacted and processed to become a fuel stock for power supplies. There are others that specialise in scenery salvage, so if you're working to a very tight production budget in the early stages of your career, it makes sense to check out what these companies have on offer to make your money stretch a whole lot further than you ever thought possible – remembering, of course, that you repay the planet with subsequently re-disposing of it responsibly, probably back to its source.

Occasionally, an artistic team overseeing a season of plays may take the step of asking a designer to make a semi-permanent architectural statement in their theatre by designing a standing environment which all the productions for that programme have to respond to and fit in. Known as a 'season stage', in the past this policy was often triggered by an artistic, logistical or financial need, but sustainability concerns can now also support the wisdom of a season stage: still requiring design and designers for each show, but giving them a tighter brief and demanding a response, albeit newly conceived, to this specific 'site'.

As theatre architects design increasingly visible green statements into their buildings and spaces, stage designers will both be expected and hopefully willing to reflect these messages and methods in their own work, whether obvious to the audience's eye or not. Theatre buildings are becoming more flexible in their forms, and stage designers are now asked to respond progressively to their environment, both architecturally and ethically, so even if the scenery changes, eco issues are quite rightly here to stay.

PART EIGHT

Help!
Agents, Unions and Societies

Designing is now almost exclusively a freelance occupation and periodically feels both fabulously liberating but also solitary. You will, over time, build a circle of professional friends who will advise you when asked, but beyond that support group there are organisations that have amassed a lifetime's experience of tackling different challenging situations. For more details on the precise nature of these organisations, you can also refer to the Useful Organisations, References and Publications section in the Appendices. Agents, unions and societies all have roles that overlap to a degree, but they came about to serve different aspects of a designer's professional life and to do that on a variety of terms.

In brief, then, the distinctions are as follows:

- *Agents* representing designers operate in almost identical ways to agents who represent actors, directors and other theatre, TV and film professionals. I will expand on their role in detail below; suffice to say that the relationship you would form with an agent should be viewed more as a one-to-one, symbiotic partnership. The designer employs the agent to fulfil particular business tasks, but agents can provide far more than that based on a high level of rapport and mutual trust over a long period of time, and that in turn suits the investment that the agent makes in the designer's career.

- *Unions* are professional associations that provide frameworks for negotiations between management groups and stage design as a sector – for either publicly or privately financed projects. Theatre and film-based unions are no different in terms of the charter of the Trades Union Congress than, for instance, electricians or civil servants. Union representatives have regular rounds of talks with reps of the three theatre management groups[39] to set pay minima and employment conditions that are then incorporated into standard-issue contracts. Benefitting from direct full union support requires the designer to be a subscribed member: the fee for membership being calculated on your income from designing.

- *Societies* are organisations that provide a more holistic network of design-led interests including exchange of experiences and wisdom throughout the profession. They promote design both nationally and internationally, provide directories of contacts and issue advice to designers at whatever stage of their career they're at. Again, to gain full benefits you need to be a member and pay an annual subscription – but there is also a student rate.

I will concentrate chiefly on representation by agents in this chapter but with reference to the other two groups when apt.

1

Before the Job

Let's be crystal clear and dispel one or two of the myths about agents that are, to be honest, unfairly perpetuated and exaggerated by comic characterisations on our screens. Firstly, agents rarely find you work – and neither can they, although they will be listening out for possibilities and will make sure their clients are considered for a job if they are a) right for the content of the project, or b) properly available and it's a project that will have longer term benefits, however speculative or slow-burn that may be. An agent might get you a meeting, but *you* get the job. Secondly, the agent is rightly working on *your* behalf, and so, for *you*. To that end, an ideal agent should be a good listener and a straight talker, but also tactful. They should have a reputation for securing terms for you that are not necessarily the best, but the fairest – this is obviously often a matter of, and subject to, the sometimes wildly subjective opinion of designer, agent and management, but it's the agent's job to gauge where the common ground will be, and seal the deal. In the long run, it's to the advantage of no one that negotiations are cut-throat for short-term gains. The theatre world is a relatively small one and a once-bitten producer or management with a long memory can so easily shy away from offering you future work, or be at least wary of an agent-designer combo with a reputation for playing extreme hard ball.

To begin with, not every designer needs an agent – at least not all the time, although most agent-designer agreements are 'all or nothing': in other words, designers can't pick and choose which projects they would like an agent's help on and those they feel they can handle themselves. Both are in it for the long haul, and it's only by building a rapport through a variety of projects that both can assess the partnership's mutuality. Indeed, agents themselves spring from a vast variety of backgrounds and learn through experience (there is no meaningful training other than that on the job). This experience is what designers will pay ten per cent[40] of their fee for, as even the most modest of projects can reveal a problematic surprise or two.

Many theatre-design graduates are given the impression that one of the first tasks on their professional to-do list is to find an agent, and that they may be at a disadvantage if they can't – much like actors. This is most definitely another myth to dispel. Having an agent is not a badge of honour. Most professional designers will know when they need the support of an agent, and it's often (hopefully before) the initiation of a project that they realise the financial angle will be an impossible burden and a distraction from their true business of designing. Many designers do look after themselves well, but those that have had the benefits of an agent will rate highly the fact that during the negotiation stages of a project, which also frequently overlap with the early phase of the creative process, they can concentrate on building a relatively haggle-free collaboration with producers, managers and directors.

Glib though it may sound, each working relationship between an agent and their client is different. Each designer will have a different need and the agent will hopefully respond to it. Some designers are remarkably good at understanding the implications of a contract and able to negotiate one very successfully, although they may feel they just don't have the time to fit it into each project. Others may have their head and heart totally committed to the work and will rely on the agent to value what they do in the context of a project.

Being an agent is definitely personality driven. You've got to like working with people. If you do your job properly you should be in the background quietly working away on your client's behalf. Any agent who has a desire to raise their own profile shouldn't be one – agents work for other people and should enjoy success through theirs.

Alice Dunne, agent for TV, theatre and film production

When the time comes for you to look for an agent, you will sense or know it. Here are the factors that might prompt you:

- You simply don't have time to handle the contract.

- You feel you can afford it.

- You have very little idea about the usual fees for this genre of project.

- You find yourself involved in a project of a vastly bigger scale, or in a more complex professional environment, than ever before.

- You are designing a project that involves negotiating with more than one manager.

- Your project has the prospect of further, but perhaps unpredictable, commercial use

- You are very unsure how to negotiate your conditions simply because you have less experience than that of the management.

- You suspect the terms you will work under are either not orthodox, or plainly, in your view, not fair.

Any or all of these circumstances may well form enough of a reason to take the step of securing representation, but it will most likely be after having built up something of a track record of working on productions that you have been able to negotiate for yourself. Through these experiences you are more likely to have known not only why you now need an agent but also what aspects they could specifically support you with and who, temperamentally, would best suit you as an agent and share in the next phase of what is your vocation.

Financially speaking, it is unlikely that you will make large amounts of money in the early years of your career, so you will have to think carefully about how the cost of an agent can be sustained over the medium to long term. In special circumstances, it may be the case that you are just caught off-guard by an aspect of a project on which you need some advice but that you are not yet ready to hook up with an agent on a permanent basis. Rest assured that some agents may offer to take a look at the terms of your contract as a one-off, and that may serve as an introduction for a more lasting future working partnership. In this circumstance, however, don't be surprised if your prospective agent gives you the news that the conditions of your contract are sound and your deal is close to the market rate – you will have to be happy that the agent's role here has been one of reassurance. You may have just needed good advice rather than formal representation, so consulting fellow designers could have been a simpler route.

Let's assume then that you have reached the point in your career when you are convinced that you need a more permanent form of support. You can start your search by either picking through a resource such as the publication *Contacts*, or ask around. The Society of British Theatre Designer's directory is an excellent starting point, in that there are two registers, one of agents that also list their designers, and then one of designers that also includes their agent. By looking at both, and with your knowledge of the business, you can identify designers that you may wish to emulate, see which agencies represent the designers of the work you would like to be akin to, and do some homework on them before making a possible approach.

You will notice that the agents you are interested in are either part of a larger agency, or a sole trader. There are pros and cons to both. As part of a larger agency you will hope that your particular agent will be able to swap notes with other people in the profession who are represented by that company – so you may want to look at not only the designers who are represented by that firm, but also potential collaborators and routes to employment, such as, naturally, directors. You will also hope that you won't be swallowed up or in some way ignored over time: a small fish in a big sea. In contrast, an individual agent with their own clientele, or perhaps a 'boutique' agency, may give you the perception at least of a more bespoke service – bigger fish, small sea. Again, the best way of taking the plunge one way or the other is to line up a few meetings with different agents and take advice or recommendations from your fellow designers.

When you meet your prospective agent for the first time, remind yourself that you are attempting to discover whether you want to work together collaboratively. *Are they going to be a positive force in your professional life?* You will inevitably take along your folio in some form, and although the agent is not viewing your past productions with the same eye and criteria as would a director, personal taste (whilst also understanding the constraints you have been working under) will play a part in whether they believe they are best placed to support your ambitions. Likewise, it will be for you to imagine and anticipate how their manner might be applied to their dealings on your behalf – after all, they will literally be *representing* you – so find out as much as you can about their background and opinions.

It is perfectly normal that, once you have found your match, you will both need a probationary period of perhaps six months during which you can both assure yourselves that it's working out or not.

2

On the Job

Your working relationship with an agent should ideally be minimal through the span of a project, other than the normal maintenance of 'radio contact'. If you and your agent have successfully negotiated your deal to your mutual satisfaction and to the satisfaction of the management, the rest of your financial and contractual dealings should play out as planned. If not, something out of the ordinary rather than something unforeseen has probably happened to cut across the agreement. An agent is primarily in place to buy you the space to just do the work in hand from the word go, but occasionally something, either technical or personal, will need to be resolved mid-term. Your agent is then on hand to give you advice or, if necessary, to step in on your behalf. Instances of this happening are so varied that it's impossible to cite any useful trends, as the most common sources of potential frustration, conflict or confusion should have been covered in the distinct but generic clauses of your agreement (see Part Seven).

Over the longer projects, there are always likely to be one or two grey areas, usually in your conditions of employment, that may need adjusting as the production takes shape. In my experience, these tend to be clustered around situations in which both you and management need to agree on an extension of the provisions in the original agreement. For example, you may have agreed to a certain number of trips to the venue away from your home that required train tickets, flights or overnight stays, and due to the demands of the show (importantly, as distinct from any personal opinions), you may need to agree that management will pay for the extra visits. These are most commonly for production meetings, costume fittings or trips to the scenic workshops... not everything can be solved by an email or a Skype call. During the design phase of a project, the number of rebuilds of your model may require extra assistance and therefore obviously a little more expense, whilst, at the performance end of the project, I've been in situations whereby all concerned realise a little more work needs to be done after the press night (and receipt of your final fee). Probably the most common and potentially ugly instances of having to call on your agent after the show has opened is in the renegotiation of terms, including further royalties, should your production have an afterlife. Somehow, when the show is a known quantity, valuing it can be more problematic and opinionated.

More extreme problems can need legal representation. These include tortuous cases of copyright infringement, major technical foul-ups causing cancelled performances and therefore major financial loss, or instances in which someone on a production may have been seriously injured. Although some of the larger agencies have legal advice on tap, or even a permanent legal department, other smaller operators might only be able to give more casual advice, and it's in these circumstances that unions can be called upon to mount a sustained defence of a member's rights.

In terms of strategic professional promotion, an agent can give you useful pointers as to how to structure your website to send the right message to the world. From a working knowledge of how designers successfully landed work and made successful partnerships, your agent can lead you to examples of clients' folios that did the trick. One or two top designers also have a publicist in tow who can promote the cultivation of a professional aura, shoehorning their clients into as many publications or events that elevate their profile as possible. As backstage artists, it's rare that stage designers either want or feel the need for such exposure, but there's no doubt that in some instances, and for some personalities, it's worth the financial and emotional investment.

Finally, your agent should be a sounding board for your work. Although, of course, they will instinctively have a positive bias, it's important that they are also prepared to give you their impressions from a slightly more objective vantage point than that of your friends and colleagues. Other than from the audience, how else are you going to know how effective your production is, and particularly how (although not necessarily how *well*) you played your part?

Top tip: *You'll need to find some common ground when meeting a prospective agent for the first time, so be prepared to talk about theatre practitioners that you 'rate', from directors to other designers, to writers and the theatres or companies that produce the sorts of work you'd want to do.*

PART NINE

Your Workplace

1

In the Studio or Workroom: What Building? What Equipment? What Environment?

You will have noticed that even in the title of this section there are different words to describe *where* designers form their ideas. The notion of this place of work being a 'studio' is founded on the artistic characteristics of design, whereas a 'workroom' reflects the designer's material output. Whichever you call this place, and I regularly veer between the two, it's important that you get it right for yourself – you'll spend a lot of time there. I will not the attempt to suggest bright ideas and solutions for setting up your space, but only aim to suggest the challenges you may face in creating it – so often a studio *or* workroom evolves into an extension of each artist and designer's inner psyche as much as their industry.

On a college course you may have been given a workplace to make things in or at, but this will most likely be akin to an open-plan office rather than somewhere for more solitary reflection associated with the traditional depiction of an 'artist's studio'. It is more and more the case, however, that fine artists are working in communal studio spaces, so the somewhat nostalgic image of an artist being defined by isolation in some romantic garret is long gone – even if it was ever there other than in the movies. Artists choose their studio space to accommodate what they make and that can vary, of course, between the extremes of painting a miniature or making an epic public sculpture. Theatre designers, on the other hand, however experimental they may be in their use of processes, methods or materials, will need to generate objects, models and drawings that adhere to an established industrial norm. The criteria for finding your ideal workplace, alongside that of the theatre itself, are:

1. Cost.

2. Domestic situation.

3. Location.

4. Scale of operation.

Your approach to prioritising these things will be both personal, pragmatic and most certainly financial: generating a matrix of conflicts in your mind that can be hard to untangle. I suggest, if little else, take the designer's approach to your own situation by listing the pros and cons, and perhaps even drawing your ideal workplace, so as to be able to take a cool and objective look at your wants and needs, and to be able to share it with others. For example, with regard to cost, when starting out it is unlikely that you will be in a position to buy a studio space, so the space you use will most likely be cheek by jowl with your living space. Cheaper urban living spaces tend to be more interconnected internally nowadays, so it may not be possible to tuck your workroom away; however, you may find this an interesting challenge – 'living your work' – and so not be unsettled by it. You should consider comparing the cost of renting a larger living space to accommodate a workroom with that of renting a studio in a separate building. Some folk enjoy separating their domestic lives from their professional ones – or indeed need to do so – and consider travelling to work as a way of helpfully decoupling the two. If you are in the fortunate position of owning property, you could consider reversing the work/life separation and decide that building the workspace into your property (a loft extension or a converted garage are obvious solutions) will be a good investment, as well as serving your work/life balance. Then again, you could contemplate maintaining some separation between the two by building a more temporary but substantial studio space in the garden (if you have one!).

All artists and designers will be constantly reappraising and on the lookout for the Shangri-La of workplaces. What most are looking to establish is a comfortable environment which also either stimulates the imagination or leaves space for it, rather than being a temple of Fordian efficiency. Of course, designers have to function in it, but how workrooms are set up can vary hugely depending on how you yourself function – in other words, you have to know and account for *how* you work as well as *what* you have to do. Some designers will always need assistants, so your workspace will need to reflect your relationship with the help you anticipate requiring. In the contemporary designer's workspace, there is a balance to be struck between digital and analogue processes. Designers still have to make some form of physical three-dimensional architectural model, which can be bulky, but, as outlined earlier, these are now generated by drawing on computers; so, you will need clean, screen-based space coupled with a far more adaptable workbench. In the not-too-distant future, the digital printer will also be a common addition to your suite of appliances.

You will never have enough tabletop space, that is 'a given'; and you will have to move models to make space for drawing and vice versa, so although a traditional drawing board may be handy at times to make more accurate drawings of smaller props, for example, I would not recommend investing in a freestanding board: rather acquiring a large but portable foldaway version.

The same is true of shelving: you will begin to amass an enormous quantity of materials that may have only been used for one project and are now consigned to some form of 'stock' that you may never reuse, cannot recycle, but feel compelled to save. Alongside this, your regular materials for model-making, such as sheets of card, foam board, wood, wire, plastics, glues and paints, should be kept both close to hand and orderly.

A proliferation of books will also need to be accommodated, and your collection will become your friend in times of need, perhaps even a joy, but will no doubt vie for much-needed space to make things in.

Light, power and regulated heat are all essential to a comfortable, efficient and safe working environment. There is a somewhat fetishistic attitude to the sources of natural light in an artist's studio, and this can be totally justified for a theatre designer if, for example, you still prefer to make costume drawings or renderings by hand and perhaps on a larger scale than just the notepad. Much of this work is now created on the screen, however, and so the need for natural light is far less important. Indeed, large windows can be a menace, causing reflections of either the room or your own face. Nevertheless, lofty natural light[41] for most people is preferable to some form of bunker as a working environment given that you may spend the majority of your day (and sometimes night) here, and that it can begin to impinge on your spirits and could therefore impact on the character of your work – or at least your attitude towards it.

2

In the Theatre:
A Survival Kit

Much of this next section could be regarded as completely facile and complaining. Of course, you are very welcome to skip over it, but if you take only one or two tips from it, you will most likely reduce your stress levels a little or – at least, if you're the strong, silent type – avoid one or two occupational hazards of the theatre designer.

As previously outlined, the fit-up of scenery before the production week will usually begin on a Sunday. It is often the case that some of the rigging of lights will have been prepared on the preceding Saturday after the last performance of the previous show to get it up into the flies and out of the way as the set is assembled. So the designer, having made the effort to arrive at the theatre at an agreed time (as outlined previously in the production-week section), confronts their first hurdle – how to get into the theatre when, from the outside, the building appears as quiet as a morgue. Theatres have a stage door, of course, but there may well be no one on duty on a Sunday and the front of the building including the box office will be firmly shuttered shut. The solution to laying siege to this fortress is ensuring communication with your production manager. Agree how you will make contact on your arrival beforehand (the obvious answer is by mobile phone, but theirs may be switched off in the heat of the moment or out of range in a subterranean theatre). Circling the building for thirty minutes and contemplating breaking and entering will not get you off to a good start. Alternatively, find out when the set is likely to finish loading in, because at this point you may be able to saunter through the load-in doors and all will be well. In fact, you have every incentive to be there as early as possible, because major decisions about the position of your set may be made very early on in the process of the get-in.

Once you're in the building there will be no welcoming party – everyone will be preoccupied with installing the main elements of the set and ensuring that it is stable and everyone is safe in the process. Remain as detached (but not aloof) as you can because you will be a useful objective observer of the focused business on stage, although you must speak out if you see the installation of your work going off-track. Choose your moment to speak to your production manager, conscious of the fact that they may have other concerns and responsibilities that change from minute to minute.

As mentioned previously, there will be no design department or even a designer's room that you can call 'home' for the period of your 'guest appearance'. Along with others in the creative team, including the director, you will be consigned to the traditions of an itinerant worker. Your carrier bag will be your kingdom and an auditorium seat your throne. However, once things have settled down a bit and you are on first-name terms with the technical team, seek out the *resident* technical or production manager: they may be able to provide you with some form of improvised table that you can call your own for the production week. The production electrician can also be your saviour: they will have already equipped the lighting designer and programmer with a generous table for all of their equipment, and importantly, power (in all senses of the word) and an extension lead of your own can provide the means of a crucial lifeline to the outside world.[42]

The next most vital facility is access to wifi. You will be submerged in darkness and miles from home for days on end, possibly entombed underground and beyond a mobile-phone signal, so the internet and email can keep you up to date with the other aspects of your busy life.

Once you have 'set up shop', be prepared to take notes on everything that strikes you as important, right through to opening night. You will have to be clear and concise to everyone supporting you, the design and production at large, so it is vital to have a systematic approach to recording your thoughts and knowing who to pass them on to. Many still choose good ol' pen and paper while others use anything techno from tablets to Dictaphones. If you have an assistant of some sort with you, you can continually rattle off your notes to them and meet later at the end of a session to draw up a priority list. Whatever the mechanics, it will be important to categorise your thoughts, after which you can aim the note at the appropriate person to sort the problem out. I tend to preface each note with a coding letter such as:

c   Costume matters (for costume supervisors).

PM   Scenic matters (for the production manager).

P   Props issues (for the props coordinator or stage-management team).

LX   Lighting notes (both artistic and occasionally technical).

SFX   Sound issuses (often to do with the installation of equipment).

VFX   Video issues (for the video designer).

SM   Setting notes (positioning props on stage).

PT   Painting notes (for the scenic artist).

D   Thoughts for the director (or any less holistic notes, such as staging a chorus, for the AD).

CH   Thoughts for the choreographer.

Rationalising the diversity of your many notes will help efficiently target your requirements at the 'tech notes' session,[43] usually at the end of each day during the production week and after preview performances.

Make sure you have access to your original drawings: both elevations and plans, either as a paper copy or 'in programme' on your laptop. They are the result of your carefully considered, original thoughts when you probably had far more time to both rationalise and fantasise, so now on stage, when decisions often have to be actioned instantaneously, you will rely on those drawings as an aide-memoire of the pledge you made to yourself and with others. You may also need factual information to hand when suggesting any precise changes to the size or position of any element now in front of you, in what appears to be two-dimensional visual space from the auditorium, rather than three-dimensional dimensional space on stage.

Keep a small drawing pad with you: designing doesn't finish until right up to the last moment, and you never know when verbal references and adjectives will fail to adequately express your thoughts whereas a hasty but clear diagram or impression will do the job better – particularly for costume and props. I've also found that one of those laser torches can be really handy to point out impossibly high or otherwise inaccessible features that need attention – gaps in the masking, for example.

During rehearsal sessions, I recommend sitting midway between the stage and the director (who is usually halfway back and near the lighting designer so as to discuss light levels and cueing). Each designer will have their own attitude to how hands-on they are at this point, but I make sure that I stay close to the stage so that I'm ready to go up and talk to actors or others in the many pauses about anything from a wig adjustment to the use of a prop. In proscenium theatres, a temporary set of steps are usually installed for the creative team to do this, so I'll establish my 'camp' within easy reach of these.

In contrast to all this, make sure you take breaks, because, in common with many of the production team, the designer has to attend every minute of rehearsal on stage and then can only catch up with both off- and backstage business during breaks. Look after yourself. As with most intensely focused manual or intellectual activity, a few minutes' distancing from the work, some daylight and a breath of fresh air can help you take a more objective view of your work, and assume a perspective not unlike that of the audience.

Don't forget your camera for the technical and dress rehearsals – there should be plenty of chances to take some good shots of your work in the many pauses during the process. You will probably find that your camera phone will not be up to the job, as the lighting conditions coupled with movement will be impossible to control and difficult to compensate for. You may well be offered the photos that are taken by the production photographer for publicity purposes. Although they can be of wonderful quality and capture a moment in the production, they will invariably be focused on actors only, and very often just the top halves of their bodies at that. As an all-round theatre designer you will be just as interested in how the whole stage picture is composed; so there are two strategies to compensate for the customary absence of the 'long shot', and I would have both these bases covered.

Route one is to take your own photographs, and as I've already said you will need a camera of reasonable quality. The only drawback to this is that in a dress rehearsal, which is the only time you can take these shots, you ought also to be looking at what the audience will see, and making notes judged on that experience. It's hard to have your attention split between the viewfinder and your design responsibilities.

Route two is to make friends with the production photographer the moment they walk into the auditorium, develop a rapport with them, and ask if they can take a long shot or two. Some photographers have two cameras on the go at one time that are linked to each other: one on a tripod further back in the auditorium and one in their hands taking the close-ups. If so, you'll have plenty to choose from and most photographers are happy for you to use their work for your own promotion if they are properly credited. Bear in mind, though, that there is the advantage of your taking the photographs yourself in that you will have insider knowledge of particularly photogenic moments that you, as a designer, would like to capture and that would represent you best in your folio or on your website.

PART TEN

Promoting Your Future and Building a Legacy

1

Web-Based and Hard-Copy Folios

Whether the 'shop window' you create to advertise your work – and hopefully you get more as a result – is a hard-copy folio, a disk or a website, there are some basic principles to adhere to. You must concentrate on both clarity and brevity. Anyone viewing your work will have limited time and, like most of us, a limited attention span.

The first rule of thumb is to transport yourself into the shoes of the viewer and ask yourself: '*How often would I spend longer than thirty seconds looking at any image?*' Your folio may have fifty of these. '*Would I seriously spend a total of twenty-five minutes scrutinising all the images in one person's folio?*' The same goes for words. It is a waste of time, both yours and the viewer's, to add over-wordy descriptions of why or how you made a piece of work. Annotate it; but don't over-explain it. My advice is to ensure that the nub of your folio or website can be 'consumed' in about ten minutes, but with other layers, pages or depths (such as process sketches) available to the viewer as an optional appendix, should they want to know more about you or your work.

The second principle I would recommend is that the display of your work has some form of narrative. If you are a theatre designer of any worth then this must surely play to your strengths; in other words, the way you structure your folio will say as much about how you go about work as what's in it. This visual storytelling should aim to lead the viewer on and want more. Here, you can interpret the word 'story' in a number of ways.

It could be structured by the use of any of the following:

- Colour (from monochrome to something more vibrant?).

- Time (from your earliest to latest work?).

- Theme ('lighter' weight to 'heavier' weight subjects?).

- Form (from naturalism to abstract?).

- Genres (from drama to music theatre?).

As you build up even a short string of productions, you may, through your experience and how your work has been recorded visually, see aesthetic or thematic patterns emerging. You might focus your folio in either of two contrasting ways:

1. Promoting yourself as either approaching work in a chameleon-like manner, adapting to your environment, be it in relation to a varied use of theatre/performance conventions or the subject matter you have tackled.

2. Acknowledging and foregrounding some distinctive hallmark that a director might want to apply to their production.

There is no lack of integrity in the first, or dogmatism in the second, but the safest bet is probably presenting evidence of both. In either case, don't 'headline' or preface your folio by explicitly declaring one or other of these, but let the way you arrange your work do the talking for you and allow the viewer's observations to prompt a conversation about your work, including why and how you make it.

The advantage that any form of folio has over a website is that you can, to a certain degree, tailor it to the needs of a potential director, producer or agent. A hard-copy folio is best kept in loose-leaf plastic sleeves that can be removed or reordered to tell a subtly but significantly different story each time you edit; disks likewise. A website is, of course, more interactive, and so the way you structure it will be more a matter of suggesting a narrative than your imposing one. When building a website, unlike a folio, you will have open access to both the best and the worst examples. There will undoubtedly be a fine line between making the site as visually interesting or exciting as possible and it adhering to the ten-minute rule. The last thing that you want is that someone significant to you becomes either bored or frustrated and clicks to leave. Again, the advantage of the folio is that in a meeting you can be in control of what the viewer sees and, to a degree, for how long.

Cynical though it may sound, it in fact stands to reason that there is little or no relationship between a great piece of theatre and a great production photograph. Neither does a memorable live theatrical moment have any impact in a photograph, or a breathtaking photograph record the actual experience of being there. For a start the photographer is never sitting stationary in a seat and, unless promenading, the audience are not equipped with a zoom lens, but a snapshot can capture the essence of a performance or the 'soul' of a character[isation]. Your choice of images, then, has to be judged at face value, disaggregated from your memory of the performance, and with each shot reviewed as if you were never there – but so they wish they had been! With this perspective you are more likely to see your folio work as others will.

Opinion is divided as to whether original drawings or copies have more impact in a hard-copy folio. There are concerns that a copy of a drawing (and I include painting in this category), and particularly of a collage, will flatten its surface, rendering it somewhat sterile and reducing its qualities. On the other hand, if you are intending to put the same work on your website it is more than likely that this will have exactly the same effect, and so, for consistency's sake, it's better to use scans for both digital and actual folios, keeping the original for your archive, for exhibition purposes or even for sale. For practical purposes during a production period, the drawings will most likely be copied several times over for distribution to makers, rehearsal and for inclusion in the costume supervisor's 'bible'. Because these prints become what I'd call the 'working original', many designers make drawings with this process in mind. So, for example, the original may have subtle tones and lines that might be enhanced by manipulating the scan in Photoshop, with other digital processes adding to the final image. This enhanced image then becomes the 'original' that can take its place not only in the process but also in your folio and your website. I would advise not putting the real originals in a folio simply for security reasons – many a folder has been left on a train, in the back of a taxi, dowsed in water or even caught in a fire! The digital 'original', although at risk of being duplicated without your permission, will always be safe in somebody's laptop or storage device. Personally I think that these copies, whether on paper or on a screen, can sharpen up (dare I say 'sex up') an image, and can also be placed in a controllable slideshow sequence, giving the viewer a truer sense of the whole production passing by, cat-walk style, and preventing them from dwelling on a particular drawing that may just be your weakest.

Having advised that you keep words to a minimum, I don't think it does any harm to preface your work with some form of 'statement of intent', reflecting your philosophy or ethos. Fine artists would call this an 'artist statement' – and perhaps there isn't a theatre-design equivalent – but let's call it your 'agenda' or, grander still, your 'manifesto'. It would state, as simply as possible (in about two hundred and fifty words), your attitude to theatre-making, design or scenography, and why you have selected these projects or images to represent your practice. You might want other people to contribute to this in that they may have a clearer idea of the character of your work, and how it might be contextualised,

than you do. For example, you could ask someone to interview you and the answers could form the basis of the
statement. You would most likely headline your website with
something akin to this anyway, and if your work were
included in a theatre-design exhibition, you would be
expected to articulate your position, at least in relation to a
particular production.

2

Exhibitions

Theatre-design exhibitions are an intriguing curiosity for the theatregoing public that visit them but cause dilemmas for the designers that show their work. Art exhibitions are usually full of objects that were made for that purpose, but exhibitions of design are a sort of value-added extra to the original project. Theatre designers have to both reinvent the ways in which their ideas are presented, and often reignite their enthusiasm for the work that has long since gone.

There are notable exceptions to this, one being architecture, in that proposals for projects can take the form of an exhibition but with the contributors competing for a commission. Theatre-design exhibitions can include models, drawings, props, puppets, costumes, documentary videos and theatre architecture projects: retelling the story of how the work was made in a totally different context, to be received by a totally different audience.

What the exhibition viewer finds absorbing is that they are given a glimpse of what (to the lay-theatregoer) is still something of a shrouded art form. It represents an echo of what had been a collective live experience in terms of reproduced visual images and largely inanimate physical objects; but this displacement seems to only add to the exhibition-goer's engagement with the rituals, conventions and mysteries of performance. The paradox of being beguiled by a scale model that miniaturises the environment in which a larger-than-life experience has happened expands the viewer's imaginative interpretation of what the event might have been, or, if the viewer has actually seen the show itself, concentrates, rekindles or relocates the memory of that event. Costumes, represented in a close-up reality, rather than distanced by the proscenium or other fictional space (even if originally viewed close-to), without the actor to wear them, almost invite the viewer to put them on – to be active rather than passive, to have a textured, even haptic[44] experience rather than a cooler, optical one.

Professional exhibitions are often curated by following the thread of a theme, whereas a theatre-design course's 'final show' exhibitions, being student-centred, and therefore more individualistic. Again, there are exceptions: the postgraduate biennial Linbury Prize is grouped into projects with particular theatre, dance and opera companies, while the national student exhibitions the world over which then progress to the Prague Quadrennial are often pulled together under some form of conceptual umbrella. The exhibition catalogues, which serve as a snapshot of the period covered by the show, are fascinating to look back at to see how the scope, language and technique of design is evolving through each generation's response to their Zeitgeist.

Much like the rules of making a folio, remember that an exhibition, among many things, is also a consumer product. You will need to tailor your work to what you judge to be the average attention span of the viewer here too. Put yourself in their shoes: how long do you spend in front of any exhibit and its accompanying text, such as something you'd find in the Natural History, V&A or Science museums? If you hold viewer for five minutes, you'll be lucky. So, to that end, you first have to 'grab' your audience – make them stop and then keep them in front of your work. The 'wow factor' that will pull someone across the room can come in very different guises. It could be any of these:

- Colour (particularly lighting).
- Contrast (also involving light, such as strong silhouettes).

- Movement (mechanics or animatronics).

- Minimal, stark images.

- Large, magnified or other faces/bodies.

This last possibility works on the same principle as a poster, in that faces, and eyes in particular (for obvious reasons), fix the viewer and lure them in. Having at least one large image will pull the visitor towards more subtle elements of your work that need close attention or more time to absorb.

What should you write in the way of captions or commentary, and how much can the viewer digest? This is an ongoing challenge for many exhibitors and curators. An exhibit should be explicit in that it should tell its own story and be in an accessible form, however complex the ideas. Like your folio pages, a verbal account of how you did something, what you were aiming to achieve when you approached the project and what it finally was as an experience for an audience, is hard to nail down, but you have to be rigorous and disciplined about this task. On the other hand, if your attitude is 'Well, you just had to be there!', leave it visual.

You may well have a chance to expand your thoughts in a catalogue of the exhibition, and you can always hedge your bets by having some form of handout near your work, but if you're tempted to do this, you have to first ask yourself, '*Who am I doing it for?*' If your motivation for entering the exhibition is to attract attention from a director, I doubt that an essay will be effective – viewers know their own taste and, person to person, you'll either have 'that' ingredient they're looking for, or not. Most theatre designers participate simply because it feels good to be part of a fraternity, 'in the swim'; and, frankly, these are one of the few times that this disparate breed of theatre animal actually drinks at the same watering hole.

There is an aspect of theatre-design exhibitions that, thankfully, is being gradually challenged – that of the framed proscenium model box. Often tucked away along endless corridors and behind bland screens with rectangular holes to peer into, fine individual work can sadly be rendered battery-farmed. Designers and the designers of exhibitions are now thinking 'out of the box' and often using integrated technology (such as Pico mini-projectors) to animate three-dimensional work. My advice is to give your set designs a new lease of life from the rigours and function of their original purpose. Instead, think of them as sculptural forms as much as possible, perhaps physically connecting them to real-scale objects from the original show and reinventing them for their new context (see photograph overleaf). In an effort to connect with the onlooker, there is also now a proliferation of flat-screen presentations to enrich the work in form of televisual documentaries. Beware though: the same 'rules of engagement' apply. Keep it punchy: TV or film trailers and commercials are likely to be your best role models here.

If nothing else, a forthcoming exhibition is a good reason to hang on to an original model or drawings. So if you think a project may have a future life in an exhibition, make sure everyone knows that you want to *save the model* before you launch into the production process. Delicate scale models have a nasty habit of being 'deconstructed' by technicians and builders to (not unreasonably, but all the same maddeningly) take a closer look at whichever element they're particularly interested in. Before you know it, that precious and expensive perfect miniature world is broken up and scattered to the winds – a sometimes hopeless situation, rendering any sort of retrieval impossible, or at least doubly costly. In any event, saving your model is good practice as, if nothing else, you might want to recycle anything from materials to model furniture for future use.

Exhibit of the author's design for *Richard III* at World Stage Design
2013. It incorporated the original model box, a short edit of music from
the show, video projection into the model to animate the scene changes
and was (literally) supported by an original puppet prop: the Prince's
severed heads in a jar of liquid. The costume designs scrolled in a
digital photo frame. (The rendering for *Richard III*'s set is in Part Four.)

An even more challenging notion is coming to terms with what you do with these objets d'art after the exhibition. They tend to be bulky and you were probably much relieved to have released it from your already cramped studio to make premium space for your current work. It's at this stage that you will question what will be useful to your (and the) future. Do you have an audience, unknown to you now, in years to come?

3

Archiving

When you are starting out as a theatre designer it's hard to imagine why you might want to keep every last stick of model, scrap of drawing or scribbled note. You will probably be filing most of your first projects into the 'putting it down to experience' category, and so, apart from making the most of your material for your current folio, the other stuff may seem to be completely surplus to the ongoing requirements of your career. Digital media in this context are a blessing in terms of being able to make a compact and orderly organisation of recent past projects, but the nature of our communication by emails, texts and other instant messaging render them easily deletable in contrast to what would have been a stack of notebooks, diaries and letters. Having said that, older archives of designer's work in the pre- or early digital age may only contain the one incoming half of a dialogue with, say, a director, rather than the two-way (or more) 'threads' that we now have available.

There are important reasons for you to save your work process and product in as practical a form as possible. Perhaps the clearest and most immediate of these is that you will never know whether the project has actually reached the end of its lifespan or whether it may have future possibilities. Sometimes the resurrection of a project can happen not only months but years after its original performances. In this case there are two good reasons for keeping as good a record as you can.

The first is that you may simply forget what you did the first time round and that you may also need to use some of the material (drawings and models) again. Also, a production's 'second wind' gives you an opportunity to retrace your steps, including your thought processes, in order to develop 'unfinished business' or apply your original ideas to new circumstances.

The second and medium-term reason for archiving is that contemporary theatre-design exhibitions are now often curated thematically, and both the organisers and the viewing public are hungry for a greater analysis of *why* the work was created in a particular way as well as *what* the final result was, along with possibly *how* it was made. Representing your thinking and methods often requires a little critical distance, so you will need your archived material to help you relive a sequence of events, including collaborative decisions, that would otherwise have been lost or submerged. The process can be a revelation. You can almost guarantee that the perception of your work executed in the present will be transformed by an unknown future retrospective view. It places us all in a timeline that stretches back to the ancient Greeks and, over the course of a few short years, reveals the conceptual strands and visual signatures that characterises your work as in some way unique. The more rigourous you can be in analysing and possibly contextualising your work, the more likely it is that your exhibit will engage the viewer beyond that instantaneous 'wow factor', and be an attractive proposition for the exhibition's cumulative impact.

Lastly, we are all the product of our experience, tempered by our genes and circumstances. Taking the long view, for most of us there is a fundamental human need to leave something behind – a legacy. The ephemeral nature of live performance can, over time, frustrate that need. Designers have an advantage over others in a creative team in that they can retain more hard evidence as confirmation of their part in an act of theatre-making – particularly the process that leads to it. Directors, for example, know that their hours of work in the rehearsal room can simply evaporate. To give any sort of urgency to conserving your working material in the long term, I believe you have to picture who you are keeping things for: seeing your art through the viewfinder of your future scope. It may be simply for family, to pass on your experiences to another generation, the unknown student, or otherwise to calm the occasional bout of angst over your mortality. The renowned Buddhist monk Venerable Beop-jeong, a plain-speaking pragmatist and philanthropist, advised that we give our worthwhile possessions to the next generation while we are still alive as they are less likely to refuse them!

It's easy to say to ourselves, '*I'll save that when the time comes*', but time, of course, exists in and of itself; neither coming or going. It's the people, things and images within time that appear, and can just as easily disappear. We have become accustomed to speaking of theatre-making in terms of ephemera or transience, and have indulged in its imme-diacy in an inconstant world that we cannot predict. Theatre acts themselves provide the perfect existential metaphor, but most practitioners and scholars of theatre will now agree it's our artistic and social responsibility to hang on to at least the traces of what we've produced, none of which devalues the power of the original theatrical moments.

Epilogue:
Where Does Theatre Design Go from Here?

Educating the mind and training the hand

The days of theatre-design courses in higher education being run by top-flight designers are over. It's unlikely that we'll see the likes of Ralph Koltai, Philip Prowse or Alison Chitty leading a programme that has its foundations set firmly on professional experience handing on a legacy from designer to designer, generation to generation. Formal design education is now largely in the grip of university traditions and, as such, is bound by increasingly structured academic regulation and an emphasis on following a practice to think *through* its activities rather than think *of* them. Gone, too, is a face-to-face engagement with a 'school of thought'. These tangible and influential timelines are being consigned to the history books that are now emerging from new scholarly interest in how theatre design has evolved in recent decades. The picture is not a gloomy one, however: like all theatre-making it's just evolving, and that's what has kept it alive for millennia.

The theatre-design student of tomorrow will undertake their apprenticeship through increasingly mixed means. They will find their learning and training in a pick 'n' mix of short courses, workshops, masterclasses, placements and internships alongside the established further- and higher-education routes. Postgraduate courses will be where the autonomous theatre-makers devise a strategy for themselves but are also offered opportunities to make interdisciplinary partnerships that can lead to longer-term collaborations.

[333]

Technology in the studio will continue to change the relationships between director and designer, and designer and assistant. The close working relationships will most likely dissipate, like stars in an expanding universe, still affecting each other but not in the tight orbits they once had. Models and drawings will continue to play a major role in the discovery and communication of ideas, but the increasing sophistication and speed of technology will leave fewer and fewer opportunities for reflection together, and for the wonder of actual things being actually made – the interpretative act by craftsmen and women. Designs will flow from machine to machine, from vector to grain of plastic to CNC cutter, without the human touch – efficient (perhaps) in its process, but adding less to the possibilities of thinking through manual dexterity and therefore perhaps also to the substance of theatre as a humane, tactile activity.

Technology in, for and of performance

Writing in the second decade of the twenty-first century, it's more tempting now than ever before to view the future in terms of technology either dominating or at least being a threat to the medium of theatre. For instance, a decade or so ago, many designers believed that by now we would be strapped to our computers exclusively making models onscreen. That's proved to be not the case (as yet); not because we can't but because the collaborative processes through which we develop designs need to have elements of live, one-space interaction, in order for us not to forget that that's what the medium of theatre relies on to distinguish it from conventional cinema – so the physical model in one form or another lives on for now.

There is no doubt that video imagery in live productions is rapidly on the increase. It lends itself to theatre in that what audiences come to see is an experience with a rich and fluid layering of overlapping worlds – simultaneously fictitious but also physically present, framed and shaped by design. Projected video, whether live feed or recorded, and when used well, simply deepens that richness and adds to theatre's complex visual language. What will be interesting is how that mix of media is folded back to the cinema, giving purely mechanical media an immediacy and richness approaching theatre – von Trier and Tarantino have touched on it in differing ways.

The streaming of live performance to cinemas will also probably proliferate in years to come. Massive advances in the technologies used to record it from the stage, particularly sound, have made the event's reception far less alienating and displaced. Its success now relies on what the audience want from it. Yes, it's live, but then so are sporting events on TV – perhaps that's what it's closer to than the essence of theatre. If you are going for a good story, you'll be none the poorer for being in a cinema and it will probably be a lot more comfy, but you'll be *consuming* the event rather than being immersed in or experiencing it, and you'll be giving up your editorial privileges of choosing to gaze at something else on stage, or even the fascination of people-watching in the audience: of being part of the human zoo. Designers will have to be a little more savvy about how these transmissions 'work', the camera angles, the detailing, etc. The greater sophistication of these production values in the pursuit of greater authenticity will, paradoxically, make the viewing of them (for all we can do is view) more cinematic. What is to be applauded is that it may nudge people towards the theatre that might rarely go or simply can't afford to, and that's particularly true of opera (live from New York's Met, for example), but in a country and community as small and concentrated as the UK, it mustn't absolve major companies from touring live shows, *live*.

Collaborative futures

Designers in the UK collaborate with more people than any other member of a production machine – so communication and its many interfaces, including the best traditional means (talking and drawing), is the 'engine oil' of a stage designer's work. The efficient generation of information suggests linear consumption of it, but good theatre design and a good theatre experience can't travel on a 'one-way ticket'. A conversation prompts a sketch, a sketch grows to a proposal, a proposal to negotiation and the result fills the stage for our audiences – the audience then responds in the ever-increasing voices of blogs, online journals, tweets and Facebook. The process is cyclical, and it's revolving with widening and increasing velocity.

Ensemble companies, or groups that aspire to an ensemble ethos, will become more common – the sense of unity of experience for both performers and audience is what will be unique for the theatregoer in an increasingly detached, screen-based entertainment industry. Design will play its part in securing that: making spaces and presenting images that continue to bind people and places together using what is fast becoming a worldwide visual vocabulary. The term 'ensemble' is often overused because its ethic is not easy to accurately pin down. There are probably as many definitions of the word as there are practitioners. Here are some that I've heard, most of which come close to describing an aspect of the experience of working in one or watching the work of one, but none managing to be definitive:

'All the performers are on stage all the time.'

'The whole story is told by a chorus.'

'All the performers have an equal voice in the rehearsal process – it's "democratic".'

'It's a "collective" – all the actors are paid the same.'

I have always been struck by the more far-sighted interpretation of the word, which is common in North America: 'ensemble' includes all contributors, from backstage technicians to the box-office staff. Here I'll restate the one that comes close to articulating its ethos, I think...

'The whole production is greater than the sum of its parts.'

The possibility of the 'ensemble' being not only the privilege of actors in a rehearsal room but also embracing everyone in the entire organisation, is now a real possibility if we want it... *do we?*

Mighty technological leaps have been made over the last decade in the production of lighting, sound and particularly video projection for live events. The creative possibilities have multiplied not only because of the relative cost-reduction of sophisticated hardware and software, but also because of the increase in rapid-response time that designers and technicians have in their relationships with directors, choreographers, composers and performers. Fluid communication can promote transparency and inclusion, as distinct from hierarchical, director-led methods – a more equitable sharing of the creative process is beginning to happen in UK theatre.

The traditional design presentation to a company can now be filmed and podcasted for the duration of a changing creative process. The Dropbox folder gives an autonomy to the design team that relieves the director of continuous command, although not, perhaps still, ultimate authority. Orchestras, however, are known to not need a conductor.

Digital media are now a vital part of the twenty-first century's need for empathy in a progressively interdependent world across an increasingly compact population. Making theatre is a consummate model of productive dependency, and it has been said that a theatre company is a world in microcosm, with all its contradictions of utopian promise and dystopian tragedy.

> We live in what is, but we find a thousand ways not to
> face it. Great theatre strengthens our faculty to face it.
>
> *Thornton Wilder, author and playwright*

If this has a grain of truth, the steady infusion of digital processes within vividly designed theatrical experiences will no doubt play its part in fostering a greater common understanding and respect of each other's diverse cultures, disciplines and, both literally and metaphorically, viewpoints.

Appendices

Endnotes

1. For example, The Blue Blouse agitprop troupes that proliferated throughout the Soviet Union and subsequently toured to Erwin Piscator's theatre in Berlin, thereafter making an impact, throughout Germany, on the turbulent political and social climate of the late 1920s.
2. It's frustrating to note, however, that, according to a *Guardian* survey in 2012, although theatre-design training is populated by a vast majority of women, only 23% of creative teams in England's top publicly funded theatres are women.
3. I've used the term 'scenography' sparingly throughout for similar reasons, but mainly because of the book's (refreshingly) straightforward title. I wonder how many people would have picked it up if it were called *So You Want to Be a Scenographer?*
4. In the heyday of regional repertory theatre, the turnover of productions was high and so actors often made a personal contribution to the acquisition of costume elements, such as spectacles, shoes and even facial hair.
5. For example, *Les Demoiselles d'Avignon* (1907).
6. This notion was later tested and developed in a series of performances by Tadeusz Kantor (1915–1990): the most celebrated of these being *Dead Class* (1975). You can read more about related ideas in his *The Autonomous Theatre* (1963) manifesto.
7. For example, Shen Teh's doubling as her 'cousin', Shui Ta, in *The Good Person of Szechwan*.
8. For example, *Triadic Ballet* (1922).
9. Using tones and rhythms, the aesthetics of music speaks to us through abstract messages. Over the twentieth century, visual art increasingly abandoned representational, figurative and other observational views of the outer world

to use form, structure, line and colour in the exploration of inner responses to matter – expressing this through painting and sculpture, and when fine artists worked in the theatre, stage design.

10. This true of all theatre design – creativity must finally drive logistics! The paradox is, of course, that sometimes 'the exception proves the rule' and logistics can prompt if not art, then innovation. In opera, particularly, a designer will often not be aware of what can be technically and therefore financially achieved in another country and for that matter, in another currency.

11. Sometimes you and the production manager have to agree on where to include sound baffles in the design or above stage to bounce the voice into the auditorium.

12. Opera is an incredibly expensive business. Opera companies can't hope to cover their costs from ticket sales, so all administrators can do is to make sure their losses are kept to a minimum – they are usually very heavily subsidised by either the state or donations, or a combination of both.

13. Dramas are, of course, filmed, but that usually only reveals what the audience saw, rather than how and why the production worked.

14. In classical ballet, this depends on the traditions of how the dancers are trained, but is chiefly concerned with effortless extension, elevation and the line through the body. Diaghilev, for example, worked from that tradition and tested its boundaries, having a huge impact on how ballets were designed both physically and visually.

15. Contemporary-dance traditions, concerned with the physical connection to the ground, weight, gravity and pushing against something, can also be recorded by formal notation, e.g. Kinetography Laban or Benesh Movement Notation (dance script).

16. A 'personal drawing' in this context means simply a drawing to explore the space. This may not be an expert representation in the classical sense, but more a discovery and recording of its detail, which will include its past, from creation (or before!) to present, its original designer's aspirations, any subsequent human marks, and general wear and tear.

17. Sidi Larbi Cherkaoui and Antony Gormley's *Sutra*, entered for PQ11, is a good place to start exploring recordings of contemporary artists involved in dance works.

18. I'll exclude singers' voices as they are usually assisted by a sound system.

19. Other related theories include those of cognitive anthropologists Jean Lave and Étienne Wenger (Communities of Practice). If how this works psychologically interests you as much as sociologically, you might try dipping into Gestalt theory.

20. I know this for a fact as I have seen design ideas that have seemingly emerged from our 'unique' relationship appear a few days later in another show of theirs... and I've diplomatically kept the observation to myself, knowing that all artists borrow and develop the ideas of others: often unconsciously.

21. Frustratingly at times, however, a fleeting moment of inspiration, a press cutting or downloaded video clip, can sometimes have a longer-lasting effect!

22. Read more about the Linbury Prize for Stage Design in the Useful References, Publications and Organisations section elsewhere in the Appendices.

23. There are always exceptions to these statements, of course! I'm mindful of, for example, Rae Smith's animated drawings projected throughout the production of *War Horse* that so eloquently connected the performers, puppets and scenic world through the idea of a diarist's sketchbook come to life.

24. 'A sentence is but a cheverill glove to a good wit: how quickly the wrong side may be turned outward!' Feste in *Twelfth Night* explains the manipulation of words that is also a (rare Shakespearean) hint for a costume idea.

25. If you do want to find out and practise the techniques of single- and two-point perspective, as well as the use of tonal shading to depict depth through aerial perspective, there are plenty of 'teach yourself' books and videos on the market or free on the web. It is a fascinating topic that is now rarely taught in art schools and, with a bit of patience and dedication, can certainly inform your free-hand confidence and skill. One of the best online resources can be found at www.perspective-book.com.

26. Sometimes called 'gridding up', this is an ancient method of transposing a relatively small image to a much larger one through overlaying a measured grid of squares onto the original and then applying the same number of squares and their contents to a larger area. By distorting the second grid, weird exaggerations can be made of the original image, such as a fish-eye lens effect or a view through water. Try it… it's *wild*!

27. One the very best is Gary Thorne's *Technical Drawing for Stage Design* – clear, authoritative and peppered with both industry-based and more general but useful geometric exercises.

28. Although we, in Europe, may regard Brecht as one of the earliest advocates of stripping back the stage to its essence, Thornton Wilder integrated 'open staging' into the central fabric of his play *Our Town* in the late 1930s, lending it both a striking dignity and radical humanitarianism.

29. Simon Higlett's drawing (page 148) has many attributes. It not only has a vivid sense of characterisation, it is a working document: it stresses the designer's priorities and you can also see, halfway down the jacket, a visible change made to its length after collaborative discussions.

30. The most well-preserved of these can be seen in the Czech Republic at the castle in Český Krumlov and another, an opera house in Sweden, at Drottningholm Palace, both built in the mid-seventeenth century. A fine original example of a later rococo proscenium theatre is the Confidencen, also in Sweden at in the Ulriksdal Palace in Solna.

31. From the excellent but now out of print *Designing for the Dancer* (1982).

32. The counter position is best summed up by Thornton Wilder, 'I regard the theatre as the greatest of all art forms, the most immediate way in which a human being can share with another the sense of what it is to be human.'

33. See the Useful References, Publications and Organisations section elsewhere in the Appendices.

34. A noteworthy citation from Jones's inspiring (if a little 'wordy') book, *The Dramatic Imagination: Reflections and Speculations on the Art of the Theatre* (1941) in this context is, 'A stage setting is not a background; it is an environment.'

35. Guidelines and regulations for the frequency and duration of these, for performers, stage management and technicians, are established through periodically updated agreements between the unions (Equity or BECTU) and theatre managers' associations (SOLT/TMA/ITC).

36. Actors, like dancers, rely on repetition to fix much of their physical performance in their muscle memory. Health and safety assessments of risk to actors and others factor in rehearsal as a form of training to surmount the possibilities of harm, so disrupting this is both irresponsible and unprofessional.

37. There are instances of critics having a stab at playwriting, and they've also mischievously been challenged to direct productions (although to my knowledge never to design one – perhaps because they don't care enough about it), but these efforts have rarely been received with anything close to critical acclaim. Incidentally, the irony has not escaped me that I, as a designer, should be *writing* this book.

38. I stop short of saying 'art work' here in the context of permanence or semi-permanence. Whether it is or not depends on each person's criteria for art, be they a lay-theatregoer, gallery visitor or professional. After over a century, Edward Gordon Craig's definition of art in both performance and design contexts (Gordon Craig, E. (1911) *On the Art of the Theatre*. Ed. Franc Chamberlain. Routledge, 2008) still holds up as both a viable but endlessly debatable position.

39. These are, in a sliding scale of economy, Society of London Theatres (SOLT), which deals with commercial West End and opera productions, Theatrical Management Association (TMA), which deals with larger regional repertory and touring companies, and the Independent Theatre Council (ITC), which deals with smaller fringe venues.

40. This is the standard agent's rate. The occasional project may vary from this, but it's a rarity. The procedure is that your fee, paid in installments as outlined above, is sent to your agent who extracts ten per cent of the gross amount and also deducts VAT. This net sum is then sent to you. The business logic runs thus: if your agent has managed to improve the fee (and other payments) than you were initially offered by

that ten per cent, then they have, in effect, paid for themselves. You can also offset their commission against income tax.

41. Studios are usually more constantly and softly lit if the main windows face north (assuming you live and work in the Northern Hemisphere).

42. There are many apocryphal tales of lighting designers installing fridges and other 'creature comforts' into their desk – perfectly understandable, of course: lighting, sound and video designers are, more than anyone else in the creative team, metaphorically nailed to the spot.

43. It's often a good idea to keep the notes for the scenic painter separate or draw them up as a separate list later, since the scenic artist is often not present during the technical or dress rehearsals, preferring to have a dedicated 'paint call' while the stage has little or no activity (often overnight or early in the morning) for all the reasons covered previously, so they will need an accumulated to-do list of their own.

44. Haptics is any form of non-verbal communication involving touch.

45. Valid at the time of writing (2015).

46. I am all too aware of my own use of these terms in this book – and the same conditions apply!

Glossary of Theatre Design and Other Stage Terms

ABOVE To move upstage (e.g. Hamlet sat *above* the grave).

ACT DROP A scenic cloth flown in at the end of an act.

AD LIB An improvised action (usually spoken) during a show.

ADVANCE BAR A lighting bar hung in the auditorium very close to the stage.

AMP An abbreviation for equipment used to amplify sound (not to be confused with 'amp', a unit of electricity!).

APRON A section of stage extending beyond the proscenium towards the audience.

ARENA A type of open stage – three hundred and sixty degree or thrust.

ASM Assistant stage manager.

AUDITORIUM Where the audience's seats are.

BACKCLOTH OR BACKDROP A 2D flown cloth, usually behind 3D scenic objects.

BACKING FLATS Flats behind a scenic element or space.

BACKLIGHT A light that illuminates objects or actors from behind.

BACKSTAGE A part of theatre building to the side of or behind the stage.

BAND CALL   A rehearsal for an orchestra or musical band.

BAND ROOM   The musicians' changing room; also an offstage playing space.

BAR (BARREL)   A metal tube used for hanging scenery or lanterns.

BAR BELLS   The warning to front-of-house and bar staff that the interval is ending.

BARN DOOR   A device of four flaps to adjust the spread of light on a Fresnel lantern.

BASTARD PROMPT   When the prompt desk is on the actor's right (stage right), whereas it is usually stage left.

BATTEN   1) The length of wood attached to cloth to keep it taut; 2) A group of floodlights.

BAUPROBE (opera)   A rehearsal of scenic elements moving in theatre light.

BEGINNERS   The call given to cast/crew at the start of a play.

BELOW   To move downstage (e.g. Hamlet sat *below* the grave).

BIBLE   The complete record of costuming a show, compiled by the costume supervisor.

BIRDY   A sort of small lighting instrument with no focus – very handy in tight spaces.

BLEACHERS   Stepped seating blocks that can be retracted for storage.

BLOCK/BLOCKING   The composing and recording of movements on stage.

BOARD   An abbreviation for the lighting-control board.

BOOK   The script or prompt book (prompt copy), compiled and used by the DSM.

BOOK FLAT   A hinged couple of flats or screens.

BOOM   A vertical lighting bar.

BORDER   A flown scenic element used in masking.

BOX SET   An architectural interior set built from scenic 'flats'.

BOUNCE CLOTH   A white cloth used to reflect light onto a material, usually a rear projection screen.

BRACE   A diagonal piece of strengthening material.

BRAIL/BREAST   The adjustment of flown bars, up- or downstage, by tensioned ropes.

BREAKING DOWN   The artistic process of ageing costume, props or scenery.

BRIDGE   A catwalk above auditorium or stage, often used as a lighting position.

BUILD   An increase in sound or light levels.

BUSINESS   Actions often invented and performed by actors.

BUTTERFLY TABS   Curtains fixed at top and drawn in from sides.

CAD   Computer-aided design.

CALL   1) A scheduled rehearsal; 2) An abbreviation for a curtain call.

CANS   The headphones used by the backstage technical team.

CARPENTER (SCENIC, DEPUTY, MASTER)   Makers of scenery.

CENTRE LINE   An architectural line, shown on ground plan, that bisects the stage space.

CGI   Computer-generated image.

CHANNEL   A connected circuit in a lighting or sound system.

CINEMOID   A type of lighting colour gel.

CIRCUIT   The means by which a lantern can be identified and connected to a dimmer.

CLAMP   Normally used to attach lanterns to bars.

CLEAT   A hooked metal fixing used for tying sash lines.

CLOTH   A complete scenic canvas backdrop or perhaps gauze.

COLOUR CALL   A list of gels for a lighting design.

COME DOWN   When the event ends.

COMPANY CALL   When everyone's needed for a rehearsal or meeting.

CONTROL ROOM/BOX   From where lighting and sound is controlled.

COSTUME CHAT   The meeting of designer and costume supervisor (and sometimes director) to discuss character and costume.

COSTUME PARADE   A costume check of the whole cast, on- or offstage.

COSTUME PLOT   A spreadsheet with a matrix of characters and scenes.

COSTUME RAIL   A mobile frame on which to hang costumes in labelled groups.

CRADLE   The carriage in which stage weights run up and down in the counterweight system.

CROSS-FADE   A change when lighting/sound levels are increased, while others are lowered.

CROSSOVER   A passage for actors to get across stage.

CSM   Company stage manager.

CUE   A verbal or physical signal for an action or effect to begin.

CUE LIGHTS   A system of lights used to give 'cues'.

CUE SHEET   A list of effects.

CUE TO CUE   A rehearsal during which action is reduced to technical cues.

CURTAIN   At front of the stage, called the 'tabs'.

CURTAIN UP/DOWN   The beginning and end of a performance.

CUT   An edit.

CUT CLOTH   A collaged 2D scenic piece with open or semi-transparent areas.

CUTTING TABLE   A large table to cut costume pieces on – usually at standing height.

CYCLORAMA (OR 'CYC')   A cloth or vinyl backing used to accept light as pure colour or a sky.

DEAD   1) The marked position of scenery or equipment; 2) Anything no longer needed.

DECIBEL (dB)   A measurement of sound.

DE-RIG   See RIG.

DESK   1) The prompt desk – operated by the person running the show (usually the DSM); 2) A sound desk – the sound operator's control console.

DIFFUSION GEL   Also called 'frost': it softens light.

DIMMER   A device that controls electricity passed to lanterns.

DIPS/DIP-TRAP   The hatches/troughs/channels at side of stage containing sockets.

DISTRESSING   See BREAKING DOWN.

DOCK   The area at side or rear of stage for storing scenery.

DOCK DOOR   The door or shutter that gives access to scenery.

DOUBLE-PURCHASE   A system of blocks and ropes that gears a counterweight to half that of the scenery it is supporting.

DOUGHNUT REVOLVE   A moving circular inner platform with a secondary outer one that can revolve at different speeds and directions.

DOWNSTAGE   The area of stage nearest the audience.

DRENCHER   A perforated pipe that, in the event of a fire, will spray water onto the back of the safety curtain.

DRESS CIRCLE   The raised balcony seating immediately above stalls.

DRESSER   A crew member who helps with dressing actors – particularly during quick changes.

DRESSING A SET   Placing objects in a precise place.

DRESS REHEARSAL   A full run of the event with costume, lighting and sound.

DSM   Deputy stage manager.

DUB   To reproduce sound from one recording to another.

EFFECT   As in sound/lighting/scenic effects: something significant to the event.

ELECTRICIAN (CHIEF, DEPUTY, ASSISTANT)   Responsible for lighting.

ELEVATION   A technical drawing showing side view. See also FRONT ELEVATION.

ELEX (OR 'LX')   Electrical things or the lighting department.

ELEX (OR 'LX') TAPE   Tape available in various colours.

ELLIPSOIDAL   A type of reflector used in profile spots.

ENGINEER   Usually 'sound', but can also be 'lighting'.

ENTRANCE/EXIT   A point in a script/physical space where performers come/go from view.

EQ   An abbreviation for the equalisation of sound.

FADE   A diminishing light or sound.

FADER   A means of controlling the intensity of lights or sound.

FALSE PROS   An addition to the proscenium arch, making it smaller.

FEEDBACK   When a mic picks up its own signal from a speaker.

FITTING   The trying on of a made, found or hired costume.

FIT-UP   The installation of equipment and scenery.

FLAME-PROOFED   Treated with a flame-inhibiting substance.

FLASH UP   A method of testing lanterns.

FLAT   A unit of hard scenery.

FLIES   The area above and to one side of the stage where flown scenery is kept.

FLIPPER   A small piece of flat scenery hinged to a larger piece.

FLOAT MICS   The microphones placed along front of stage.

FLOATS   The footlights.

FLOODS   Lanterns with no lens and therefore not focused.

FLOOR CLOTH   A painted soft flooring, usually canvas.

FLOWN   Scenery or equipment that has been 'flown' into the flies.

FLY   To raise scenery above audience sight level.

FLY FLOOR   The technical gallery where the flown scenery is operated from.

FLYMAN   A crew member operating flying equipment.

FLY (OR PIN) RAIL   A heavy rail on the fly gallery equipped with cleats for the ropes.

FLY TOWER   Structure above stage containing flying equipment, such as pulleys.

FOCUS (SESSION)   The adjustment of lighting/projection equipment.

FOH   Abbreviation of front of house.

FOLDBACK   Sound returned to the performer.

FOLLOW SPOT   A large profile spotlight with an operator (used to be a 'lime').

FORE-STAGE   The area in front of the tabs.

FRENCH BRACE   A collapsible brace hooked to the back of a scenic flat.

FRENCH FLAT (FRENCHMAN)   A large solid scenic flat.

FREQUENCY   The number of times a sound vibrates.

FRESNEL   A spotlight with Fresnel lens that gives soft edge.

FRONT ELEVATION   A drawing of a scenic element (or the entire set) as seen from the front.

FROST   See DIFFUSION GEL.

FX   Abbreviation for 'effects'.

GAFFER TAPE   A strong fabric-based tape.

GAIN   The 'master' volume control on sound mixer.

GATE   Optical centre of profile spotlight.

GAUZE   A meshed scenic cloth or vinyl used with light for 'vanishing' effects.

GEL   A sheet of coloured lighting film inserted in front of a lantern (originally made from gelatine).

GENERAL (opera)   A dress rehearsal with orchestra and invited audience.

GENIE TRAP   A mechanised trap where the actor shoots up through a stage floor.

GET-IN   When a company installs the set and lighting for a show.

GET-OUT   When a company removes the set and lighting for a show.

GOBO   A metal slide placed in the gate of a lantern that throws a shadowy pattern.

GODS   The highest balcony of audience seating.

GRAVE (GHOST) TRAP   A body-length trapdoor in the stage.

GREASEPAINT   A generic term for stage foundation make-up – removed by cold cream.

GREEN ROOM   The cast/crew recreation room.

GRID   Frames in the fly tower from which flying equipment is suspended.

GROUND PLAN   Bird's-eye view technical drawing of stage.

GROUNDROW   Floodlight battens placed on stage.

(THE) HALF   The half-hour warning given to cast/crew thirty-five minutes (30 + 5) before curtain-up.

HANAMICHI   From kabuki, a catwalk-like jetty from the stage into the auditorium.

HEADER   A horizontal flying piece.

HEADS (UP)!   A warning shouted if anything is dropped from above.

HEMP   A type of natural rope used in theatre for flying.

HEMP/HEMP SET   A traditional method of flying using hemp ropes and no counterweights.

HOUSE   The auditorium and/or audience.

HOUSE LIGHTS   The lights illuminating the audience.

HOUSE (also 'FRONT-OF-HOUSE') MANAGER   Supervising ushers and audience.

HYDRAULIC LIFT   A platform that rises out of the stage floor using pistons.

IN-THE-ROUND   An audience seated on three hundred and sixty degrees of the stage.

IRIS   A device in the lantern gate that allows a beam size to be altered.

IRON   A fireproof metal safety curtain flown between the scenery and audience.

IRON LINE   The line on the stage where the safety curtain falls.

KEEL   A metal guide that keeps a moving scenic truck in its track.

KILL   The instruction to stop an action or effect.

LADDER   A framework in the shape of ladder; can be for lanterns used for sidelight.

LANTERN   A stage light.

LEG   A flown cloth or flat, masking side of stage.

LEVEL   The intensity of light or sound.

LIFT   A platform that usually rises out of the stage floor.

LIGHTING BOX   A cabin at the back or side of the auditorium where the lighting operator sits.

LIGHTING PLOT   Lighting-cue description.

LIMES   Old term for FOLLOW SPOTS.

LOSE   To turn something off or remove from set.

MAKE TO FINISH   Costume construction without a fitting, from maker to stage.

MAQUETTE   Another word for a scale model; often a term for an early, rough version.

MARK OUT   The temporary objects/lines on a rehearsal-room floor used to describe a set/stage.

MARK THAT   The instruction to record position of performer/object on stage.

MAROON   An electrically triggered pyrotechnic device giving the effect of explosion.

MASK   To hide from audience's sight.

MASKING   Flats/cloths used to 'mask'.

MASTER   The lever/slide which controls groups of lanterns or all light or sound.

MD   Musical director.

MIC PACK/POUCH   The elasticated sling holding a mic transmitter close to the body.

MILLIPUT   A type of modelling plastic used to create model figures and scaled shapes.

MIXER   A desk or software for mixing sound.

MODEL   A model of a stage design.

MODEL BOX   A basic model of the theatre space in which the set-design model is housed.

MULTICORE   A thick cable containing many (usually lighting) cables.

MUSLIN   The American term for a TOILE.

OFFSTAGE   The outside performance area, but not necessarily out of view.

OMNIDIRECTIONAL   A wide pick-up pattern of a microphone.

OP   Opposite prompt side, i.e. usually stage right.

OUT   A piece of scenery that has been 'flown out' to a particular height.

OVERTURE   A musical passage that starts a musical performance.

PA SYSTEM   The public-address system or any designed sound system.

PAGING   To make a call over the backstage relay.

PAINT FRAME   The frame on which cloths and gauzes are vertically stretched for painting.

PAN   To move light or sound from one place to another.

PANCAKE   A water-based stage make-up, applied with a cosmetic sponge.

PAPER A HOUSE   To give away tickets to fill an audience.

PAR CAN   A type of lantern containing a PAR lamp.

PAR LAMP   A fixed-beam lantern (Parabolic Anodised Reflector).

PASS DOOR   A door allowing access to front of house from backstage.

PASSERELLE   A walkway across or around a sunken area (e.g. around the pit).

PATCH PANEL   A panel where lighting circuits are connected and changed – 'patched'.

PERCH   A lighting position concealed behind proscenium.

PERIAKTOI   A three-sided flat that can revolve to show different painted scenes.

PERSONAL (PROP)   Small prop, retained by actor.

PHOTO CALL   A session for either posed production shots or for press photographers.

PIN HINGE   Hinge jointed by a removable pin, so that the two halves can be separated.

PIPE   An informal term for a flying bar.

PIT   The area at front/beneath stage where musicians sit.

PIT LIFT   Mechanical lift that lowers to create pit.

PLOT   Any list of cues.

PORTAL   A unit of masking or scenery that frames a space or image.

PRACTICAL   A working object onstage, such as a door or window.

PRESET   The position of scenery and effects at the start of a performance or scene.

PRESS NIGHT   The official opening of a show when the critics review it.

PRODUCTION MEETING   The meetings for staff involved in production.

PROFILE SPOT   A lantern which can be focused to produce hard or soft light.

PROMENADE   A performance with no set seating for audience.

PROMPT   The lines given to actors who have forgotten the script.

PROMPT COPY/BOOK   The master copy of the performance, including all blocking, effects and cues.

PROMPT CORNER   A place where prompter was traditionally placed, but now usually where the DSM is positioned, at the 'prompt desk'.

PROP   An abbreviation for properties. Any items used onstage that are not costume or scenery.

PROP BOX/SKIP   A place to store props.

PROP TABLE   The table situated in wings on which props are placed.

PROPS ROOM   Room for construction of props by stage managers or property master.

PS   Prompt side, usually stage left.

PYROTECHNICS   Bombs, bangs, flashes, etc.

(THE) QUARTER   The quarter-hour warning given to cast/crew twenty minutes (15 + 5) before curtain-up.

QUICK-CHANGE BOOTH   A space with chair, table and mirror constructed for fast changes in the wings or substage.

RADIO MIC   A personal microphone without power lead.

RAIN BAR   A perforated suspended pipe to make a rain effect. Fed by a mains or recycled water supply.

RAKE   The incline of the stage (or any) floor.

READTHROUGH   Usually the first meeting/reading with the full company and director.

RECORD   The plotting of a lighting cue by saving it to the lighting board.

RETURN   A recessed plane at ninety degrees to another.

REFLECTOR   A shiny surface in back of a lantern which helps throw light.

REVOLVE   A circular platform on or in the stage floor that revolves at a variety of geared speeds.

RIG   The positioning of lights (the DE-RIG is removing them).

RISER   The vertical front on a step.

RP   A rear projection screen, sometimes used as a cyclorama. (Also a B ('back') P screen.)

RUN   1) Putting scenes together in rehearsal; 2) Number of performances in production.

RUNNER   1) Used to hold down carpet edges; 2) Someone who gets anything the technical team needs.

RUNTHROUGH   A rehearsal that 'runs through' an act or the play.

SANDBAG   Used to add ballast to a flown line.

SCENIC ARTISTS   The people who paint scenery. 'Scenics' also sometimes sculpt objects.

SCISSOR LIFT   A platform that rises out of the stage floor using pivoted cross members.

SCRIM   See GAUZE.

SETTING LINE   The line past which no scenery, props or furniture may be set: usually just upstage of the safety curtain (see IRON).

SFX   Sound effects, as designed by a sound designer or, in film, a foley artist.

SHIN BUSTER   Low sidelights.

SHOE ROOM   The repository of shoes, boots and slippers in a major company.

SHOUT CHECK   A detailed check carried out by stage management to ensure all is ready.

SHUTTER   A device in a lantern used to shape the beam.

SIDE ELEVATION   A drawing of a scenic element (or the entire set) as seen from one or other of the sides.

SIGHTLINES   The angles of visibility to the stage from the audience's seats.

SILL IRON   A narrow strip of half-round metal connecting the bottom of a door frame.

SITZPROBE (opera)   Often the first rehearsal of orchestra and singers rehearsing together. The equivalent Italian term is *'prova all'italiana'*.

SIZE   A glue made from animal bones, traditionally used to harden canvas on framed flats.

SKIDS   Small solid nylon feet that help a large object be pushed across a polished floor.

SLIDERS   Screens that move across the stage on tracks in the stage floor.

SLIPS   The raised seating areas to the extreme sides of the auditorium.

SLOTS   A side-lighting position in auditorium walls.

SM   Stage manager.

SOUNDCHECK   The time on stage when recorded or live music/sound is balanced.

SOUNDSCAPE   The live or recorded underscoring of action or dialogue.

SPARK(IE)S   The lighting crew.

SPECIAL   A tightly focused lantern rigged to illuminate an actor or object in a specific position.

SPIKE   To nail something to floor.

SPILL   Unwanted light on the stage.

SPOT LINE   A line rigged from grid to fly a specific item, e.g. a lampshade.

STAGE AND ORCHESTRA (opera)   The technical rehearsal sessions dedicated to conductor, orchestra and singers.

STAGE AND PIANO (opera)   The first technical rehearsals on stage for everyone but no orchestra.

STAGE BRACE   An extending support for scenery.

STAGE CREW   Someone employed to move/operate scenery.

STAGE LEFT   The left-hand side of the stage from the actor's perspective, usually the side where the prompt is (see also BASTARD PROMPT).

STAGE RIGHT   The right-hand side of the stage from the actor's perspective.

STAGGER-THROUGH   An acting company's first runthrough of part or whole of a play in the rehearsal room.

STALLS   The seating on ground floor of auditorium.

STAR TRAP   A mechanised trap where an actor shoots through stage floor.

STRIKE   To remove object or scenery from stage.

STROBE   A pulsating light that can be fast or slow.

SUPERNUMERARY   An actor playing a variety of non-speaking roles; an 'extra'.

SWAG   Curtains with a fullness, sometimes rigged to open by ruching up.

SWING   An actor or dancer who understudies/replaces one or more parts.

TABS   curtains that can also run on a 'tab track'.

TEASER   A masking leg or short flown border.

TECH   A technical rehearsal.

TECHNICAL FITTING   A costume fitting for makers rather than the designer.

THROW   The distance between lantern and object.

THRUST STAGE   A stage with at least one back wall and with audience usually on three sides.

THUNDER SHEET   A large suspended steel sheet that sounds like thunder when shaken.

TOILE   A prototype for a constructed costume, often made from a basic cheap fabric.

TOP AND TAIL   A rehearsal in which dialogue is reduced to technical cues.

TORMENTOR   A substantial masking leg just behind the proscenium.

TRAVERSE   A staging with audience facing each other.

TREADS   Steps or stairs.

TRI-LITE   A lighting/scenic metal truss section made from triangular alloy or aluminium.

TRIM   The level of a piece of suspended scenery at the right height.

TRIPE   A thick bundle of cables from a lighting bar to offstage.

TRUCK   A platform with wheels.

TURNTABLE   See REVOLVE.

UNDERSTUDY   An actor who learns another's role in order to replace them at short notice.

UPSTAGE   The furthest area on stage from the audience.

UV   Abbreviation of ultraviolet, paint or light.

VOMITORY (OR 'VOM')   Ramped or stepped entrance onto the stage, sometimes through the audience.

WALKING UNDERSTUDY   An actor who is dedicated just to covering another's role.

WALTER PLINGE   The traditional name for an actor with more than one role.

WARDROBE   The department where costumes are maintained.

WARDROBE MAINTENANCE   The washing and repair of costume.

WARNING BELLS   Warns of interval.

WINGS   The masked sides of the stage.

WIPE   A scenic piece that continuously moves across stage to obscure an object or actor.

WORKING DRAWINGS   Process drawings made in addition to the final design.

WORKING LIGHTS   Lights used by stage crew to aid work.

Useful References, Publications and Organisations[45]

Professional Organisations

Association of British Theatre Technicians (ABTT)
www.abtt.org.uk

The ABTT campaigns on behalf of the theatre industry to ensure that legislation is appropriate to the industry's needs, and that regulations are suitably drafted and enforced. It has a training programme and produces *Sightline*, an industry journal that announces the latest innovations in technology and theatre architecture. The ABTT is the also UK centre of OISTAT (see below).

Equity (Theatre Designers) www.equity.org.uk

Equity is a trade union usually associated with protecting professional theatre and film actors, but for over twenty years it has also represented designers. It secures basic conditions of employment, minimum fees and other concerns, such as copyright protection in the case of further use of a design. It has a legal department that can represent you if a dispute finds its way to court.

Equity negotiates nationally recognised contractual terms with the three main theatre-management organisations that cover smaller fringe and more modestly funded theatres (ITC, Independent Theatre Council, www.itc-arts.org), regional repertory and major subsidised theatre companies (TMA, Theatrical Management Association, www.tmauk.org), and the commercial touring sector, including London's West End (SOLT, Society of London Theatres, www.solt.co.uk).

Annual membership is by subscription based on your level of income from contracted theatre and film work.

Society of British Theatre Designers (SBTD) www.theatre-design.org.uk

The SBTD grew out of designers' need for their field to be more fully recognised, both within and beyond the theatre industry. It soon became a lobby group for change in designers' working conditions, but in the late 1970s its members realised that a more powerful advocate in such matters would be a fully fledged union. The Society therefore secured Equity to represent their members, and this gave its leading lights the time and space to concentrate on promoting the art and culture of stage design, both in the UK and abroad. A team of now experienced members design, coordinate and fundraise for the UK and PQ (Prague Quadrennial) exhibitions.

The SBTD produces the *Blue Pages*, a quarterly magazine that helps keep members in touch and includes news, articles, guidance notes and advice on contracts and working practices, as well as details of events, exhibitions and publications.

Their website has a comprehensive directory of set, costume, lighting and other specialist designers, their agents and supplementary pages for assistant designers to advertise their skill sets.

Annual membership is by a fixed-sum subscription.

Academic Theatre-Design-Related Courses in the UK

These are the principal specialist courses in colleges, conservatoires and universities. Most of them are affiliated to the Association of Courses in Theatre Design (ACTD, actduk.wordpress.com) that meets regularly to coordinate strategic thinking for the field across the UK.

The ACTD also encourages publications and organises, in collaboration with the Society of British Theatre Designers, the student displays of work and performance events that partner the professional national and Prague Quadrennial (PQ) exhibitions.

Birmingham City University www.bcu.ac.uk

BA (Hons) Theatre, Performance and Event Design

Arts University Bournemouth aub.ac.uk

BA (Hons) Costume with Performance Design

Bristol Old Vic Theatre School www.oldvic.ac.uk

MA Professional Theatre Design

Cambridge School of Art www.cambridgeschoolofart.com

BA (Hons) Film, Television and Theatre Design

Central School of Speech and Drama, London
www.cssd.ac.uk

BA (Hons) Theatre Practice

MA Scenography

Central Saint Martins, London www.arts.ac.uk/csm
BA (Hons) Performance Design and Practice
MA Performance Design and Practice

Croydon College www.croydon.ac.uk
BA (Hons) Design and Craft for Stage and Screen

Edge Hill University (Birmingham) www.edgehill.ac.uk
BA (Hons) Design for Performance

Edinburgh University www.ed.ac.uk
BA Performance Costume
MA/MFA Performance Costume

University of Leeds www.pci.leeds.ac.uk
BA (Hons) Performance Design

Liverpool Institute for Performing Arts (LIPA)
www.lipa.ac.uk
BA (Hons) Theatre and Performance Design

London College of Fashion www.arts.ac.uk/fashion
BA (Hons) Costume Design for Performance
MA Costume Design for Performance

Nottingham Trent University www.ntu.ac.uk

BA (Hons) Theatre Design

MA Puppetry and Digital Animation

Northbrook College (Brighton) www.northbrook.ac.uk

BA (Hons) Theatre Arts

Royal Academy of Dramatic Art (*RADA*) (London)
www.rada.ac.uk

PG Dip Theatre Design

Rose Bruford College (Sidcup) www.bruford.ac.uk

BA (Hons) Theatre Design

Royal Welsh College of Music and Drama (Cardiff)
www.rwcmd.ac.uk

BA (Hons) Theatre Design

MA Theatre Design

Wimbledon College of Arts www.arts.ac.uk/wimbledon

BA (Hons) Theatre & Screen: Theatre Design

BA (Hons) Theatre & Screen: Costume Design

MA Digital Theatre

MA Theatre Design

Theatre Production Courses

Bristol Old Vic Theatre School www.oldvic.ac.uk

FdA Costume for Theatre, Television and Film

Cleveland College of Art and Design www.ccad.ac.uk

FdA Costume Construction for Stage & Screen

Liverpool Institute for Performing Arts (LIPA)
www.lipa.ac.uk

BA (Hons) Theatre and Performance Technology

Royal Conservatoire of Scotland (Glasgow) www.rcs.ac.uk

BA Technical Production Arts

Wimbledon College of Arts www.arts.ac.uk/wimbledon

BA (Hons) Theatre & Screen: Costume Interpretation

BA (Hons) Theatre & Screen: Technical Arts and Special
Effects

Non-Academic Training

Many of the universities and colleges listed above offer short
courses in stagecraft. They are usually a few days in duration and frequently operate in the summer months, taught
by educators and professionals who have connections with
longer validated courses.

International Organisations

International Organisation of Scenographers, Theatre Architects and Technicians (OISTAT) www.oistat.org

OISTAT aims to support, promote and maintain a global network of specialist practitioners, students, educators and researchers in the live performing arts. It has centres in many regions of the world and has a strong presence at the PQ every four years (see below).

OISTAT is fundamentally an organisation to exchange knowledge, share innovation, encourage experimentation and promote international collaboration in the development of live performance, its associated technologies and spaces.

On the OISTAT website, there is a useful directory of two thousand international stage terms, called 'Digital Theatre Words', in the form of a downloadable app.

Prague Quadrennial (PQ) www.pq.cz

The PQ was first created in 1967 and, as the name suggests, is based in the Czech Republic – although, along with the more recent World Stage Design organisation, reaches across the globe through regularly inviting representation from theatre artists in over seventy countries. It aims to explore and present contemporary scenography, costume, lighting, sound, architecture and the explosion of perform-ance design forms.

By mounting its ambitious four-yearly exposition in central Prague, it has continued to map the latest trends in con-temporary scenography and its applied forms in other fields. This international exhibition is the world's largest event devoted to scenography and theatre architecture. It now attracts more than 40,000 visitors over two weeks, and includes international symposia, workshops, publications databases and online projects.

United States Institute for Theatre Technology (USITT)
www.usitt.org

USITT has provided an environment for backstage theatre professionals to connect, create, share, and communicate their craft since 1960. Their office is in Syracuse, New York, and it is also the US centre of OISTAT.

USITT offers an annual award to support young designers and technicians at the beginning of their careers.

UK Organisations to Help New Designers

Jerwood Young Designers scheme

The Gate Theatre in London's Notting Hill Gate is specifically funded by the Jerwood Charitable Foundation to employ four designers per season. The idea of the scheme is to support designers in the early stages of their career. The Gate currently produces five or six shows a year, which means that Jerwood designers design most of their shows. Some designers are recent graduates from design courses, but others may have been trying to make a start in design for as much as nine or ten years but lack a significant professional profile or platform. The definition of the 'early stages' of someone's career can be somewhat nebulous and subject to opinion, but essentially the scheme exists to give a young designer the opportunity to make fully funded work. Jerwood pay the designer's fee and the production's design budget. This enables the Gate theatre to produce sets and costumes on a budget not unlike that at, for example, the Royal Court Upstairs, and fulfils the Gate's flair for impressive and ambitious visual work.

The way that the Gate sources design candidates is more ad hoc than, say, the Linbury Prize for Stage Design (see below). However, they do try to meet each designer that applies or writes to them, or they may headhunt specific designers who may be emerging through their practice or whose work may be visible through the Linbury Prize exhibition. The possible designers are then discussed with the Jerwood to determine their eligibility or potential for support.

There may be a number of reasons that the designer has crossed the boundary between 'emerging' and 'established' – it's a fine line, but the debates are rigorous and fair. When the Gate's season of productions is planned, designers will be asked onto projects that suit their aesthetic or interests, thereby introducing them to directors who they have not worked with before, which in turn enriches their network and helps a new partnership to form.

For more information on this scheme:

www.gatetheatre.co.uk/about-the-gate/jerwood-young-designers

www.jerwoodcharitablefoundation.org/the-gate-jerwood-young-designers

Linbury Prize for Stage Design

This, as the name suggests, is a design competition for which the main prize is a commission for a production – there are four of these offered each time by the various theatre, opera and dance companies involved. However, all twelve finalists have their work showcased in an exhibition mounted in the National Theatre's Lyttelton foyer, and that in itself is a worthwhile reward for the substantial effort put in by entrants.

'The Linbury' has been running since 1987 and is a biennial event that is open to the most recent graduates of UK design courses, including those who graduated in the 'gap year' between competitions. Application is by folio: the criteria are published on the web. Applicants go through rounds of folio review as well as a meeting with a panel of eminent designers and the directors/choreographers from the four theatre or dance companies in the scheme that year. The final shortlist will then be elected to compete for each company's favour.

The winners are announced at the opening of the finalists' exhibition, and there is an additional one-off cash prize, the Jocelyn Herbert Award, for design potential.

Many of the finalists have gone on to make a name for themselves in the top flight of the profession. Some the winners' experiences after the competition have been not altogether positive as they confront the pressures of making realised work to commission and when the territory of the project may have shifted from the original brief for one reason or another, but the scheme as a whole is unmatched and continues to motivate a growing number of hopefuls in a profession that has very few such opportunities for emergent designers to take flight.

For more information on this scheme:

www.linburyprize.org.uk

www.nationaltheatre.org.uk/discover/platforms/the-linbury-prize-for-stage-design-getting-started

National Theatre Studio

The NT Studio, located adjacent to the Old Vic theatre, is the experimental wing of the organisation. It promotes writers, directors, performers and designers by offering short residencies that can last anything from two weeks to three months. It's a chance to meet other creative theatre-makers and bench-test embryonic projects through a sustained period of research and development using the building and organisation as a supportive base.

Applications are invited on a project-to-project basis, and the best way to start is by contacting the studio directly on the 'contacting the studio' page of the NT website.

For more information on this scheme:

www.nationaltheatre.org.uk/discover-more/about-the-national/studio/what-we-do

Young Vic Director/Designer Network

This is a way of meeting the next generation of directors through an ongoing scheme supported by the Genesis Foundation since 2003. The Directors Program is the only scheme of its kind in the UK and, although centred on helping directors establish themselves, is also useful for young designers to ride on the their coat-tails. You have to register as a member, and the scheme also manages sessions, at which directors and designers are introduced to each other to share ideas and folios – a sort of speed-dating event.

The website also provides a resource which young directors can use to source young designers to collaborate with. Designers in return can use the site to find out about job opportunities or events available at the Young Vic and other theatres.

For more information on this scheme:

www.directors.youngvic.org

Old Vic New Voices

This scheme aims to nurture young talent in many areas of theatre production. It was started in 2001, and has an excellent track record of placing people in the industry. They produce education packs in parallel with the Old Vic main-house productions, which include sections on design.

www.oldvictheatre.com/oldvicnewvoices

Other organisations that can give you sound advice about how to achieve and maintain a life in the creative industries at large are:

IdeasTap (www.ideastap.com)

Stage Jobs Pro (www.stagejobspro.com)

Arts Jobs (www.artsjobs.org.uk)

...and for funding an arts project using small grants:

Esmée Fairburn Foundation (esmeefairbairn.org.uk)

The Leverhulme Trust (www.leverhulme.ac.uk)

The Wellcome Trust (www.wellcome.ac.uk)

Artsadmin Bursary (www.artsadmin.co.uk)

Publications

There is a growing and deepening interest in theatre-design practice, particularly the processes and methods by which visual ideas for the stage evolve in the mind and through the hand of the designer. 'How-to' books have a lengthy heritage, but these are now being complemented by many orbiting publications and websites that contextualise past work or provide an intellectual springboard for the diversity of twenty-first-century design for performance.

Designers often need answers to problems or inspiration at the drop of a hat and tend to smash 'n' grab source material, so, in order to make this far from exhaustive bibliography more user-friendly, I have loosely grouped the entries into thematic areas. The areas cross over, of course. Thus, designers often think through making, and so the more technical and manual-like publications are often imbued with profound ideas; likewise, concepts have an impact on practical methodology and visual language.

The list is by no means exhaustive, but it includes one or two esoteric backwaters, particularly of performance and costume. The depth of your interest in performance theory and performance art is very much dependent on your specialist interests or tastes, and the costume section cannot begin to cover the range of knowledge and reference required throughout a career of stage design, but it does offer a selection of general historical surveys or periods of clothing that are commonly referred to. The truth of the matter is that you will build your own library in response to your needs from project to project, and much of the visual material can be found online.

I still value, sometimes treasure, books, in that they concentrate the mind on a subject in a structured form in contrast to the 'cherry-picking' habits of surfing the net. Books may indeed finally outlive websites, or at least the rather haphazard and vulnerable means we have of cataloguing what we come across on the web each time we change a device. Ageing books also draw one's attention to the fact that we are all a product of our time so, for example, the terms 'modern age' or 'contemporary'[46] in a title almost certainly mean the book, though up to the minute when first published, will now be a historical document – but is certainly nonetheless fascinating for that.

Designers and their work

Spencer, C. (1978) *Leon Bakst*. Academy Editions.

— (1994) *Cecil Beaton: Stage and Film Designs*. John Wiley & Sons.

Georgiadis, E. (2004) *Nicholas Georgiadis: Paintings, Stage Designs* (1955–2001). Oklos.

Courtney, C. (1993/7) *Jocelyn Herbert: A Theatre Workbook*. Art Books International.

Christov-Bakargiev, C. (2004) *William Kentridge*. Skira Editore.

Backemeyer, S. ed. (2004) *Ralph Koltai: Designer for the Stage*. Nick Hern Books.

Pinkham, R. (1983) *Oliver Messel*. V&A.

Aronson, A. (2014) *Ming Cho Lee: A Life in Design*. Theatre Communications Group.

Unruh, D. (2006) *The Designs of Ming Cho Lee*. Broadway Press.

Mullin, M. (1996) *Design by Motley*. Associated University Press.

Durbin, H. & Krueger, B. (2014) *The Designs of Ann Roth*. USITT.

Scarfe, G. (1992) *Scarfe on Stage*. Hamish Hamilton.

Blumenthal, E. (2007) *Julie Taymor: Playing with Fire*. Harry N. Abrams.

Unruh, D. (2012) *The Designs of Tony Walton*. USITT.

Safir, M.A. (2011) *Robert Wilson from Within*. Flammarion.

Hetzer-Molden, K. (2000) *Erich Wonder, Bühnenbilder/Stage Design*. Hatje Cantz.

Interviews with designers and other online resources

Arts and Humanities Data Service (AHDS)
http://www.ahds.rhul.ac.uk/ahdscollections/docroot/shakespeare/playslist.do

British Library. National Life Stories· An Oral History of British Theatre Design ·
http://www.bl.uk/reshelp/findhelprestype/sound/ohist/ohnls/nlstheatre/theatre.html

Theatre Design/Scenography

Aronson, A. (1990) *American Set Design*. Theatre Communications Group.

Aronson, A. (2005) *Looking into the Abyss: Essays on Scenography*. University of Michigan Press.

Baugh, C. (2005) *Theatre, Performance and Technology*. Palgrave Macmillan.

Docherty, P. & White, T. (1996) *Design for Performance, From Diaghilev to the Pet Shop Boys*. The Lethaby Press.

Goodwin, J. (1989) *British Theatre Design: The Modern Age*. Weidenfeld & Nicolson.

Howard, P. (2003) *What is Scenography?* Routledge.

McKinney, J.E. & Butterworth, P. (2009) *The Cambridge Introduction to Scenography*. Cambridge University Press.

McKinnon, P. & Fielding, E. (2012) *World Scenography 1975–1990*. OISTAT.

— (2014) *World Scenography 1990–2005*. OISTAT.

Smith, R. (1990) *American Set Design 2*. Theatre Communications Group.

Theatre-design exhibition catalogues and associated publications

Burnett, K. (2007) *Collaborators: UK Design for Performance 2003–2007*. SBTD.

— (2013) *World Stage Design 2013*. RWCMD.

Burnett, K. & Ruthven Hall, P. (1994) *Make Space!* Theatre Design Umbrella/SBTD.

— (2003) *2D>3D: UK Design for Performance 1999–2003*. SBTD.

Crawley, G., Farley, P. & Jump, S. (2011) *Transformation & Revelation: UK Design for Performance 2007–2011*. SBTD.

Performance theory and practice

Alrutz, M., Listengarten, J., Van Duyn Wood, M. (2012) *Playing with Theory in Theatre Practice*. Palgrave Macmillan.

Auslander, P. (2008) *Liveness: Performance in a Mediatised Culture*. Routledge (2nd edition).

Bennett, S. (2007) *Theatre Audiences: A Theory of Production and Reception*. Routledge (2nd Edition).

Bleeker, M. (2008) *Visuality in the Theatre*. Palgrave Macmillan.

Brook, P. (2008) *The Empty Space*. Penguin Modern Classics.

Carlson, M. (2003) *Performance: A Critical Introduction*. Routledge (2nd edition).

Chaudhuri, U. (2005) *Staging Place: The Geography of Modern Drama*. University of Michigan Press.

Escolme, B. (2005) *Talking to the Audience: Shakespeare, Performance, Self*. Routledge.

Etchells, T. (1999) *Certain Fragments: Contemporary Performance and Forced Entertainment*. Routledge.

Freshwater, H. (2009) *Theatre and Audience*. Palgrave Macmillan.

Jones, A. (1998) *Body Art: Performing the Subject*. University of Minnesota Press.

Lehman, H. (2006) *Postdramatic Performance*. Routledge.

Pavis, P. (2006) *Analyzing Performance: Theatre, Dance and Film*. University of Michigan Press.

Phelan, P. (1993) *Unmarked: The Politics of Performance*. London: Routledge.

Zunbrugg, N. (2004) Laurie Anderson and Meredith Monk interviews in *Art, Performance, Media: 31 Interviews*. University of Minnesota Press.

Technical theatre practice and craft

Coleman, P. (2003) *Basics: A Beginner's Guide to Stage Lighting*. Entertainment Technology Press.

James, T. (1992) *The What, Where, When of Theater Props: An Illustrated Chronology from Arrowheads to Video Games*. Better Way Books.

Thorne, G. (2003) *Stage Design: A Practical Guide*. Crowood Press.

— (2010) *Technical Drawing for the Stage*. Crowood Press.

Orton, K. (2004) *Model Making for the Stage*. Crowood Press.

Wilson, A. (2003) *Making Stage Props*. Crowood Press.

Woodbridge, P. (2000) *Designer Drafting for the Entertainment World*. Focal Press.

Theatre architecture

Ham, R. (1987) *Theatres: Planning Guidance for Design and Adaptation*. Architectural Press.

Hardy Holzman Pfeiffer Associates. (2000) *Theaters*. Images Publishing.

Leacroft, R. (1984) *Theatre and Playhouse: An Illustrated Survey of Theatre Building from Ancient Greece to the Present Day*. Methuen.

Leacroft, R. (2007) *The Development of the English Playhouse*. Methuen (2nd edition).

Mackintosh, I. (1997) *Architecture, Actor and Audience*. Routledge.

Mulryne, J.R., Shrewring M. & Barnes, J. (1999) *The Cottesloe at the National: Infinite Riches in a Little Room*. Mulryne & Shrewring.

Theatre costume

Arnold, J. (1978) *A Handbook of Costume*. Macmillan.

— (2006) *Patterns of Fashion: 1560–1620*. Macmillan.

— (1982) *Patterns of Fashion 2: 1860–1940*. Macmillan.

Baumgarten, L. (2002) *What Clothes Reveal*. Yale University Press.

Boucher, F. (2004) *A History of Costume in the West*. Thames & Hudson.

Bruhn, W. & Tilke, M. (2004) *A Pictoral History of Costume*. Dover.

Johnson, L. (2005) *Nineteenth-Century Fashion in Detail*. V&A Publishing.

Pattison, A. & Cawthorne, N. (1997) *A Century of Shoes*. Chartwell Books.

Rothstein, N. (1984) *Four Hundred Years of Fashion*. V&A Publishing.

Waugh, N. (1968) *The Cut of Women's Clothes 1600–1930*. Faber & Faber.

(1994) *The Cut of Men's Clothes 1600–1900*. Faber & Faber.

Theoretical contextualisation and research

Collins, J. & Nisbet, A. (2010) *Theatre and Performance Design: A Reader in Scenography*. Routledge.

Kershaw, B. & Nicholson, H. (2011) *Research Methods in Theatre and Performance*. Edinburgh Univ. Press.

McKinney, J. (2009) *The Cambridge Introduction to Scenography*. Cambridge University Press.

Moran, J. (2001) *Interdisciplinarity*. Routledge.

Zarilli, P., McConachie, B., Williams, G. & Sorgenfrei, C. (2005) *Theatre Histories: An Introduction*. Routledge.

Ipsos MORI (2010) *The West End Theatre Audience: A Research Study for the Society of London Theatre*. Society of London Theatre (SOLT).

Related ideas and philosophies

Benjamin, W. (1999) *Illuminations*. Pimlico.

Bleeker, M. (2008) *Visuality in the Theatre: The Locus of Looking*. Palgrave.

Foucault, M. (2001) Preface to *The Order of Things*. Routledge.

Fuchs, E. & Chaudhuri, U. (2002) *Land/Scape/Theatre*. University of Michigan Press.

Mitchell, W. J. T. ed. (1990) *Art and the Public Sphere*. University of Chicago Press.

Potolsky, M. (2006) *Mimesis*. Routledge.

Ranciere, J. (2007, March) 'The Emancipated Spectator', *Artforum* (pp. 271–280). Verso.

Useful directories

Contacts (Published by the actors' directory *Spotlight*)

Contacts has long been the bible for anyone working, or looking to get started, in the UK entertainment industry. It contains listings for over 5,000 companies, services and individuals across all branches of television, stage, film and radio.

The Original British Theatre Directory (Richmond House Publishing)

This technical directory features facts and figures of nearly all the working theatres in the UK, giving designers an instant view of a space's vital statistics and contact details. There are also sections on agents, publishing, education and training.

List of Illustrations

Samuel Beckett's *Not I* designed by Jocelyn Herbert. Photo: John Haynes/Lebrecht Music & Arts (p. xx).

Jocelyn Herbert's costume design for Dandy Nichols as Marjorie in *Home* at the National Theatre (p. 10).

Notation from the notebook of choreographer Tony Thatcher (p. 32).

Costume design by Yolanda Sonnabend for *La Bayadère* (1989) choreographed by Natalia Makarova for the Royal Opera House (p. 34).

Exit and entrance plotting system developed by designer Peter Farley for John Webster's *The White Devil* (pp. 118–191, 121).

Costume sketch by the author for Richard Harris' adaptation of Koki Mitani's *The Last Laugh,* Tokyo 2007) (p. 125).

Digital rendering by the author for Propeller Theatre's *Richard III* (UK, European and North American tour, 2011) (p. 132).

Jocelyn Herbert's storyboard drawings for Brecht and Weill's *The Rise and Fall of the City of Mahagony* at the Metropolitan Opera, New York (pp. 134–35).

Ground plan by the author for the premiere of Frank McGuinness' *The Hanging Gardens* (Abbey Theatre, Dublin 2013) (p. 42).

Costume design by Simon Higlett for the RSC's production of *Love's Labour's Lost* (2014) (p. 48).

Sketch by the author produced in the dance studio during the early phases of rehearsal for Stan Won't Dance's *Revelations* (2006) (p. 150).

A physical white-card sketch model and the equivalent wire-frame digital model by the author for Propeller's productions of *Twelfth Night* and *The Taming of the Shrew*, Old Vic (2006) (pp. 155–56).

Fully rendered model (1:25 scale) by the author for the Abbey Theatre, Dublin's world-premiere production of Frank McGuinness's *The Hanging Gardens* (p. 57).

A view of a proscenium stage from the auditorium's circle (p. 161).

A view of a courtyard space from the second balcony (p. 163).

A view of a thrust space from the left of the auditiorium (p. 165).

A view of an arena theatre from the back of a seating block (p. 167).

White-card model (1:50 scale) by the author for the Abbey Theatre, Dublin's production of Frank McGuinness's *The Hanging Gardens* (p. 249).

Scenic, character and props list for the start of rehearsal for the author's production of David Mamet's *Edmond* for the National Theatre (p. 255).

Rehearsal notes from Propeller Theatre's DSM, Ellie Randall for the production of *The Winter's Tale* (p. 264).

Exhibit of the author's design for *Richard III* at World Stage Design 2013 (p. 328).

Thanks

I am indebted to the many friends and fellow theatre professionals who have generously contributed their ideas and histories to this book. Some of the editing's collateral damage has been the accounts of how everyone I talked to had set out in life on such an unpredictable but positive voyage of discovery, and always also with an unspoken expectation of what new surprise might then be just around the corner. Theatre practitioners have intense working relationships that leave little time for calm reflection, so I have treasured these brief interludes to trade and record what we feel so passionate about.

The keyword in the book's title is '*be*' – what it's like *being* in the profession: living it. What I've attempted to put into words is a set of broadly shared approaches and principles. I've therefore tried to reassure either a newcomer to the subject, someone already immersed in it or someone reorientating their profession, however late in life, that there is a network of understood but often understated and diverse ways of being and doing, in the business – perhaps, dare I say, bordering on a collective conscience. Everyone I interviewed has had a different story to tell – all in, probably totalling well over five hundred years of experience!

Anyone who has made the theatre their vocation meanders through the business in their own way, and hearing different people's perspectives on the industry has been one of the most personally satisfying aspect of writing *So You Want To Be A Theatre Designer?* I also sincerely hope that this book has captured the voices of those who represent some of the unsung heroes and heroines of theatre-making, without whom the quality and complexity of UK theatre design would be undoubtedly and significantly poorer.

Like most professions in art and design, theatre design is both a product of its considerable heritage whilst also being in a healthy state of continual, evolutionary flux. My impression is that the recent vortex of voracious and compulsive change is currently being tempered by a real need to reconnect to at least the last two and a half thousand years of history, whether from Eastern or Western traditions. I have tried to give the younger reader a passing sense of this being a support to their creativity rather than feeling crushed, or bored, by history's baggage. We theatre designers, both young and not so young, are contemporaries at the end of a long, rich and inspiring timeline of theatre-makers. Thanks then to all the students of theatre design I have known over the last twenty years or so as this book is, in many respects, a concentrated record of the hours of discussions we've shared together.

Particularly, my thanks go out to Peter Farley for his constancy and wisdom over many years, and other contributors and interviewees, Alison Chitty, Edward Hall, Jan Bench, Geraldine Pilgrim, Grant Hicks, Alice Dunne, Chris Haydon, Douglas O'Connell, Ellen Havard, Hannah Lobelson, Laura Rushton, David Harris, Nick Ferguson, Tim Lutkin, Suzie Holmes, brother-in-arms Ashley Martin-Davis and others, no less valuable, in passing.

I decided early on that images would have to be a vital part of this book, so I really appreciate the generosity of those that have given their blessing for me to use their work – it's so easy to forget the skill and experience invested in a drawing or photograph. Thank you, Tony Thatcher, Simon Higlett, Yolanda and Joseph Sonnabend, John Haynes. Thanks too to Cathy Courtney and her work in the Jocelyn Herbert Archive at Wimbledon College of Arts (the archive now resides at the National Theatre); it was heavenly rooting through Jocelyn's extraordinarily sustained life's work over a number of Tuesday mornings.

Finally, thanks to all those who repeatedly gave me the encouragement to see this project through – particularly, Jan.

www.nickhernbooks.co.uk

facebook.com/nickhernbooks

twitter.com/nickhernbooks